Norton
650 C.C.
Sports Special
≡ £302·12·0 ≡
P/Tax £64·14·0 Extra

Norton TWIN RESTORATION

The essential guide to the renovation, restoration and development history of all post-war Norton Twins including Commando, Featherbed, Dominator and Jubilee series. Plus how to recognize parts, improve specifications and maintain these classic motorcycles

ROY BACON

NITON

Published by Niton Publishing
P.O. Box 3, Ventnor, Isle of Wight, PO38 2AS
First published in 1987 by Osprey Publishing,
Reed Consumer Books, Michelin House,
81 Fulham Road, London SW3 6RB

A CIP catalogue record for this book is available from the British
Library

Bacon, Roy H.
    Norton Twin restoration: the essential
    guide to the renovation, restoration and
    development history of all post-war Norton
    Twins including Commando, Featherbed,
    Dominator and Jubilee series: plus how to
    recognize parts, improve specifications and
    maintain these classic motorcycles.
    1. Norton motorcycle
    I. Title
    629.28'775   TL448.N6
    ISBN 1-85579-043-2

Editor Tony Thacker
Design Gwyn Lewis

Original edition filmset by Tameside Filmsetting Limited,
Ashton-under-Lyne, Lancashire
Reprinted via World Print., Hong Kong

HALF TITLE ILLUSTRATION *A not really street-legal Norton with Denis Parkinson aboard acting as a travelling marshal in the 1954 Manx Grand Prix. No doubt it flew past a good few of the real racers!*

TITLE PAGE ILLUSTRATION *Earls Court late in 1966 with Bill Smith presenting Giacomo Agostini with a short seat and rearsets for his own 650SS. The machine is a 1967 version of that model*

CONTENTS

Douglas quayside in 1955 with John Surtees, Geoff Duke and wife Pat. John is on a model 88 of that year and the lorry behind has nothing to do with the author

Acknowledgements

It can hardly be any great surprise that the third book in this restoration series should be on Norton twins and follows ones on Triumph and BSA, as this is just the same as in the earlier Osprey Collector's Library. Again it is written in response to a call for more detail on restorations and, as with the others, seeks to aid identification as well as provide a guide on the techniques used when working. As with the other titles, the basics of dating, colours and specifications are included along with much more.

Once more I have to thank my good friend Don Mitchell who supplied most of the basic data from his stock of second-hand motorcycle literature. Other material from Richard Negus of Norton Motors filled up some gaps.

The most important help I received with this book came from two well-known Norton Owners Club members who looked closely at the manuscript. One was John Hudson, who paid particular attention to the large twins, and the other was Andy Sochanik, who dealt with the small ones. Both put the text under close scrutiny and came back with corrections, alterations and, best of all, many useful additions based on their extensive experience of the marque. We are all in their debt.

The pictures and line drawings came mainly from the EMAP archives which hold the old *Motor Cycle Weekly* files, for which my grateful thanks. Others were from the *Motor Cycle News* files, courtesy of editor Jim Lindsay, and a number from Amal and Lucas material originally.

A number of the pictures carried the imprint of a professional and photos used came from Cecil Bailey, Court Studio, Dennis Dobson, K. G. Jones, Donald Page and Publifoto. As usual all the pictures were returned to their files after publication and I have tried to make contact to clear copyright. If my letter failed to reach you or I have used an unmarked print without realizing this, please accept my apologies.

Finally, my thanks to Tim Parker for conceiving the idea of this series and to Tony Thacker, my present editor, for bearing with me and helping to bring this one to a conclusion.

Roy Bacon
Niton, Isle of Wight
December 1986

Our policy

This book is written on the basis of a restoration back to original factory specification for the model and year. It is appreciated that not every reader will want to aim for this, but it is the only practical way to write the words.

Restorations can range from a mild check-over to a concours standard rebuild and further to add features and a finish never seen on a production machine. Alterations may be carried out and these again can range from discreet rider improvements to accepted changes to update the specification, or even total rework into a hardtail chopper. A common change for a Featherbed Norton is for another engine to be fitted, and the most usual is the Triumph twin to create the Triton.

In all cases and regardless of the final aim it is hoped that this book will assist and guide the reader to produce the machine of his or her dreams. It is also hoped that the result will be sound in wind and limb, and every endeavour has been made to offer advice which is helpful and safe. However, the onus is always with the reader to ensure that any machine he or she works on or rides is in a safe and legal condition. If you decide to carry out a modification you must make certain that it will work properly.

Neither the author nor publisher can accept any liability for anything contained in this book which may result in any loss, damage or injury, and the book is only available for purchase or loan on that basis.

Note It is worth remembering that each chapter of this book contains both general principles and specific information. The first can really apply to any make or model, while the second is very much only applicable to particular cases, such as a part made for a model that was only available for one year.

The distinction is important. The reader will invariably find the principles in other material, but the particular appeal of this book is that it gives you the specific details that relate the general principles directly to your machine.

Machine year

Chapter 1 gives details of the way in which models are dated, which causes, for example, 1958 models to run from late 1957 to late 1958. It also covers the habit the industry had of using up 1957 stocks in early 1958 models to clear the bins at the factory. Because of these points the text will use the model year without constant repetition that the feature or model was introduced late in the previous calendar year. Thus a late-1957 model is referred to as 1958 because that is the specification to which it was made.

The use of old parts is ignored by the Norton factory parts list and by this book. By definition they had to interchange by form and function so any notes on parts have to bypass this area. Some further possible confusion was caused by Norton, who changed the form of the part numbering system more than once so that identical items can be listed under two totally different numbers. This means that it is possible for an all-original machine with known history to be fitted with an incorrect part according to the parts list. It is the owner's decision as to whether to keep it or change to the correct listed part.

Engine and frame numbers take precedence over model year in determining when a change took place and have been noted where necessary. Parts lists, coupled with these numbers, are always the correct way back to original specification.

Scope

This book sets out to deal with production road models from 1949 to 1977 specification.

The data quoted applies to standard UK specification machines as these are the basis from which any factory variations were derived. Thus, while the data will assist when dealing with a machine to USA or any other overseas specification, it cannot be assumed to be exact. The same applies to all machines built for the police as these had their own specification and could vary in detail from one force to the next.

Norton also complicated matters when they became part of the AMC group by producing a series of models using their engine in an AMC frame. This began with the Atlas scrambler but in time led to the G15 series, the 33 AJS, the N15, plus the P11 and P11A. In general the Norton parts are covered but not those from AMC, and the content varied from model to model. A very tricky five years to get involved in.

Neither prototypes nor one-off specials are mentioned. If you are lucky enough to have such a machine, I am sure you appreciate its rarity and will look after it without my help.

Your skills

This book is not a workshop manual and neither is it a primer on being a motorcycle mechanic. It has to assume that you know how your machine works and have a good idea as to how to maintain it. Also that you have a degree of mechanical aptitude and have worked on motorcycles to some extent.

In many cases a good restoration is a combination of skill, available tools and knowledge of techniques and tricks that get the job done. Together they equate to experience and no book can give you that. It can only advise that you don't attempt more than you can cope with and add the suggestion that with the right information, care and attention to detail this could be more than you think. Proceed slowly but with confidence.

Address list

Always a problem in a book as they tend to be out of date by publication.

If in difficulties the 'agony' columns of the specialist magazines are there to help, so you can send them your query as long as you include some method of return postage.

Specifications

Many books of this type carry extensive tables of data to the fourth decimal place which have been compiled from endless hours of research. This does not, as much of it is in *Norton Twins* (Osprey Publishing) and the rest in workshop manuals.

Before any restoration is attempted, it is recommended that data and information are collected to cover your model and its year. In many areas the four-figure dimensions are of little moment as parts are reamed to fit and made to size. Part of the art is knowing which ones matter and no book can teach that, any more than it can show you how to paint a masterpiece or write an opera. Well, not one that is any good.

So there are no endless lists of bushes and bearings, gaps and settings, or tolerances and gauges. The figures and data that are provided are there to back up the manual you should have and to help you sort out what you may have bought.

Note

To avoid constant detailing the twins will be referred to as big or small. The former covers any of the 500 to 850 cc models as all are based on the same engine design. Subdivisions of this group may be referred to as Dominator, Featherbed, hybrid or Commando. The small twins are the 250 to 400 cc, unit-construction lightweight models.

1 To begin

The Norton twin was announced in the motorcycle press in November 1948, so it came a little later than others following in the steps of the pre-war Triumph Speed Twin. For all that, it had a good engine and inherited the legendary Norton roadholding. The engine began life as a 500 but in time was to be stretched to 850 cc, although always as a separate unit from its gearbox.

For 1959 the existing range of big twins was joined by a 250 cc lightweight and this, in time, was built in 350 and 400 cc versions. These were all of unit construction but the larger models did use some cycle parts from the heavier range.

The greatest change in the big twins occurred in late 1967 when the Commando was launched. This used the existing mechanics but the frame was all new and featured the interesting Isolastic principle.

Over the years the electrics changed from dynamo to alternator and the cycle side varied, but all the twins had overhead valves and a Norton line.

History

The first parallel twin was listed as the Dominator model 7 and its basic design was the same as that of the last Commando. It was of 497 cc and first shown at Earls Court late in 1948, where it appeared in the plunger frame used by the singles but with a revised form of the traditional Norton gearbox. This was the laid-down pattern later adopted by the range and it tucked in better under the oil tank and behind the engine's timing chest.

At first there was little change, but late in 1951 public demand for a twin in the Featherbed frame was answered by the appearance of the model 88. This was an export-only machine initially, and to appease the home market the 7 went into a pivoted-fork frame for

The start of the line in the form of the 1949 model 7 Dominator with an engine design that was to run on for nearly 30 years

1953. The next year saw both models with a bigger front brake, and 1955 brought an alloy cylinder head and round tank badges.

That year saw the end of the model 7 but for 1956 there was a larger Featherbed twin, the 596 cc model 99, which shared the cycle side and much of its engine with the 88. During that year the gearbox was changed again to the AMC type which remained with the big twins from then on.

At the time, the Featherbed frame was not thought to be up to the strains of a sidecar, so for those customers who had to have three wheels the model 77 was introduced for 1957. This was, in effect, the pivoted-fork model 7 frame fitted with the 99 engine. It was only listed for two years as in 1958 the great Eric Oliver showed just how good a sidecar outfit the 88 could be, and from then on a sidecar kit was available.

The 77 parts were also used to create the Nomad off-road model in 1958, using a twin-carburettor version

of the 99 engine fitted with magneto ignition but an alternator for the lights. This went on to the 88 and 99 for 1958, but in their case there was a distributor in the magneto position and coil ignition. Early in the year a twin-carburettor conversion went on the options list.

The year 1959 saw the advent of the first small twin, the 249 cc Jubilee with an enclosed tail, and this theme was taken up by the larger models in 1960. That year brought the 'slim-line' version of the Featherbed frame and the two machine sizes listed in standard and de luxe (with rear enclosure) forms.

The number of models increased for 1961, and among the newcomers was the Manxman which had a larger 646 cc engine with twin carburettors and was built for America. At first it was assembled in a US style but later took on the same cycle parts as the smaller models and was listed simply as the 650. The Jubilee was joined by a 349 cc version called the

ABOVE *Early signs of the Featherbed in the form of Dick Clayton's 1951 ISDT mount. Note the massive front brake and sprung mudguard*

LEFT *The drive side of a 1950 model 7 with characteristic Norton chaincase and footrest*

Navigator, and both were listed as de luxe in the original style with rear enclosure, and standard without it. For the sporting rider, two new models appeared in the spring as the 88SS and 99SS, both with twin carburettors and other useful items.

The 88, 99 and 650 were all listed in standard, de luxe and SS forms in 1962 to create nine models, although records suggest that only four standard 99 machines were built. The lightweights also continued, as they did for 1963, with the addition of the 383 cc Electra which had electric start but no rear enclosure. The three 99 models were dropped late in 1962 along with the other two large de luxe machines, but during 1963 another large twin was introduced. This was the 745 cc Atlas, and in the autumn of that year the first signs of inter-marque breeding appeared with an Atlas scrambler version. This kept the Norton engine, forks and wheels but used an AMC-type CSR frame to create a hybrid.

At the end of 1963 the de luxe versions of the Jubilee and Navigator were dropped, as were the standard 88 and 650. This left the two SS models, the Atlas (now with 12-volt electrics), the three smaller twins in standard format and the Atlas scrambler which became the N15CS'N' during 1964.

From then to the end of the 1960s the main and true

Norton line-up was simple, but alongside it ran a confusion of hybrids. The three models with the Featherbed frame continued as they were until late 1966 when the 88SS was dropped. The Atlas went at the end of 1968, while for 1969 the 650SS became the single-carburettor Mercury. This was finally dropped during 1970. The three lightweights became one by the end of 1965, with only the Jubilee continuing for a short while until it too went in July 1966.

On the hybrid front, the first event to follow the 1964 appearance of the N15CS'N' scrambler was the advent of the Matchless G15 and G15CSR in 1965. Both had the Atlas engine in an AMC frame but with Norton wheels and forks. Later in the year there came the AJS models 33 and 33CSR.

These four models continued alongside the Atlas for 1966 and 1967 when they were joined by the N15. This was simply the Matchless G15 fitted with a Norton tank. Early in the year the Norton P11 appeared. This differed from the other hybrids in that, while it retained the Norton Atlas engine, it used the Matchless G85CS frame with AMC forks and brakes. A month later the G15CS'N' was revised and relisted as the N15CS, being built as a trail machine or street scrambler.

By the end of 1967 the AJS models and the N15 had gone, but for 1968 the G15 became the G15 Mk II, and the P11 the P11A; the G15CS and G15CSR continued as before. Late in the year the N15CS came to an end and the P11A was renamed the Ranger, but it failed to make it into 1969. During 1969 the various G15 models went out of production and the whole untidy mess came to an end.

This was just as well, for back in late 1967 Norton had launched the Commando model with its unique

frame. Into this went the Atlas engine, tilted forwards a trifle, and the faithful AMC gearbox, but the style was fresh. A new series was off and running.

The first production machine reached the public early in 1968 and a year later was given the name Fastback. At the same time it was joined by the R model with conventional seat and rear mudguard, and the S model which had twin waist-level exhausts on the left. The R was short-lived and disappeared about September 1969 when the Fastback gained a timing chest containing the points, as was standard on all the S models. March 1970 saw the first Roadster version, which was an S with Fastback exhausts, while three months later the S was dropped and a hotter engine, called the Combat, was made available.

From September 1970 the Fastback became the Mk II, but not for long as from January 1971 it was the Mk III while the Roadster became the Mk II. The year 1971 also saw the introduction of other models, the first being the Street Scrambler, followed quickly by the Fastback LR (or long range), the Production racer

and the Hi-Rider. The Street Scrambler only lasted a few months before being dropped.

In January 1972 the engines were revised and the Fastback, Fastback LR, Roadster and Hi-Rider all became Mk IV, while the Production racer continued and the range was joined by the Interstate. This had the Combat engine and front disc brake as standard, and by the middle of the year these were also common to all the other models. However, there were untold troubles with the Combat engine which took the rest of the year to overcome.

Early in 1973 the two Fastback models went and the Roadster, Hi-Rider and Interstate continued in Mk V form. A month later all three were also available with the engine taken out to 829 cc, which was to be its largest production size. In September 1973 these three became known as Mk I models and were joined by the Mk IA versions of the Roadster and Interstate.

A month later the machines with the 745 cc engine came to an end, and in November the 850 line-up was joined by the John Player Replica model. This arose

from the road-racing sponsorship enjoyed by the firm and the result was a delightful, faired café racer. While it was usually fitted with the 829 cc engine, it could also be had with a short-stroke 749 cc version.

From January 1974 the Roadster and Interstate Mk I models became Mk IIA types, but the IA versions also continued. The Hi-Rider became the Mk II. In February 1975 the last major change took place with all the IA, II and IIA models being dropped along with the JPR. In their place were just the Roadster and Interstate in Mk III form with electric start and left-mounted gear pedal. These continued unchanged until the end of the line in 1977.

Model choice

The range of Norton twins offers the owner plenty of choice in model types, engine sizes and years. That which is chosen is down to the individual and is his choice alone. Selection can be determined by a past memory, a wish for a particular model or to complete a collection, but for most it is settled by the money they have and the machines on offer.

Spares for all may be a problem. The situation varies from model to model, part to part and day to day. Items that are impossible to find at the date this is written could be readily available when you read the words, or the reverse may be true. Because of this

LEFT *Prototype scrambles model built by Ron Hankins and used by Les Archer but here seen at the 1954 Services trial*

BELOW *A 1958 Featherbed produced that year as the 88 and 99 model. Headlamp, tank panels and hubs had by then all moved on from the first version*

variation the text is written on the basis that spares are to be had, but that while the mechanics should be available, with occasional lapses, the cycle side could be much harder to find. However, they may be easier to re-create by one means or another.

Remember that some models were only made in small numbers, so their spares could be harder to locate. Also that export-specification models can pose problems even in the country they were destined for and worse outside it. A further pitfall arises if an attempt has been made to create a rare model from a more prosaic one or to convert from one specification to another. Very rarely will the change be complete, causing yet more headaches.

An added complication with the Featherbed models is that many were used to create Tritons and other specials, and as a source of parts need to be checked with care. Many parts may well have been changed or modified to make the special and thus will no longer be suitable for use in a Norton assembly, unless returned to their original condition.

The Norton can be obtained in many ways, but purchase from a dealer, following up small advertisements in local papers or specialized magazines, by word of mouth, club grapevine or personal contact are the more usual methods. Alternatively you may already have one you wish to restore or improve in some way.

You may not actually start with a complete machine but with a box of parts bought at an autojumble or from a local source. Often such are the hardest to complete as invariably parts are missing. The box is on sale because the last owner allowed enthusiasm to run ahead of resources, stripped the machine and then gave up or was forced to stop. He is sure it is all there but has forgotten various parts already missing, lent, lost or strayed—every one a problem for the new owner.

The restorer must also decide what is wanted and what is possible, which may not be the same thing. A concours model may not be everyone's desire but all should aim to put the machine in good running order so that it is reliable in use.

Aims can vary and may simply be to correct the faults of a machine in poor condition so that it is a pleasure to ride, even if its appearance is nondescript. They could be to repair damage to reach this standard or might include changes to enhance performance, reliability or appearance. More usual is the ambition to restore to original condition or, in some cases, beyond that with more chrome, polish and sparkle than even a Bracebridge Street show model.

The decision on the standard and style of restoration belongs to the owner just as the machine does. Whether all chrome, all original or all bituminous black, it is your choice and no one else's. The decision on what to do depends on many factors which can include time, money and facilities as well as the owner's wishes.

TOP *A Triton, typical of many and in this case built by Alf Goodwin using a 1958 Manx frame and Triumph T120 engine*

RIGHT *The launch of the 1959 Jubilee model at the Earls Court Show held late the previous year*

Assets

Motorcycle restoration or repair requires time, money and equipment, and it is necessary to have some amount of all three. Possession of a large amount of any one reduces the need for the other two but will never remove them completely. Thus, given plenty of time, the highest restoration standards can be reached using limited facilities and at minimal cost. A deep purse will allow the project to be farmed out and finished in a short time without the need for much equipment. The ultimate on this road of just handing over the machine and money to a professional may sound easy but can still call for decision making and organizational skills. Finally, anyone with really good facilities can complete a restoration cheaply and quickly by making or refurbishing the parts and tools needed. It has to be noted that all three assets do have to be present to some degree.

Abilities

The Norton restorer must try to make a realistic assessment of his or her abilities. Some of us are less well blessed with manual skills than others and it is very important to realize one's limitations early on

and to plan ways around them. This can be equally satisfying as the object is to complete the project by the means that are available to you.

An example lies in the use of special tools. You must use these in certain instances and they can be bought or made. Alternatively, your parts may be taken to someone with them. The method you choose depends on the money, facilities and time already mentioned.

A person's level of skill varies from job to job, and this also must be allowed for. Your expertise in some areas may be to a very high standard but in others may be lower, so accept that fact. You must judge in which areas you have the required competence and those where help will be needed.

One answer to this problem is to lower the standard of the restoration. If you cannot do certain jobs and don't want outside help, then the only answer is to

BELOW RIGHT *One of the last machines to gain a special number plate as this really is a 650SS model. It is from 1962 and the mark was issued by East Lothian CC*

BELOW *The de luxe version of the 1960 model 99 showing the rear enclosure from the Jubilee and the new tank badge*

settle for less than a concours finish. It is likely to be more satisfying to rebuild a basket case into a reliable machine than to attempt perfection and miss it due to personal rather than financial reasons.

A further factor to consider is the timescale of the job. The machine may be wanted by a particular date, in which case the planning must allow for some mishaps, as they always occur. For your first restoration it is much better not to have any deadline, as even with the experience of several it can be hard to estimate when a project will be finished.

It is much better to allow for delays, particularly if you are aiming for a concours standard. If a straight rebuild is being done, it is easier to keep to a schedule as more of the work will be under your own control. Planning ahead can often reduce delays. A series of tasks that depend on one another and which run in sequence should be started early to prevent a hold-up later on.

Wheels are a classic example as you have a whole series of jobs that can only be carried out in one set order, each task depending on the one preceding it.

Thus the first stage of the restoration is to decide on a machine and determine the degree of restoration to be carried out. It pays to think this through before committing oneself—proper planning not only saves time and money but makes the work more enjoyable and turns a job into a hobby.

Receipts

It pays to keep the paperwork in order from the start. This is dealt with in more detail later, but it cannot be over-emphasized that you must be able to prove that you actually own the machine which sits in the garage, shed or front hall depending on your workshop habits. Thus it is essential to obtain a receipt for the machine or, if it is built up from boxes of parts, receipts for them and for all the major purchases you make. It won't do any harm to keep the till slips of even minor items and to log all these in your records.

This will help prove ownership, be a useful record should you wish to sell (showing a prospective buyer exactly what has gone into the machine) and may even frighten you at the size of the cost of a restoration.

Workshop

This has been the subject of many articles which seek

ABOVE *The 88SS in 1966, its last year, not really very much changed from the first Featherbed*

TOP *The Atlas with high bars in 1964 and rather different in appearance to the 88 thanks to them and other details*

to describe an ideal arrangement, but for most restorers it is either their garage or garden shed. Some lucky people have better premises and some much worse, but the work that comes from the shop may bear little relation to its size or facilities.

It is possible to produce a concours Norton in a small draughty shed, and many people have done just this. However, the job of restoring a machine is not an easy one and, since the exercise is supposed to be an enjoyable hobby, it makes sense to be able to work in comfort at least.

There is seldom much you can do about the size of

your workshop, but the smaller it is, the more you need to have it well organized. Whatever the size it must be clean, dry, warm and well lit. The first job is to stop the roof from leaking; the next to check the floor and consider sealing its surface. Aside from the dust problem, which sealing greatly reduces, it also makes finding anything dropped on the floor much easier. Normal concrete is gritty and locating small screws can be difficult.

With the roof and floor in order, the walls can be seen to. A coat of white emulsion brightens the atmosphere no end and helps the efficiency of the lighting. This must be good and fluorescent tubes are essential. They should be the daylight white type and may need to be supplemented by a bench light and a hand torch or wander light. It pays to wipe over the tubes occasionally as they tend to get dirty in a workshop, and any reduction in illumination is a handicap. If likely to be knocked at any time, they should be protected by a guard.

Some people share a workshop which can be a great help, but only if you get on well and can work side by side. For some jobs an extra pair of hands will save a lot of time and trouble, while discussing a problem will often solve it.

Just as important as sharing with another person is sharing the restoration site with another machine. If the same shed has to garage a machine in daily use then sooner rather than later it will come in wet and dirty. Not impossible to live with but a factor to remember when deciding what can and cannot be attempted at home.

Equipment

The workshop has to be fitted out and the first need is a bench to work on. This must be solidly built and firmly fixed in place. Next on the list is a machine bench with a means of running the motorcycle up on to it; finally come shelves of various sizes for the storage of parts, tools, equipment, spares and consumables such as oil and grease. Don't forget a place for a large, shallow box in which to store your gaskets.

The bench needs a vice and you may also wish to make up an engine stand. This can be constructed of wood or metal, its purpose being to stop the unit from falling over on the bench and possibly damaging itself. To be really useful the stand needs to be clamped to the bench and the same effect can be achieved by holding the engine, or gearbox, in the vice. This leaves both hands free to do the work but does emphasize the need to fix vice and bench securely. Needless to say, the vice must be fitted with smooth jaws to avoid marking the castings.

A pleasant young lady with a 1965 Atlas. The engine size is indicated by the breather in line with the camshaft

Hand tools are best stored on a board so they are easy to reach, but keep files beneath the bench to avoid any chance of metal particles getting into the works. Your hand tools are likely to have been accumulated over the years and may be of variable quality. Now is a good time to get ruthless with them and separate the good from the rest.

Spanner types are legion but the rules are to use only those that fit and are made from a high-quality steel. My preference is for combination spanners, open at one end with a ring at the other, both being of the same size, a set of $\frac{1}{4}$ in. drive sockets which give me feel on most motorcycle fixings, and a selection of $\frac{1}{2}$ in. drive sockets. Mine have been bought as needed to suit specific jobs so that, thanks to the changes from Whitworth to Unified to metric threads, a fairly full set is to hand. But it took many years to acquire. Nortons used Whitworth fixings until the Commando which also had Unified threads on all its cycle parts.

The $\frac{1}{4}$ in. drive is thought light by many but its slimness is an asset in many situations. Often a nut may be slackened by a heavier tool and then run off with the smaller one which will tuck in better.

A 1967 Atlas with twin instruments and a rubber bung in its chaincase

In addition to hand tools for taking things apart, you will need some for making things. It is at this point that you have to decide how much work you will attempt and what to farm out as the equipment becomes more specialized and expensive. Possession of a good electric drill is taken as read, and it is not too difficult to adapt this to a pillar drill or a bench grinder for sharpening drills. A flexible shaft will also help with port work. The next items, however, are in another league.

There are two pieces of equipment to consider and their relative importance depends, to an extent, on the work you intend to do. If you will be making spacers, machining parts and working to a greater degree on the mechanics then a lathe becomes essential. With a good set of tools and attachments, a wide range of possibilities opens up and parts can be made at a speed undreamed of. Should you intend to concentrate rather more on the cycle parts, then welding equipment is essential for you. Standard oxy-acetylene gear enables parts to be brazed, welded, filled, loosened, bent and re-formed. An alternative, which helps with the engine and a good deal of the cycle part work, is a butane torch. In all cases when using a mobile heat source, be careful where you point it and remember what items you have heated up. A fire extinguisher is a good investment.

Although a great deal is possible without a lathe or welding gear, for serious restoration both are needed. One area where they can help is in making special tools for working on the machine in general and the engine in particular.

A further piece of specialized equipment well worth considering is a hydraulic press, which can be constructed using a car or lorry jack. Remember to disconnect the overstroke release, if it has one, as otherwise you can lock the press up solid and it will stay that way until a seal goes.

Also worth putting on your shopping list is an air compressor. It does not have to be new, and often the compressor and motor to drive it may be bought separately, but it can be very useful even if you have no intention of doing any paint spraying. What it will do is enable you to check oilways, pipe lines, carburettor jets and the like for obstructions. Also, an air-line will blast cleaning agent from the parts as they

LEFT *The excellent Norton Owners Club showing a 1969 Mercury. Membership is more than just a good idea for any owner*

BELOW *The Nomad 99 model of 1958 with special exhaust and frame which was to lead to other off-road hybrids*

are finished and can save lots of time spent drying with a cloth.

The equipment you decide to acquire will depend on many factors and relates to the earlier assessment of your abilities. There is no point in having more tools than you can handle but don't confuse lack of confidence with this. If welding or machining is unfamiliar to you, read about them, consider attending an evening course at the local college and, above all, practise before working on anything expensive or hard to replace.

Data

Just as important as tools for the workshop is data for the mind. Before laying a tool on your Norton, there is a good deal of information to be collected if you want the best results. Even if you are only after a good working machine you still need certain basic engine settings, while for a concours job the data needed is far more detailed.

In all cases the first step is to establish what you have by checking engine and frame numbers for year and model type. The latter can be checked further against the machine specification and often this will reveal discrepancies. It is all too easy to switch Norton twin engines around, so it is as well to check that engine and frame numbers match as they should and that the year letter codes and model marking numbers all tally. All manner of changes can occur to a machine during its life and some may date from long before the classic machine revival.

Hybrids are a common problem with any make that stayed in production for a long time with few changes to basic dimensions. This is especially true of Nortons

ABOVE *Show model Commando pictured in September 1967, still with a few badges missing*

ABOVE RIGHT *Two 1972 Commandos with an Interstate on the left and a Roadster with it, both with the Combat engine (bad news) and disc front brake*

RIGHT *A 1974 John Player Replica with the 829 cc engine. This one has been fitted with a dualseat rather than the usual single*

due to the Triton influence. A Feathered frame is not quite the same thing if fitted with a single-cylinder engine, and many Tritons were based on the 350 cc model 50 frame. If the Triumph motor has gone, the rolling chassis could give major headaches when a twin engine is offered up. Aside from the Norton variations, there could also be those introduced when the special was first created. Not at all easy to unravel.

So it pays to be wary and to check with the data as the interest in original-specification machines has inevitably led to some being built up from spares or parts from many sources. In other cases items may not match due to an engine blow-up sometime in the past.

The magazine agony columns indicate that all this is common with most makes, so it is always something to be aware of and to check. For the machine to be a hybrid may be a good thing, rather than bad, as the changes may be a worthwhile improvement. The important matter is knowing exactly what you do have.

Dating is complicated by the British industry's

tradition of starting its model year in August or September. Like most confusion, it arose from good intentions and came about because the works switched to making new models when they returned from their annual holiday. Thus production was well under way, with stocks in the warehouse or at the dealers, when the new models were announced in the press during the run-up to the Earls Court Show in November. In theory, at least, you could view in London and collect your new machine from a local dealer the next day.

With the maker's year out of step with the calendar, it is quite possible to find a machine first registered in October of the year *before* its model year. Further complication for the restorer lies in the change-over of parts which may not coincide with the start of a new model year. Often stocks of old parts would be used, where feasible, until run down, before the new ones were phased in. In many cases changes are internal and out of sight, but some are on the outside and can cause real confusion.

The only answer is to work from the engine and frame numbers using the relevant parts book. This is a most useful publication and really an essential for the restorer with a workshop or maintenance manual. In some ways, the parts list is the more important for anyone striving for originality, as it lists every part used on the machine with its part number and quantity.

Other literature that will help, and which can be obtained from specialist book dealers, are the rider's handbook (this may add to the data in the manual) and a sales brochure, often the only indication of the colours of the machine and its component parts.

A marque history is well worth having as it will fill out the background, and I am biased to recommend *Norton Twins* as I wrote it. You should also be reading the specialist magazines *Classic Bike* and *The Classic Motor Cycle* for older machines, and *Performance Bike* which covers modern techniques. These will provide addresses and articles that could be useful to you. The addresses to note are any that look helpful—those close to you and the ones offering any special services likely to be needed. Plating, painting, wheel rebuilds and crankshaft regrinds are common needs, but you may also need someone to help with seat renovation, electrics or instruments. *Classic Bike* publishes a supplier list in the autumn, usually in the October issue, and this is something well worth keeping to hand.

Firms of this type are not listed here for two reasons. The first is the general need for them to be local. It is one thing to send a dynamo away for repair but quite another if you have 40 items for stove enamelling. The second is that firms comprise people and their expertise. A good reputation may be due to the owner ensuring it is so or the workforce being skilled, or a combination of the two. This can easily change if one or more men leave, so recent recommendation is the best guide.

It will also be useful to join the Norton Owners Club as they offer a unique combined experience. No other body has quite the same outlook, and members are in the best position to carry out very real evaluation tests on machines, modifications and their effects. There is also the Vintage Motor Cycle Club in Britain (with others elsewhere) which offers a further source of data, a marque specialist, and from their work has come a transfer scheme available to all.

Yet another source of information is the show in its various forms. This may be a straight exhibition which includes older machines, a classic machine show, a rally or a race meeting with events for older machines. All provide an opportunity to study other machines, talk to owners, gather information and find out where to get parts. Autojumbles, which are often combined with other events, can become an important part of the restorer's life for they offer the opportunity

RIGHT *A Commando with some French police extras but not that far from stock*

BELOW LEFT *The Thruxton Club racer for 1975 with Frank Perris aboard*

to seek out elusive spares, data and services. Local and not so local ones should be attended, dates and venues being found in the pages of the specialist press.

Work plan

This is the grand title for you tearing the engine out and apart in the first flush of enthusiasm. Unfortunately, come winter, this fades and the mix-up of parts now spread between many boxes, bags and tins becomes very unattractive. Before long another basket job hits the ad columns, which is both sad and unnecessary.

Before you pick up the first tool take a long look at yourself, your facilities and the machine. *Think*, painful though it is. Make sure that you have decided what *you* want to do and that this is within the capabilities of yourself and your equipment. Now think again and decide how that happy dream of a concours win, sweet-running machine or whatever is to be reached.

In essence you have to decide whether to deal with the machine as a whole or by major parts. The first is usually quicker but requires more fortitude. Once apart, there will be a vast number of parts all needing attention, and long before you get to the assembly stage you may run out of interest. The alternative is to take a major assembly and renovate that alone. It will take longer to complete the whole machine, but this method does reduce the storage space needed and you do feel that you are getting somewhere as each major lump is completed. Whichever way you go you need

notes, photographs and sketches in large numbers. If you are going to rely on photos alone, you will need to take plenty and they must be good close-ups. It is possible to do this with a very basic camera, but for the best results you really need a decent SLR which can focus down to three feet or less. Unless you can get that close you just won't record the detail you need. Good lighting will help in obtaining good photos, and a wide-angle lens could be useful.

Notes and sketches are a good alternative and mean that you can safely proceed without wondering if your film is going to develop satisfactorily. A pad of paper should be kept handy in the workshop for rough notes and these tidied and written up cleanly the same day. It is all too easy, especially with cycle parts, to forget the order in which parts fit on to a stud, which way round a bolt goes or even where the horn is fitted when you come to put things together months later. Plenty of labels and plastic storage bags will make life easier.

Even if the assembly you start with is wrong, it is useful to record it as a basis to work from. Do not think that you can remember it all as you cannot; neither is it always obvious as to how the parts should be. Mudguard stays in particular can cause problems; often the apparently same part is used on both sides of the machine and can be fixed in four alternative ways in each position. Four? Yes, as it can be turned over or end for end, but only one way and one position will put it back where it came from. In theory this may not matter, if all the stays are the same, but in practice they always seem happier if replaced as they were. No doubt this arises because of small distortions that the parts have accommodated and if switched round they will have to begin again.

If you start with someone else's disaster as a basket case then the problem becomes more difficult as you will have to determine what each part is, where it goes and if it needs attention or was made in its present shape at the factory. A common difficulty with basket cases is rogue parts from another machine that have crept in and can give you hours of fun and frustration. Identifying these may be no trouble for you if they are stamped BSA or Triumph but they could prove a minor headache if marked AMC. If you have a late Norton they may belong—or they may not! A major headache is the appearance of real Norton parts which happen to come from a single, or another model twin not compatible with yours.

You must also beware of parts that changed in detail over the years but remained very similar in appearance, changes of thread form from Whitworth to Unified, changes brought about by metrication and some pattern parts. Of the last, some are very, very good but others can be awful.

Another headache can be proprietary parts which were common to many British machines and some of which happened to fall in with your basket. A handful of petrol taps might be useful but not if they all came from some other machine.

Lists

Some people live by lists, others abhor them, but in restoration they really are an essential and should

Ray Petty (left) and Mike Jackson with a final, last, late Commando in 1982. More could always appear at some time in the future

form part of your note-taking. Starting from a complete machine, parts can be listed as they are dismantled with notes as to whether they need to be repaired, treated or both. By working with a parts list, missing items can be highlighted and a shopping list compiled. This should include consumables as well.

When starting with a basket case a parts list is invaluable, and one or more photocopies are well worth obtaining at the start. Using one as a master, the parts can be checked off one by one down to the last nut, bolt and washer. What is finally left on the list becomes the shopping list and any parts not identified are, or ought to be, rogue.

While checking the list you can begin to establish the work needed on the parts you have, depending on how much you are short and how essential the missing items are. How you fulfil the shopping list depends on your aims, money and the items themselves. You may have a good selection of nuts and bolts that would be fine for the job even if not correct to concours standard. If your aim is a good working machine then use them; the same philosophy can apply to many other items.

At the end of this operation you will have dismantled the complete machine and listed all the parts that require your attention or their purchase. This may have happened in stages if that is your way of working, but happen it has. With this knowledge the restoration work will be easier to organize and the assembly straightforward to carry out.

Security

Classic motorcycles and their component parts are valuable and in some cases nearly irreplaceable. One professional restorer is quoted as saying, 'What man has made, man can make again', which is perfectly true, but only at a price.

Therefore security has become a point to bear in mind. This is especially true if you are forced to use a lock-up garage as your workshop, and the necessary steps should be taken before the machine is on the premises. Avoid publicity as the word can quickly get about, so don't leave the doors open if the premises face on to the street.

Working at home reduces the problem but may not remove it, so discretion is a good idea. It could also avoid an argument with the local council through a neighbour thinking you are using your home as a repair business.

A method used by some restorers, at least to cut down their risk once a machine is partly dismantled, is to store the parts in different areas of their home. This is a particularly useful way of protecting the smaller, more delicate, rather expensive and fairly universal items. These minor assemblies, such as magneto, dynamo, speedometer and carburettor, lend themselves well to this arrangement and benefit from the household heating.

2 First steps

Clean machine

With the 'before' pictures safely taken, work can begin on your project but not in the workshop. The very first thing to be done is to take the machine outside and give it a good clean to remove dirt, grime, grease and oil. There are a number of cleaning agents to help with this task, the aim being to get the bulk of the dirt washed away and the machine dried before it enters the working area.

Transfers

While this chore is in hand, care must be taken not to damage the finish or any transfers as reference to them may be necessary. In fact, once the machine is clean and back in the workshop, it is a good time to go round it and make notes of the exact positions of all the transfers with measurements taken from fixed features.

If you are just overhauling the machine, the transfers are unlikely to be of any major concern, but for a full restoration they are. The position of the oil tank level, for instance, is a fixed dimension from some other point and for a concours job should be correct.

First removals

The initial steps are to remove the parts that are fragile and easily damaged, or which impede access to the major items. The first step is the fuel tank, but before touching it have a look at the control cables and note how they run; whether they are to left or right of the steering head and above or below the fixing lugs.

On some models you cannot remove the tank without taking the seat off first, so if this is the case tackle it that way without forcing anything. If any of the bolts involved hold something else as well, you must note the order of the parts and which way round the bolts go.

Note also the run of the petrol pipes while the tank and taps are in their correct location, and watch the handlebars as you shift the tank. It is all too easy to catch the front of it on something and have the bars swing round and clout it to produce a dent or a nasty scratch.

Now set the machine up on the bike bench and make quite sure it is secure. If it is on a stand check that the feet cannot slide off the edge of the bench even when you lean on it with a tool. Check what will happen as you dismantle the machine. Most with a centre stand will keep their front wheel on the bench top, but if there is any doubt force a piece of wood under the back tyre to ensure stability. To have the whole machine rock back just as you try to lift the engine out can really put you off your stroke and cause you to drop something. Or worse still, you might dive to save the bike and knock it over.

So aim for stability until you have the major weighty items out, then jack up the front and take out the wheel. Do it the other way round and you will have too much mass balanced on too short a wheelbase for safety. Remember this when you come to assemble it again.

With the bike up in the air and secure, continue with the dismantling by removing the exhaust systems which might fall away or could stick. If the latter occurs don't tip the bike over while hauling on the pipes, just try to work them off a little at a time.

Tackle tight systems from the rear, a section at a time. Leave the pipe fixings tight and remove the silencer bolts and clips. Work at the silencer to ease it back and off, then move on to the pipe which should respond to the same treatment.

Now attend to the fragile items, starting with the headlamp rim, its glass, reflector and bulb. Place something soft over the front mudguard on which to rest the assembly while you disconnect the wires or pull out the bulb holders. Store with care, adding the rear light lens and bulb.

Next is the speedometer, and rev-counter if fitted, noting which is to left or right. Watch the bulb holder fitted in the back of the instrument and remove the bulb itself. Tie the parts so they stay together at the end of the wire and don't slide off into the main harness. The same trick is often worth doing with the instrument drive cable to restrain the knurled end fitting, and a clothes peg can be used temporarily. Note the run of the cables.

ABOVE *The gold-plated 1961 Jubilee on show at Earls Court*

ABOVE LEFT *Using a spanner and screwdriver in place of an impact driver on timing-cover screws. The machine is a 1956 model 99*

BELOW LEFT *Drive side of a 1957 model 88 fitted with Armstrong rear units*

Remove the carburettor(s) and float chamber, drain out the petrol and store. If a complete strip is intended, the slides are best removed from the cables and kept with the carburettor until attention is turned to that item.

The wiring is next on the list along with the control cables, for they may well be linked by clips and tape holding them to the frame. More notes are needed before they are released. Then disconnect the battery and remove it. Don't hide it as it will need immediate attention if it is to act as a case, or regular attention if it is to be used further.

The cables, suitably labelled, come off first. The label should indicate which end is which if not obvious. The wiring is usually best detached working from the rear of the machine forwards to the headlamp switch. Depending on the year of the machine, it may be best to detach it from the switches and other electrical parts or it might be simpler to leave it connected and take the parts off it. Some, a dip-switch is an example, don't leave you any choice. More notes, of course, but also check along the harness as you

remove it for any points where it has been rubbed or shows signs of damage. These are areas to do something about on assembly to prevent problems occurring.

It is likely that the rectifier will have been removed during this operation but not necessarily the regulator, if one is fitted. This is fragile so take it off for storage.

With the delicate details and the tangled mass of cables and wiring out of the way, the machine will look a lot cleaner and be easier to work on. You can now see what you are doing and can get at the machine without fear of damaging something fragile and costly. No reason not to take care, of course.

Basket case

When your Norton has come in boxes, start the restoration with the assembly of shabby components. It is well worth cleaning the contents of each box as this will make them nicer to work on, but nothing special is needed at this stage as they will need a lot more work and another, more thorough, clean before final assembly.

What you have to do is build up your collection of parts, each checked off against the parts list, into a complete machine. There are three problems in doing this. First is that it may not all be there. If the missing items are mainly bolts and fixings, anything from stock can be pressed into temporary service, but if you lack structural items it becomes more tricky. Secondly, some parts may be damaged and ill-fitting, even distorting other parts. Allowance must be made where this occurs. Finally, there are rogue parts which may throw you off course.

ABOVE *A 1960 model 99 showing the engine and gearbox plates and other details common to the models of that era*

LEFT *An Atlas, fitted with the optional rev-counter alongside the speedo, on road test in 1964*

At this stage keep everything; in fact, this is a sound move with any part from any older machine. No matter how tired or worn it may be, at some time you or someone else will want to use it because it is the best one available. If you don't use it yourself you may be able to swap it for something you need, and many a rebuild has been completed on this basis. Sometimes the swaps involve three or four people but usually all will finish up with the parts they need—often at little or no cost.

With a basket case you have to build up the machine as you get the parts. It is valid to leave out, say, the gearbox internals as their space is defined, but beware of any assumptions with the cycle parts. It is only too easy to think all is well, begin final finishing and have to undo that effort with further fitting work.

This is why a basket case always takes so much longer to complete and tries the worker's patience, as it can be ages before any progress at all seems to be made.

From this first assembly exercise should come a list of missing parts and those needing attention. Once you are satisfied that it is all there and will all go together, you can continue along the same lines as someone fortunate enough to start with a complete machine.

You can now take it all apart again.

Restoration

This is another word for repair and is closely linked to service and maintenance. The philosophy is the same whether you have a 1949 Dominator or a 1977 Commando; the work involved and techniques used are similar or the same for both machines. The problems will vary enormously with no regard to the age of the machine, and only the availability of spares will relate to the years to any degree.

The essence of the job is that the machine is reduced totally to its component parts. That means studs out of castings, spokes from wheels, seat cover from frame and so on, until you are down to a single piece of metal, rubber or plastic for just about any item. Ball races and rectifiers should not be dismantled if you want them to continue working, but most assemblies will break down to individual pieces.

Each piece has to be checked and then mended or replaced. This may be as simple as running a die down a thread or as complex as metal spraying followed by grinding to a very close tolerance. A specialized welding process might be needed plus careful free-hand cutting using a flexible drive followed by a machining operation.

Replacement can be by a new spare or by an uprated part from a later machine which improves the performance. Or it can be by a modern component that does the job in a better way; tyres, shock absorbers and electronic ignition are just three examples.

After repair or replacement comes finishing which may be paint, plating or polish. In all cases the finish mirrors the base material and reflects its preparation. You can then put it all together again.

The 1964 scrambles model Atlas with its special frame and open pipes

ABOVE *The 1967 Atlas still in the Featherbed frame and with that unique Norton line*

BELOW *A hybrid with a Norton engine in an AMC frame as the G15CSR with swept-back pipes*

This Commando for the show late in 1967 is missing some badges but has the 745 cc engine and Isolastic mounting

Dismantle

There is a special technique for taking things apart and if you want to restore successfully you need to learn it. The first step is to soak things in paraffin or penetrating fluid. If anything is stuck this is the opening move—and time. Let the fluid soak in well, give the part another dose and come back days rather than hours later.

Try to move it. If there is any sign of a shift, you are winning; give it another soak, more time and bit by bit it will come. Rush the job and it will snap.

Stubborn, well-rusted nuts and bolts holding cycle parts together call for another method. If they are too far gone for further use, if they hold solid sections and if the parts are none too strong, don't try to undo them. You can easily do real damage to nuts, bolts, the major parts and your fingers, either with spanners or a saw if you resort to that method. You will not be able to hold the fixing still to saw it and inevitably will damage the parts.

The answer is to do them up. Get out a ½ in. drive socket and wind it on until the bolt goes bang. If the bolt is largish, drill a hole up its centre first, but don't try this on bolts fixed to tapped holes—ever.

Timing cases often respond well to an impact driver, but if you go that route two rules apply. First is that the blade must fit the screw and second is to hit it good and hard. A series of taps is no use, it has to be one good blow. One of the very best motorcycle men I

have known told me once that this distinguished the pro from the amateur. The latter would tap at a puller to jump a taper apart and either shift nothing or damage parts. The pro would decide it was tight, select a four-pound club hammer and hit it once, good and square, direction being as important as the force behind the blow.

It always pays to think before playing the heavy hand as often parts won't part because you have not undone all you should have. Particular care is needed when dealing with castings or mouldings; both are brittle and respond in the same way if put under a bending strain. They crack. So if something is stuck, check against the parts list as this may indicate a screw you have missed, either because it is hidden in a dirty counter-bore or due to it assembling from the other side to the rest of the fixings.

Checking

At this point you really start to find out how much work you have let yourself in for. You need to go over each part to establish if it can still be used, if it needs mending and if it needs finishing. More lists, I fear.

Whether a part can still be used will depend on what it is, its material and whether it is bent, cracked, broken or badly worn. If in any or all of these conditions it will need mending or replacement. Bent parts will have to be straightened using heat and a press on occasion, cracked and broken ones may be

35

ABOVE *The 745 cc Interstate on show in January 1972 complete with its disc front brake*

BELOW *John Player Replica Commando with one of its styling forms for the fairing and single seat. To travel fast, travel alone!*

RIGHT *Last of the line and with long legs; a 1977 Interstate Norton in Mk III form with electric start and rear disc*

welded and worn ones reclaimed.

It is while you are checking parts that you will find the bodges that have been done over the years to keep the machine running. Often these are the greatest problem and you are left to think that if only previous owners had just repaired the machine your troubles would be minimal.

Mending

Thus you are left to return parts to their original standard, and it can often take all your ingenuity to deal with past horrors. Some of the worst concern studs and threaded holes, the first often broken off in the second. Removal means making a drill bush, drilling into the stud and using an extractor to wind it out.

One thing with cover screws is that, if all else fails, you can drill the head off to release the cover which will expose enough screw for it to be removed easily.

Threaded holes in castings or the frame are another source of problems, and thread inserts may be the solution. Normally there is enough material available to accommodate them, but for success the maker's instructions must be followed carefully.

Mending also includes getting joint faces flat. For this all the studs will need to be removed and it is worth checking round each stud hole. Often the metal will have pulled up a little so needs to be countersunk and then the whole surface made flat. Keep any machining to a minimum as modern gasket sealants can help a good deal in keeping oil where it should be.

Welding or heating equipment is often vital when dealing with cycle parts which need to be warmed up before being straightened. It also allows holes to be filled and redrilled where necessary, so is very handy for some rear mudguards. It is not unknown for

several sets of holes to exist for various pillion pads fitted in the past but all long gone, and these holes will need removal as well.

Parts may be taken individually to a shop for welding, but the need for a heat source in your own workshop may be emphasized if some assembly is out of line. Getting everything straight can call for the parts to be in place, which makes it difficult for the job to be taken elsewhere other than to a restoration specialist.

Finishing

Once you are satisfied that a part is correct and will assemble as required, it needs to be finished. This may be as simple as a coating of oil to prevent rust on engine and gearbox parts. Or it can be a complex sequence of plating, painting and lining on a tank.

Castings may be bead-blasted or polished, cycle parts are mainly painted, while details are plated. In many cases parts will need to be masked to protect threads and holes.

The specialized electrical assemblies, and others of the same delicacy, go through their own special processes as detailed later, but their basic mechanics may need the same mending and finishing as everything else.

Then all you have to do is put it all together again.

Note

From now on, I will assume you are either starting from a complete machine or have loosely hung your basket together and have collected most of the major parts needed. This is to avoid needless repetition of the assumption together with the notes relevant to it and already mentioned.

The Norton 76 built by the workforce and here on show with its cast wheels

3 The engine

Most people like to begin with the engine because it is of the greatest interest to them. It is also likely to be the easiest assembly to restore and the least boring.

The exact procedure you follow will depend on which model you have and on your working style. The first job is to take the engine, or engine unit, out of the frame and then dismantle it. Before removing it a decision needs to be made about the large, tight nuts that are used in various places.

The purist approach to large nuts is to use a suitable tool to hold the part they are attached to and undo them. However, this can be a problem because of the number of special tools that may be needed and it may govern the sequence of operations.

At this stage all that is needed is for the nuts to be loosened, and common practice is to do this with the engine in the frame and connected to the rear wheel and brake. With the machine in top gear, each nut is attacked in turn, starting at the engine and working through the transmission to the rear wheel. A combination of jammed-on brake and clouted spanner will usually prevail, unless the clutch slips.

This method means that the timing cover has to come off at what is really too early a stage in order that the pinion and cam gear nuts can be slackened. The alternatives are less messy in their approach and enable parts to be dealt with as desired. The first is to use special tools to hold parts still, and a further option, given the equipment, is to use an impact spanner. If you go the latter route do ensure that all the parts will take the shock.

Engine types

Norton twin engines divide into two basic groups, as already indicated, and are big with separate gearbox, or small featuring unit construction.

Big twins began with the 497 cc Dominator which was quickly joined by the same-sized Featherbed. The latter then grew to 596 cc in 1956 and 646 cc in 1961, while the former ran on to 1963. In 1961 the SS versions began to appear and while all the 596 cc engines went at the end of 1962, the 497 cc SS unit ran on to 1966.

The 646 cc engines were down to just the SS type by 1964 but had been joined by the 745 cc engine two years earlier. The 646 cc version remained in use up to 1970 but the 745 cc engine went into a variety of AMC hybrids and then into the Commando. There it was used up to 1973. From it came the 829 cc unit in the same year and this continued in use until 1977. It also formed the basis of a few special 749 cc short-stroke engines.

The small twins started with the 249 cc engine in 1959, which was joined by the 349 cc unit in 1961 and the 383 cc electric-start version in 1963. The two larger engines went at the end of 1965, and the 249 cc unit in the following year. All three were of unit construction.

The two types of engine had little in common, but essentially each remained unchanged for all years and versions. Big-twin changes were mainly to fit an alternator, coil ignition, alloy cylinder heads and to incorporate improvements in the detail parts. Small-twin changes were mainly to the gearbox, with a new design appearing after 1963.

Removing the engine

The exact procedure depends on the engine type, the model it is installed in and your lifting strength. The unit-construction small twins are not light, and some of the big twins are designed to come out in one lump with gearbox and engine plates. This makes them a job for two or three people, or, better still, two with some form of lifting tackle.

The solution for most people is to take off some of the heavier items while the engine is still in the frame, not that it is all that easy to remove the head of a big twin. However, with the top half, primary transmission, timing gear, electrics and gearbox internals removed, the rest becomes much easier to manage. You will have to reverse the procedure on assembly, which may not be as tidy as building it up on the bench, but at least it is an answer to the problem.

In all cases start by draining the oil tank, primary chaincase, gearbox and engine sump, remembering to replace the plugs to stop any remaining oil dripping on you and the floor. You should have already detached the control cables and wiring but if you left

ABOVE *Well-known Norton dealer Taylor Matterson's service centre in 1970 with Commando S and an interesting dohc single on the work benches*

BELOW *The first year of pivoted-fork frame for the model 7 was 1953 and this example shows the pear-shaped silencers of that time*

them for any reason, now is the time to do the job. The dynamo, where fitted, can be removed readily but the other electrics can stay, unless you plan to part-dismantle before engine removal.

Detach the main oil pipes between engine and oil tank plus the small one that feeds the rocker gear. Take care when undoing the banjo bolts that hold this in case they stick to the pipe union and try to carry it round, which will put a nasty kink in the pipe. You must hold the union to prevent this. Store the pipe with care so it does not become distorted.

Next deal with the primary transmission and, having removed the outer chaincase, undo the engine sprocket nut using a well-fitting socket spanner and jarring it undone. The clutch on all, except the Commando series, is similar and you undo the spring nuts to remove the plates. The Commando insists that you use the correct special tool to compress its diaphragm spring, which has to be done to allow the parts to be dismantled. You *must* use this tool as the spring is under a great deal of tension and could inflict serious injury if suddenly released.

With the plate out you have to undo the clutch centre nut, and to hold the centre while you do this you either rely on the rear brake or a locking device. This can be an old clutch plate with a handle attached, one plate of each type bolted together to lock the centre to the drum or a scotch made from bent steel strip. The last is not recommended as it puts all the load in one place. The centre is splined to the gearbox mainshaft and may slide off or may need to be pulled off with an extractor. If it does, take care to apply the load evenly so as not to bend or crack anything.

The same applies to the alternator, while all engine sprockets are on a taper and a puller must be used. Tricks with levers or chisels usually result in a damaged or broken crankcase. With these items detached the inner chaincase can be removed. As this comes off, check and note carefully the spacers behind it for if these are not as they should be you can easily distort or crack the case on assembly. You may well have to return to this point on final assembly in case things have altered because of other work you have carried out on the parts. This is an important point on all models.

Now move on to the top half of the engine if you intend removing it at this stage. Follow this by the timing side and gearbox internals as covered in more detail in their own sections.

This brings you to the stage of the big heave, and the exact sequence depends on the model, assistance available and method chosen to support the engine. The general principle is to remove the engine torque stays, slacken all the fixings, slide out the minor ones and then support the engine's weight on a box or a jack, or with a sling. Pull each remaining bolt in turn, removing all distance pieces and noting where they came from. A diagram with their lengths will help. Then remove the bolts fully and lift out the engine.

Big-twin dismantling

This may have begun in the frame but the essential tasks are the same whether there or on the bench. First, hold the engine in the vice by its front mountings and add a support at the rear if this is needed. Make quite certain the unit is held firmly. You can now take it apart but don't rush and be sure to observe as you go. It is well worth checking the valve timing before you remove anything, in case the markings are missing or the assembly wrong. Use a degree disc clamped to the drive side of the crankshaft, set the valve gaps as prescribed and make your notes. While you are at it and have the degree disc in place, also check the ignition timing at full advance and retard on both barrels.

The engine will come apart easily enough and on anything unknown the golden rule is to check everything, assume nothing, suspect the worst and take it all apart. It may seem less trouble to leave a crankshaft in one, but only a full examination will show if it is really fit or about to fail because the sludge trap is full.

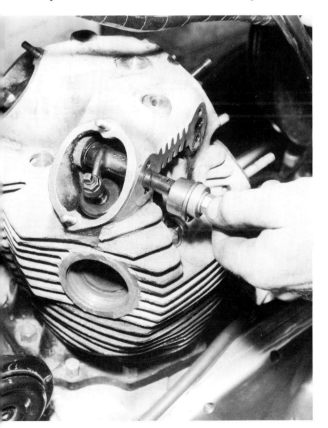

Removing a rocker spindle with an extractor tool. They are tight and need to be aligned on assembly

Start at the top by removing the inlet manifold or twin tracts plus the rocker covers. Next tackle the head nuts and bolts, leaving the centre one till last. Turn the engine to minimize the effect of at least one or two valves being open and then remove the final bolt. If the head joint does not part of its own accord, don't lever at the fins but use a piece of wood to jar up against the roof of each exhaust port in turn.

As most Norton owners know, removing the head while the engine is in the frame is tricky as the pushrods have to be worked out first. With the head off, note which way up the gasket is. Leave the head assembled for the time being as this keeps the various small parts in one place and prevents their loss.

The timing cover can be next but before removing it slacken the large, oil-system plugs or nuts. Use an impact driver, if necessary, to undo the cover screws and remember that there is likely to be some oil left inside, so position a tray to catch it. On most Commando engines you have to remove the auto-advance unit and points assembly first, and it has been suggested that you should not use the factory extractor screw as it has been known to swell the spindle tube so the advance mechanism either jams or becomes sluggish in operation. Simply loosen the fixing screw a couple of turns and tap down smartly on it with the handle of a screwdriver.

Now undo the cylinder-block nuts, set the pistons near top dead centre and lift. The joint has to be broken and the block raised a trifle to allow some of the nuts to be removed from their studs, so make sure that all nine are at least loose before any start pressing on the bottom fins. With the block raised a little, pack rag in the gap to catch debris and protect both rods and pistons. Lift off the block and base gasket.

Remove the circlips and put them in a bag labelled 'used'. Don't use them again but keep them in case you need a pattern when looking for new ones. The pistons are handed but this should not stop you marking them L and R on the inside front as this is a good habit. It is best to either use an extractor to remove the gudgeon pins or to warm the pistons so they will slide out. Drifting is another method but requires two people as the pistons must be supported during the operation.

Now you can lock the crankshaft by one of two methods. The first is by inserting a good clean bar through the small ends with supports placed across

LEFT *The Norton twin engine as in the 1955 model 88 when still fitted with a dynamo and the Norton laid-down gearbox*

RIGHT *The model 7 in 1953 in its first year of the pivoted-fork frame but otherwise little changed from its introduction*

the crankcase mouth after it has been wiped clean. The second is by placing a bar in the deepest balance hole in the flywheel rim with a pad between it and the crankcase.

The camshaft nut is the next obstacle and is only a problem because locking the crankshaft to allow it to be freed also places quite a load on the intermediate gear, which now lacks its outer support bearing. An old cover, cut away to reveal the nut and drive chain or chains, is the best answer, but in its absence steady pressure should give the desired result.

Remove the oil pump and then its drive worm, which has a left-hand thread. For this a flat ring spanner is better than a socket as it is less likely to tilt off the nut. At this stage check the pinions and sprockets for timing marks, making careful notes as to how they sit and the relevant crankshaft position. Undo the magneto sprocket assembly if fitted. If a manual magneto is in use you will need an extractor, while the distributor sprocket is held by a cross-pin you have to drive out.

Remove the camshaft chain tensioner followed by the camshaft sprocket, complete with dynamo drive gear assembly where used, which can be levered off its

key and shaft. This will allow the whole assembly to be removed. Watch carefully for any thrust washers and spacers, noting their positions.

This leaves the crankshaft pinion, for which it is best to use the correct puller. It may be possible to lever the pinion off, although this is likely to damage the oil sealing disc behind it along with the backing disc. Remember that the pinion key will not pass through these items so the pinion must come off first. Any attempt to force the shaft through prior to this will cause expensive damage. The right puller usually works out cheaper, as well as easier, in the long run.

You are now ready to split the cases, so remove all the studs and screws. The drive side will now pull away or may be driven gently using a wooden drift against the top inside wall of the case. It will release the breather parts from the end of the camshaft; don't forget to check for any shims that may be present. The timing side may need gentle levering to remove it from the crankshaft. If the main bearing stays on the shaft it can pay to warm the case so the bearing drops out easily. The outer race of a roller will need this removal technique anyway.

Now all the major parts are ready for attention.

Small-twin dismantling

This engine is very different from the big twins for it has a one-piece crankshaft and two gear-driven camshafts. Also the cylinder heads are separate and, on the Jubilee, so are the barrels. The oil pump alone followed Norton tradition. Unit construction was employed but the gearbox cluster could be removed as a unit once the clutch was off the mainshaft.

The engine has a sump plate which is best left in place for a while as you are bound to stand the unit on it at some time.

As with the big twins, a good deal of dismantling can take place in the frame, which reduces the weight you have to lift out. Again, start by draining the oil, then remove the points, the advance unit, the timing cover and the primary chaincase on the other side. The intermediate gear will not slide off its spindle until the oil pump worm is removed. Slacken the engine nut, dismantle the clutch, undo its centre nut, remove it and then go on to the chaincase inner, followed by the gearbox assembly.

On the engine, start at the top with the carburettor, manifold, stays, oil feed pipe and rocker covers. Six nuts on through-studs hold each head in place; the heads are best kept as complete assemblies until you

ABOVE *The timing chains as in a 1956 model 99. Still much the same in 1977 other than for the dynamo gear and still in need of a support for the middle gear shaft before any tensions can be truly checked*

ABOVE RIGHT *Another view of the timing chains with the magneto being moved to set its chain tension. Note the oil-pump drive as used for many years*

get to them. The pushrods lie within the cylinder head and should be held there as it is lifted. Before removing the cylinder, wind a rubber band round the top of each tappet to stop it falling into the crankcase.

The pistons of these models are the same so must be marked L and R on the inside front. They have to be warmed up before the gudgeon pins can be pushed out.

In the timing chest undo the camshaft gear nuts and the oil pump worm, which has a left-hand thread, then check the timing marks. The camshaft gears and crankshaft pinion are drilled and tapped for a bar extractor and require the correct pullers. Levers are not recommended.

The crankcase halves can be separated now, but first the sump must be removed. Most of the case fixings are external but don't overlook the two screws

in the crankcase mouth and two sunken screws in the timing chest, which need a very long Allen key. With the screws removed the drive-side half should come off. A special drift is needed to release the crankshaft, plus any shims that have been fitted, from the timing-side half. Basically this is a tube of $1\frac{1}{8}$ in. outside diameter, $\frac{53}{64}$ in. bore and $2\frac{7}{16}$ in. length with an internal radius at one end. Do not use a hammer or mallet on the end of the crankshaft as this will damage the oil-feed seal and ruin the shaft. Once more, the parts await your attention.

Crankshaft

Two basic types of crankshaft were used in Norton twin engines and both have the crankpins at 360 degrees. All big twins had a built-up assembly comprising two halves clamped to each side of a central flywheel by six fastenings and aligned by a single dowel. All small twins had a one-piece crankshaft incorporating a thin central flywheel. Both engine types had replaceable shell big-end bearings.

The first job is to remove the connecting rods, and in all cases it is essential to mark each part so you know where it came from. The same goes for the big-twin crankshaft which can be dismantled. Up to 1972 all these engines had the crankshafts clamped by four bolts and a pair of studs, but for 1973 this changed to six studs.

The bolts are always fitted from the left so their heads go on the drive side. It therefore pays to remove the stud nuts from the timing side along with the bolt nuts. Note where each one comes from as there are variations. This will release the timing-side halfshaft, after which the drive side and the flywheel can be parted. The latter should be marked and replaced the same way round; Birmingham wheels have a mark stamped in the timing-side rim to aid this.

The crankpins must be inspected for wear and damage. It is feasible to remove light scores, marks and even surface rust with fine emery-cloth, but if they are worn they will need regrinding. A micrometer or vernier is essential for checking the crankpins, but some idea of the degree of ovality can be gained using calipers and feelers to detect variations.

If grinding is needed, the reduction in diameter must be in 0.01 in. steps from the nominal to a maximum of 0.04 in. in some engines but less in others. In all cases the finish and the end radii dimension are very important and have a bearing on big-end life and crankshaft reliability.

The mainshafts also need to be inspected as they must be a good fit in the main bearings and timing-cover oil seal. Their threads need to be in good condition, and if there is any sign of trouble its cause must be located and remedied.

On all crankshafts you must clean out the sludge trap thoroughly, removing plugs and oilway screws as needed to do this. Do not try to remove the plug in the timing-side crank of the big twin as it won't come out; the part can be cleaned from the inside. It is essential to check that oilways are completely free from blockage from entry to exit, including the small crankpin holes.

The crankpins may be reclaimed by metal spraying if there is no other solution. In this process minute metal particles are heated and sprayed on to the hot surface of the parent part, fusing to it. When cool the part can be ground back to its standard size. The process requires special equipment and a degree of skill to achieve the right result but it can save parts which often seem beyond repair.

Before assembling the crankshaft check that everything is scrupulously clean, including nuts, bolts and tools. Make sure you have everything laid out for assembly in the right order and then proceed with the job. Just nip down nuts at first and then go

back to them one by one, gradually tightening them to a torque figure of 25 to 30 lb ft. Pessimists can also use Loctite and centre pop the threads to make sure. Turn up the lock plates and fit the oilway plugs, which can be sealed using jointing compound and locked by centre punching.

Once assembled, all crankshafts should be primed with oil to make sure there is no obstruction to its flow to the crankpins.

Crankshaft types

These were all much the same, and the careful restorer should inspect any unknown assembly fully to make sure it is of the correct type for the engine. There were four basic strokes made: 72.6 mm for the 500, 82 mm for the 600, 89 mm for the 650, 750 and 850, and the rare 80.4 mm used in the special, late-type, short-

BELOW RIGHT *The 1966 650SS with twin carbs at a steep angle and rather prone to flooding when cold*

BELOW *The sidecar model 77 with single downtube, its own oil tank and plain footrest rubbers as in 1957*

stroke 750 Commando. Thus the stroke is the first thing to check with a basket case.

For the 500 engine there were just two types of timing-side halfshaft, the original changing for 1961. The drive side changed twice as it had to be revised to take the alternator rotor for 1958 and was changed again for 1961. The 600 engine had the same 1.5 in. diameter crankpins and remained unchanged on the timing side but had the rotor altered on the drive for 1958.

The 650 crankshaft was unchanged and later served in the 750. The timing side remained the same part through to 1973 but the drive side was modified to suit the Commando primary drive for 1968 onwards. In all cases the big-end diameter was 1.75 in., as it was in the 850 engine for which only the crankshaft assembly was listed.

The flywheels followed a similar pattern, the 500 wheel changing for 1961 and the 600 version remaining unchanged. The 650 had its own wider flywheel and the 750 another, which did not go on into the Commando. This had a new part from 1968 to 1973 and just the assembly was listed for the 850.

The fixings varied to a degree over the years although only in detail. All pre-Commando engines had four bolts, two studs, eight nuts, two lock plates and a dowel. This last item ran through the flywheel and into each crank cheek. The studs went either side of the dowel, so their lock plates prevented it from escaping, and they were positioned nearest to the shaft centre line.

The dowel was common from 1949 onwards, as were the two studs and their lock plates. The four original bolts were reduced to two for 1957 and joined by two more of the same length, but a closer fit. These went next to the flywheel rim for better shaft alignment. The same arrangement went into the 650 for 1961, and in that engine the two nuts nearest the flywheel rim were extended in length, but not thread. This was to allow a spanner easy access to the hexagons despite the proximity of the crankpin flange. The other six nuts remained as they were, as did the arrangements for the smaller engines.

The first Commando went back to the four original bolts but kept the two special nuts from the 650 along with the original six. For 1973 the design was modified to use six studs for both the 750 and the new 850 engine, so a total of 12 nuts was needed. These came as two types in groups of eight and four. The original locking plates remained in use. Finally, the details were altered again for 1975 when the dowel was lengthened and threaded on each end for a nut and

The Dunstall Dominator with many special parts both on the outside and in the engine

washer. At the same time the studs were amended so that a common nut fitted them all including the dowel. While two studs were fitted items, the other four were not.

From 1958 on, a plug was listed for the crankshaft and screwed into the top of the timing-side cheek to blank off the end of the oilway. The part was changed for 1975 but the original item was still to be found on the small twins.

For these there was one crankshaft for the 250 and another for the 350 and 400. The former was in cast iron with a 44 mm stroke and the latter in steel with a 56 mm stroke. Each had two sludge-trap plugs but these varied from model to model. The 250 used two of one type, the 350 two of another, up to 1963, and the 400 one of these plus yet another variant. From 1964, only one plug was listed for the 350. All models had the oilway plug which was the same as the one in the big twins. The Electra crank can be identified by the two slots, cut across the end of the drive-side shaft, to take the starter dog.

Connecting rods

All Norton twins were fitted with forged, light-alloy rods having separate caps and shell big-end bearings. They must be handled with care at all times and never allowed to knock against other parts. This includes the crankcase mouth when working on the engine. All rods should be inspected carefully for any signs of damage which should be polished out. The rods may also be checked for alignment if there is any reason to suspect that they are not true. If there is any doubt about a rod it should not be used. In general, Norton rods are robust, but if one snaps it will wreck an engine, so using a suspect rod is not worth the risk.

Repair is usually only a matter of renewing the small-end bush, where fitted, replacing the big-end shells to suit the crankshaft grind and attending to the nuts and bolts. These last are best renewed in all cases although it is acceptable to reuse the bolts from standard, low-output engines. If you do this, inspect them carefully for any signs of stretching or thread distortion. In all cases fit new nuts which should be tightened evenly, and in steps, to the specified torque figure: 15 lb ft for the small twins and 500 and 600 cc engines, and 25 lb ft for the larger ones.

Each bolt is prevented from turning in its hole by means of an eccentric head and matching recess in the rod. It is all too easy to allow the sharp edge under the head to scrape a shaving of alloy from the rod as it pulls down and for this to lodge under the head. If the shaving packs down in use the bolt becomes slack. The remedies are to remove the sharp edges with a small file and to check every bolt recess in case there is already a shaving hidden there.

Rod types

The original rod was used in all the 500 and 600 cc engines and was the only one fitted with a small-end bush. The first 650 cc rod was altered to increase its strength for 1965 and again in 1966 when it gained an oil hole running from the top bearing shell to the outer flank. This was to improve piston lubrication, and the hole must point away from the engine centre. The same rod was also used in both 750 and 850 engines. It was modified for 1975 along with its cap bolts and their nuts, which had been unchanged from 1961. Originally, the rods for the 500 and 600 cc engines had

A 99SS in 1961 with siamezed pipes and splayed carbs without downdraught

a split pin to lock each nut but this went from 1957 when self-locking nuts were fitted.

At the same time the bolts lost their pin holes but otherwise continued as they were, along with the 1949 washers, up to the end of the 500 cc engine in 1966. The big-end shells were made to suit the crankpin diameter, so that one pair went into the 500 and 600 engines at 1.5 in. and another served the 650 cc and larger engines. For 1966 the original 650 type was fitted in the cap only while the top shell had an oil hole added. This arrangement continued up to and included 1972. From 1973 a pair of shells was used and in all these engines they were to suit a 1.75 in. diameter pin.

The addition of the bleed hole places more demands on the lubrication system, so the double-speed pump drive is necessary. Also the extra oil reaching the cylinder bores can be too much for the oil-control piston rings, which need to be the later type. An answer for some owners is to fit the drilled shell in the cap and avoid the entire arrangement.

The small twins had one rod for the 250 and another that served both 350 and 400 units. In both, the gudgeon pins ran direct in the rod, and the bearing shells, cap bolts, nuts and washers all came from the 500. They were common to all models and all years.

Small-end bush

There was just the one bush, used in the 500 and 600 cc engines. If worn it can be pressed out using a new bush, but line up the oil hole first. Ream the bush to give a nice sliding fit on the pin. Avoid reaming by hand, if possible, as a guided machine reamer will do a much better job. Check the oil holes again before use.

Pistons

Before checking the condition of the pistons, see if the block needs boring, as if it does, you will have to fit new ones. If you plan to keep the existing pistons they do need to be inspected closely. They must be examined for cracks in the skirt or around the gudgeon-pin bosses, while the ring grooves must be in good condition as must be the pin holes and circlip grooves.

A number of pistons were available for each engine size, some used as standard and others listed as options. This means that if there is any doubt, the pistons and compression ratio should be checked. The latter is done by measuring the combustion chamber volume and making a simple calculation. Also compare the valve head diameters with the cut-outs in the piston crown to see if they are compatible, as this provides further evidence to aid in identifying the piston type.

If you replace the pistons use a quality brand and keep to the standard compression ratio for your model. Any attempt to raise this could bring a major disaster in its train as the middle-aged or old engine objects to the added loads. Should you find yourself with a sports engine fitted with the old cast-iron head, use pistons with a compression ratio to match the head or the engine will overheat.

If you keep the existing pistons expect to renew the rings, in which case you may need to deglaze the bores with a special tool or medium-to-coarse emery-cloth. Check the gaps of the new rings and be sure to fit the taper rings the right way up or you will have a plug oiling problem.

Two types of gudgeon pin served the 500 and 600

49

ABOVE *Dunstall version of the 745 cc Commando of 1969 with balance pipe which the factory left off until the 829*

BELOW *The 1963–65 Electra with forks and wheels from the larger models*

engines, the change occurring with the 1959 models. The 650 had its own pin, as did the 750 which was modified in 1966 and 1968. The 850 also had its own pin, as did each size of the small twins.

Circlips for the 500 and 600 were altered in 1957, 1959 and 1960, the last two types also being used for all the small twins of the same years. The 650 had its own clips which went, in turn, into the 750 and 850, with a final change in 1975.

The gudgeon pins should be checked for ridges and be changed if not in really good condition. Change the circlips as a matter of course. If of the Seeger type, they should be fitted so the sharper outer edge is away from the pin as this gives the best support against end thrust. Circlip pliers must always be used for dismantling or assembly.

Cylinder block

The block, or blocks in the case of the 250 twin, needs to be checked for damage and wear. Damage may be found on the fins, the top or bottom mating surfaces or the threads. Wear occurs in the bore. The block may need to be finished to restore its appearance; all are made in cast iron.

Damaged or broken fins may be repaired by welding or brazing but it is a tricky job. If a middle fin has gone you may have to cut others away to gain access and refix them once the broken one is repaired. Be careful about heating the block and let it cool slowly. Do all this work before any reboring or machining that may be needed.

Check the gasket surfaces for burrs and distortion.

At the base these may only cause an oil leak but at the top could lead to a blown gasket, which could mean burn damage to both head and barrel. If the fault is extensive, machining may be necessary to remove it but this must be kept to a minimum. However, it must be done or the trouble will recur. If high-compression pistons are fitted it is prudent to check the piston-to-valve clearance when you assemble the engine.

All the big-twin blocks have tapped holes in the top surface, and these need inspecting to ensure that the threads are in good condition and not pulling up around the holes. If the surface is in poor condition it must be machined flat, the holes lightly countersunk and the threads cleaned up.

Bore wear is best checked with a Mercer gauge, which will provide exact measurements. Some idea of bore wear can be gained by feeling the wear ridge at the top of the bore, but careful judgement and an oily finger are needed. If you don't possess a Mercer or an internal micrometer there are alternative methods available. One is to use an internal bore gauge, which can be set to the unworn diameter at the bottom of the bore and used with feelers to find the wear at the top. Internal calipers can do the same job but a more delicate touch is needed to get accurate results without measuring caliper spring. More homespun techniques are to use the piston and measure the skirt clearance at several points, or a piston ring and check its gap in the same way.

If the bore is worn it will have to be rebored, but before this is done two other points need attention. First you must establish whether it is standard or oversize at the moment. This will indicate the size it must be taken out to. Second you *must* get the new pistons before having the bores machined in case there is a supply problem.

All the big-twin blocks, except the 850, can be taken out to plus 0.04 in. and the small twins to plus 0.06 in. The 850 is listed with only two oversizes and thus can go to plus 0.02 in. There have also been plus 0.06 in. pistons available for the 500, 600 and 650 engines, so this is a possibility as well.

All big-twin blocks have an oil drain hole behind the right cylinder. This must be checked for obstruction and cleaned out if necessary.

Finishing

When the block is mechanically fit for use it needs to be finished. This process will have begun with the cleaning it received before work started and now it should be completed. The block will need to be masked and bead- or sand-blasted for an even matt finish and to remove all the dirt from the crevices between the fins.

It then needs to be painted either black or silver, and stove enamelling is to be preferred for the tough finish required. An alternative is a modern air-drying paint, but it is difficult to get between the fins with a

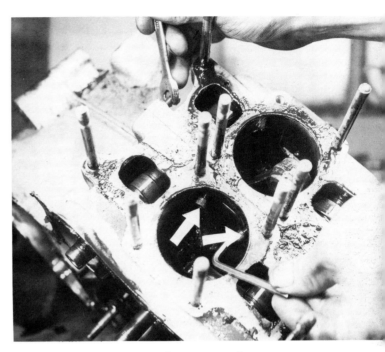

These internal screws of the small twins are easily overlooked, but must be removed along with two more in the timing chest

brush. A trick that sometimes will work is to use a piece of felt, stiffened with wire, but for best results a spray gun is needed.

Let the paint dry fully and then remove the masking, checking carefully for blasting grit in all holes. If you have masked the piece properly there won't be any, but it is as well to make certain.

Block types

The first check in determining which block you have is the bore size. Standard figures were 66 mm for the 500, 68 mm for the 600 and the 650, 73 mm for the 750, and 77 mm for the 850. The small twins were 60 mm for the 250, which had separate barrels anyway, 63 mm for the 350 and 66 mm for the 400. If you find anything larger on a big twin, it has been fitted with a big-bore kit and is special.

The 500 block has eight fins whereas the 600 and 650 have nine each, as do the Atlas and all the Commando models. In addition, the 850 block has flat sides at the base of the fins without the recessed style of all the others, thanks to its extra through-bolts.

The 500 block was modified a little for 1959, as was the 600, and it was changed again for 1960 when it gained some fin area. The same blocks were used for the SS models and this arrangement continued for these machines until they were dropped. The 650 and 750 blocks were revised for 1966 from engine 114870 when they lost their top spigots, relying on the gasket alone to contain the hot gases.

A Dunstall Dominator 650 in 1965—very much in the café racer style

The 750 Commando block was launched in silver paint, changed to black for the early production and became silver again in March 1969. For 1971 it was strengthened and for 1972 changed to a black finish for the Combat engines. The silver was retained for the standard engines and was continued on the 1973 engines, which kept the same block.

The 850 block was only changed once for 1974, but a compression plate to go under it became available as an option in 1975.

In the small twins the 250 had one pair of barrels for all years, but the 350 block was modified for 1964. This entailed the removal of the barrel spigots and corresponding head recesses plus a change of compression ratio. The 400 block was different again but was the same length as the later 350 type.

Tappet guides

These are only to be found in the small twins as the tappets run directly in the block in the big twins. An idea of their condition can be found by rocking the tappet and measuring that for wear. The guides

themselves seldom wear, which is fortunate as they are not to be had, and it is the tappets which become worn. As the guides are cast iron treat them with respect and check that they are positioned correctly with the oil drain slots across the engine. Just one type was used for all models and years of the small twin.

Block fixings

These were cycle thread up to 1971 and Unified from then on. All big twins have nine fixings and all, except the 850, have just studs. The 850 has four long bolts, which fit from the top of the block into the crankcase, and only five studs. That engine apart, there are always seven $\frac{3}{8}$ in. studs and two $\frac{5}{16}$ in. ones.

On the first engines there are just the nine studs and nine nuts to suit. From 1957 the centre front stud differed from the other six $\frac{3}{8}$ in. versions, and the $\frac{5}{16}$ in. studs gained a washer each. This arrangement continued on all pre-Commando engines. The first Commando unit used the two 1949-type $\frac{5}{16}$ in. studs and nuts together with the washers. The centre front stud continued in its 1957 form and was joined by six

ABOVE *Mk III Commando with right brake pedal and doubtful electric starter*

RIGHT *Top of an 829 cc barrel showing the four holes for long bolts which clamped it to the crankcase*

new ones, still of $\frac{3}{8}$ in. diameter. These had six new nuts with just one 1949 type remaining. The new nuts had washers under them for the first time.

For 1972 the studs and nuts changed to a Unified fine thread and only the washers stayed as they were. For the 850 in 1973 one of the six $\frac{3}{8}$ in. studs was used along with its nut and washer, but the other four were new, as were their nuts and washers. For 1975 the odd washer became common with the four used under the bolt heads.

The small twins have through-studs so there are no block fixings as such.

Lifting the head of a 745 cc Commando while holding the pushrods up to release them from the barrel tunnels

Cylinder head

You may find this a victim of misguided enthusiasm with valve seats cut back due to years of keen, but unnecessary, valve grinding. Each owner may have done this 'to put the sparkle back' with the result that the valve heads are now well masked. The only answer is an insert—a job for a specialist.

The first task with the head is to remove the valves and rockers and to clean it thoroughly. If of iron, the head can be cleaned using a caustic soda solution, but *never* use this for aluminium parts. These should be treated with a hot household detergent. After cleaning, both types of head must be washed well with hot water, dried off and the iron or steel parts oiled or greased to prevent rust.

Inspect the valve guides. If they are worn or cracked they must be replaced, and this is best done with the head heated evenly. Unless the valve seat has been damaged, the fitting of new guides is normally the only occasion when the seats need cutting. Even then a *light* cut only is needed, followed by a minimum of valve grinding, using the valves you intend to fit.

Check the plug thread and fit an insert if it is in poor condition. Check all the other holes and fit inserts if required. Inspect the head joint area for any signs of gas leakage and deal with this. Examine the exhaust port threads of the big twins as these are susceptible to damage if the pipe nuts have not been kept tight. Certain engines do have locking washers but in some cases the gasket compresses so the nuts loosen, although the tabs on the washers prevent them coming undone. In this state it can rattle enough to knock out the port threads, and then reclamation is the only cure. This can be done by sleeving or with a thread insert, which will make it better than new. The only repair considered by the works was a Helicoil insert. Keeping the nuts tight will prevent any recurrence.

Check the oil drain hole in the inlet valve well, removing any obstruction found. Also make sure there is no flash in the pushrod tunnel that could touch the rods. This has been known to occur on Mk III Commando heads and needs to be filed away.

Once the features of the head have been repaired it can be left in a natural finish or painted to match the block.

Cylinder-head types

The very earliest Dominator heads were made with an inlet manifold as part of the iron casting, but within a few weeks this changed to a separate manifold feeding the two inlet ports. The next change came for 1955 when the casting material became aluminium. The same head also went on the 600 for the following year. For 1957 the front edges of the fins between the exhaust ports were amended to run straight rather than to be concave.

In 1959 a second head appeared as an option. This had larger inlet valves and provision for twin, splayed-out carburettors. For 1960 both capacities of twin had a head with increased fin area, while the bigger inlet valve was fitted as standard. These heads increased the standard compression by about one ratio. The horizontal centres of the inlet manifold studs of both 1959 and 1960 heads were the same, but the vertical ones changed. They were 1.5 in. up to 1959 and 1.625 in. from 1960 onwards, so there are two single-carburettor manifolds and two more of the splayed type for twin carbs.

The first 650 came in 1961, and this had downdraught, parallel inlet tracts. The same year saw the first SS models in 500 and 600 sizes, and these had twin-carburettor heads but without downdraught ports in the first year. This was corrected in 1962 on

ABOVE *Measuring chain tension but note that the intermediate spindle is not supported so the reading could be in error*

RIGHT *The Dunstall kit as shown at Earls Court at the Commando launch late in 1967*

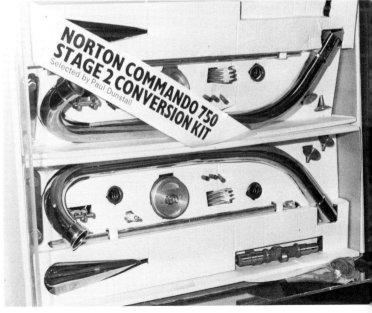

the 88SS, which featured the 650 head, but the few remaining 600 models to be built ran on with the older type. The 500 models also continued in this manner until withdrawn, while the advent of the 750 Atlas brought a new head. Both this and the 650 version were altered for 1966 when the block spigot and the resultant head recess were deleted.

A revised version of the 750 head went on to the Commando engines and was marked RH1. It was joined in 1972 by the Combat type, which took 32 mm carburettors in place of the usual 30 mm size. The original continued for 1973 when it was joined by two others after the problems of the Combat engine had been ironed out. The low-compression head was marked RH5 and the high-compression version RH6. The 850 had its own head, which was revised in the parts list for 1974 and again for 1975.

For the small twins there was one pair of heads for the 250 and another, without spigot recess, for the 400. On the 350 the original heads were modified for 1964 when the spigot recess went. At the same time the spindle clamp pin became larger and more robust. This larger pin is well worth fitting to earlier models as the first type is prone to distortion. This reduces its clamping effect and, in turn, increases the valve gaps.

Cylinder-head fixings

All big twins have the same arrangement of head fixings with one central $\frac{3}{8}$ in. bolt, four longer $\frac{3}{8}$ in. bolts either side of the sparking-plug holes and five studs with nuts. Two $\frac{5}{16}$ in. studs are screwed into the front of the block, so their nuts sit on top of the head, and three $\frac{3}{8}$ in. studs are screwed into the underside of the head. These have their nuts set in between the block fins, one at the rear under the inlet ports and the others at the front under the exhaust, the latter being long sleeve nuts.

Although this layout was never altered, the details did vary a little over the years. Parts that stayed the same from start to finish were the $\frac{5}{16}$ in. studs and nuts, although each is listed under three separate part numbers. Engines built after the move to Plumstead have washers under the nuts; Bracebridge Street versions do not.

The four main bolts were the same for engines up to the 650 but the Atlas had its own, as did the Commando engines. The short centre bolt went on all engines, with a change for 1966 onwards. All five had washers at first but not the centre bolt on the early 650 or 750, the latter having its own special washer. From 1966 all five bolts had the washers which had been introduced with the 1964 models, and this type continued on the Commando.

The $\frac{3}{8}$ in. studs were modified for 1955, when the alloy head was adopted, and were joined by three others for the Atlas. This type continued on the Commando. The long sleeve nuts at the front followed the same pattern, with a new part for the Atlas which continued on to the Commando—it was altered for 1973. The remaining nut was altered once in 1961. Again, a new part went on to the first 750 and continued on for the Commando. This nut is the same spanner size as those used for the block but retained a

cycle thread when the others changed to Unified for 1972. The latter are marked with a series of rings on one flat. As the tpi figures are 26 and 24 it is very easy to mix these and ruin both nuts and studs, so take care.

The small twins had a much simpler means of holding the head down: 12 studs, each with a nut and washer, the latter common to all years and models. The studs of the early 250 were $3\frac{7}{8}$ in. long, while those of the 350 and 400 were $4\frac{3}{16}$ in. From 1964 the longer type was used on the 250 as well.

Gaskets

Up to 1965 copper/asbestos head gaskets were used on the big twins and should normally be renewed as a matter of course. There was one type for the Atlas engine and another for the smaller ones. When the barrel spigots went for 1966, new composition gaskets were introduced with one for the 650 and another for the 750.

Next came a slightly thicker solid copper gasket on the Commando engine, and it is possible to reuse this. It must be examined for distortion or burning, but if in good condition can be annealed to soften it. First make sure it still fits cleanly over all the head studs and bolts

and that continued reuse has not materially reduced its thickness from the nominal 1 mm. Annealing is done by heating the gasket to a cherry red and allowing it to cool either naturally or by quenching it in water. The latter may produce a slightly softer material and is usual practice if you have a butane torch and the right-sized bucket. Should you have to heat the gasket a little at a time, let it air-cool as the result will be as good.

The copper gasket was later joined by a 2 mm aluminium version introduced to reduce the compression ratio on Combat engines and not recommended by those who have tried them. Both this and the copper type should be checked to make sure they are clear of the pushrods, a point to remember with all gaskets. Finally, in 1973, came eyeletted gaskets for both 750 and 850. These have flame rings incorporated in a composition material. They are marked *top* and are generally accepted as the best to fit.

The big-twin block gasket was deleted for 1973, but up to then there was one type for the 750 and another for the rest. For 1973–74 a silicone-rubber compound was used, but as owners tended to fill the oil drain holes with it this practice was stopped. For 1975 a

LEFT *Drive side of a Jubilee engine in 1964 when the massive rear enclosure had become a small panel*

RIGHT *Timing side of the same 1964 Jubilee showing the oil tank and other details*

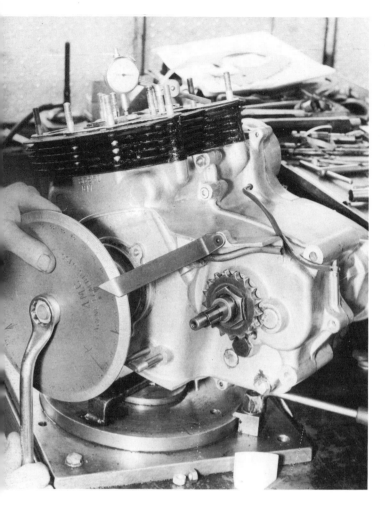

The early big twins all had a single carburettor and a one-into-two manifold. Around 1958 it was joined by an optional item that allowed splayed twin carburettors to be fitted. This continued to be available for both old and new models up to 1962 except for the semi-enclosed, de luxe versions where the panels prevented its fitment.

For 1960 the manifold was modified with wider-spaced vertical hole centres to match the new cylinder head with bigger inlet valves. At the same time the insulating pieces that went between manifold and head were changed to the type listed for the optional twin-unit fitting. This set-up continued on all single-carburettor models.

The advent of the 650 in 1961 brought in a new manifold having four fixings in a line across the head. With this came suitable insulation plates plus alloy inlet tracts or port sleeves to suit a twin-carburettor installation. The same arrangement was featured on the 88SS and 650SS models, using common parts, from 1962. However, for the 99SS and the 1961 88SS a splayed carburettor mounting, similar to the earlier option, was listed.

The Commando models all have two curved inlet tracts with corresponding insulating plates. The first machines had 30 mm tracts, but for 1972 a second tract was introduced at 32 mm which went on to the Combat engines. At the same time the balance-pipe union, which had been a separate part screwed into the tract, became an integral fitting.

The 32 mm insulating plate was altered for 1973, and for 1974 both 30 and 32 mm tracts and plates were still offered, with the 30 mm version being a new item. For 1975 the balance pipe was modified to include a vacuum take-off at its centre.

All the small twins have a single carburettor and conventional manifold. One served the 250 with its $\frac{25}{32}$ in. choke size, and another the 350 and 400 which had $\frac{7}{8}$ in. units.

Valves

These should be renewed unless in very good condition, especially the exhaust valve which has a hard time. Grind in the new valves lightly without taking too much from the valve seat.

One pair of inlets and exhausts was used in all the big twins up to 1959 when the bigger inlet was listed as an option. It was fitted as standard for 1960, being joined by another size of inlet which went into the 750 only.

At engine 125871, in 1968, the valves were made 0.1 in. longer. Thus three new items were listed: one exhaust and an inlet each for the 650 and 750. These continued for the Commando until there was a change to both for 1972. In 1973 the inlet was changed again, and in 1974 it was the turn of the exhaust.

The small twins had one pair of valves which was common to all engines and years.

gasket was again listed and, while officially for the 850, it can also be used on the 750.

It is quite in order to replace the gasket with a jointing compound but only if it is kept out of the oilways. It can always be used for the rocker covers in place of gaskets which remained the same from 1949 to the last Commando.

The small twins were simpler, having a pair of head and base gaskets for all years of the 250. The 350 and 400 had only one of each, the head gasket being common to both with one change for 1964 when the block spigot went. The base gaskets differed at first but the 400 type went on to the 350 for 1964. Four rocker-cover gaskets were used and one part served all locations, models and years.

Inlet manifold

These are all cast in light alloy and are often polished. They should be examined for damage, flatness of the mounting faces, both in and out, and for the condition of the threaded holes that take the carburettor studs. Where twin carburettors are fitted to separate stubs connected by a balance tube, the tube and its fitting should be checked for leaks.

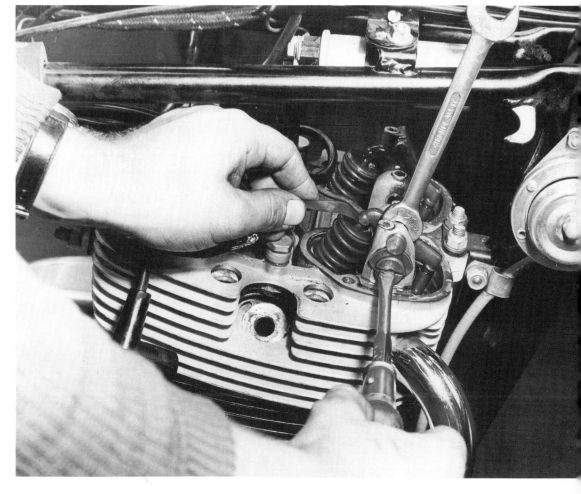

FAR LEFT *Checking timing with degree disc and dial gauge on the piston top of a 1960 Jubilee. Note the breather pipe just above the gearbox sprocket which it must clear*

RIGHT *Adjusting valve clearance on a small twin using the eccentric rocker spindle. Note the rather small clamp on this 250 which is best changed to the later 400 type*

Valve guides

As has been mentioned already, these should be removed or replaced after heating the head. For many years the guides were common to both valves, and the part only changed in 1955 for the alloy head.

It was 1972 when the next alteration occurred to the inlet for the 750 with the addition of an oil seal. This was followed by a new exhaust in the following year. That year also saw the first 850 guides, which were fatter and located on circlips rather than the flange used previously. As the 750 guides are rather thin it can be worth boring the head to take the 850 type, but this does require good machining facilities. Like the 850, the small twins also had guides located by circlips, and one of each served both valves and all models and years.

Valve springs

These should be replaced as a matter of course and all twins have dual springs. The big-twin springs were changed for 1955 and the alloy head, being joined later by a second pair which went into the 650 and the SS models. This latter pair continued in the Commando with a change of part number for 1975.

The small twins had one pair of springs for all models and years.

Valve detail parts

These comprise cups, collets, collars, heat-resisting washers and stem seals. Many of these items were common to all the big twins, while the small twins had their own set, except the seals, and these were common to all models and years.

On the big twins the collars and collets that went with them to retain the valve springs were the same parts for all years, even if both had three different part numbers. The cups that went under the valve springs changed once for 1973 when they were thinned a little.

The heat-resisting washers first appeared in 1953, and a second type was listed from 1961 for the 650 and SS engines. The latter type was fitted in all four locations in the Commando engines with two exceptions. One of these was the 1972 Combat engine and the other was the 1973 low-compression 750 head with 30 mm inlets marked RH1. For these two the washers were only fitted under the exhaust-valve cups.

Shims to fit under the valve springs were listed from 1960 but had gone again by 1964. Two thicknesses were available and they were selected to correct the installed spring length and loading. The valve stem seals were not listed until 1972 when they were added for the inlet guides only. They were changed for 1975.

All these small details need to be cleaned and inspected for any signs of damage or cracking, replacement being the only answer if any are found. Be sure there is no sign of collar collapse or collet pull-through.

Rocker-box details

All Norton twins have the rocker box as an integral part of the cylinder head with access covers to assist assembly and valve-clearance adjustment.

The covers need to be checked in the same way as any other alloy part for cracks, damage or poor mating surfaces and repaired as necessary. The detail parts will require inspection for cracks, damage, poor

threads, wear or obstructed oilways. While it is possible to inspect the parts during a service without dismantling them, this is not good enough for a restoration if you want to be sure that a failure is not imminent.

This means that the rocker spindles will have to come out, and on the big twins they are a tight press fit in the head. Some form of extractor will be needed, the spindles being threaded internally to assist this. Note the order of the washers on the spindle and how it is located by the plate that keeps it in place.

The earliest engines had spindles integral with the outer plate so only needed a single gasket. The bolt holes in these plates were tapped to enable jacking screws to be fitted to assist spindle removal. Soon this was changed to a design having a groove across the outer end of the spindle, a plate that locked into that groove, an outer plate and two gaskets.

Many of the parts used on the big twins remained the same from first to last but not the four rockers. These changed once for 1966, at engine 114870, when

they were shortened. The spindle lost its oil grooving to become plain at engine 116372, also in 1966. The rockers changed again for 1971 when they were listed complete with ball end. This last item continued to be available separately and, along with the adjuster and locknut at the other end of the rocker, it remained the same for all models. The only exception is that some nuts have an AF hexagon size, rather than the earlier Whitworth, although the thread is the same for all.

The plates and gaskets that retained the rockers went unaltered along with the thrust and spring washers on either side of them. However, the retaining bolts did change, first for 1955 and the alloy head, and second for 1972 when they also gained copper sealing washers.

The covers remained the same but became polished from 1969. Their studs only changed for 1955 and the alloy head, and in the rear location for the 650 and SS models. From 1957 a dowel was added to locate the rear cover. All gaskets were common to all years. The retaining nuts were common for all at the front and only varied at the rear for the stud.

The small twins had common rockers, covers, gaskets, shims and thrust washers for all models and years. The rocker spindles were eccentric for valve-clearance adjustment, being handed left and right. A special nut and bolt clamped each in place, and new spindles, nuts and bolts were introduced on the 400, appearing on the two smaller models in 1964.

Note that the rocker spindles of the big twins have a flat machined on them. Factory instructions for the earlier engines were for these to point away from their respective valves, but on Commando units this is reversed to avoid an oil build-up in the valve wells. This change also applied to earlier engines from 116372 in 1966.

Rocker-box oil pipes

These feed into banjo connections sealed with copper washers which need to be annealed by heating and then being allowed to cool. Avoid using jointing compound as it can easily block the small feed holes in

LEFT *First year of the Jubilee in 1959 with full enclosure and built-up frame*

RIGHT *A 1967 Atlas still much as the first 88 of 15 years earlier but now well stretched*

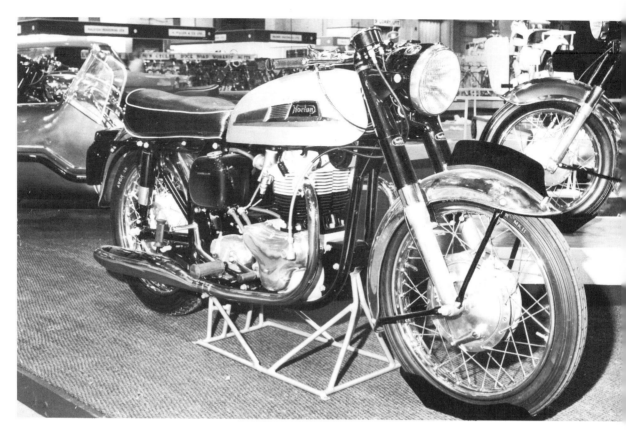

the banjo bolts. Don't use a locking compound, either, or the bolt will snap off rather than come out again.

Check the pipes with care as from engine 116372 the Atlas and Commando engines have a tapping from the pressure side to feed the rockers, and any leak is serious. This is much less so on earlier engines fed from the return line at a low pressure. In either case, any pipe repair must be done properly using silver solder if possible, or ordinary solder if not. Flux-cored solder will not be good enough. Better still is to change to the black plastic pipe used on late Commandos.

Finally, and just in case, check that the banjo bolts do not have a restrictor in them. These were used on engines prepared for production racing and could well have moved on to others by now.

Tappets

These should be examined for wear and fit in the guides. The big-twin tappets are hollow and the interior of each needs to be investigated in case it still carries a remnant of casting sand. Any found must be washed out. Also check that the bevels on the front tappet edges still allow the oil draining from the head to pass them on its way to the sump.

Unlike the big twins, the small twins have tappet guides and these have slots along their length to allow for oil drainage. Check that the slots are clear and are orientated across the engine.

Tappet wear in all big twins usually only occurs on the foot and, depending on the degree, the part may be reclaimed by grinding or replaced. The small-twin tappet also wears on the stem and is usually the cause of a lot of the mechanical noise in these engines.

The same tappet went into all four locations on the early big twins with a change for 1953. In 1957 they became handed and were revised in 1960 to have flat feet and thus a quicker valve movement. From then on this pair was used for all engines with just a part number change in 1975.

The big-twin tappets were held in place and prevented from rotating by a plate sitting between each pair and held to the block by two screws, wire-locked in place. The screws were common from start to finish, but the plate was altered for 1972 when it became much shorter and no longer extended across the width of the tappet. Check that it does not hinder tappet lift with your particular combination of camshaft and valve gear.

The small twins used one tappet and one bush type for all locations, models and years.

Pushrods

Check that these are straight by rolling them on a flat surface such as a sheet of glass. Examine the ends for cracks, undue wear or any signs that the ends are coming loose from the centre. If the cylinder head has had any significant amount machined from it, the pushrod ends need to be removed, the centre sections

LEFT *The 1965 650SS on show at Earls Court with optional rev-counter added*

RIGHT *Top half of a 1962 650SS showing the twin carbs and intake balance pipe*

reduced to suit and the parts reassembled. Some Combat engines were built without this having been done, so the rocker geometry is not as good as it might be.

The early engines had all-steel pushrods but from 1957 this was changed to an alloy centre section, though with the same steel ends. The ends remained the same for all years and models of the big twins, but a new pair of assemblies came in for 1957 to go in the 600 as well as the new alloy pair for the 500.

These were joined by two more pairs in 1961 with barrel-shaped alloy sections which were for the 650 and 88SS models. In 1968, at engine 125871, the 650 pushrods were shortened by 0.1 in. at the same time as the valve stems were lengthened by the same amount. These pushrods went into the Commando engines with just a part number change for 1975.

The small twins had one rod type for the 250 and another for the larger models. Both used the same top cup as the big twins but another form of lower end.

Camshaft

There were several types of camshaft used in the big twins, and in all cases they need inspecting for wear on the cams and the bearings. Make sure the keyway and sprocket-nut thread are in good order with no obvious damage.

Note that, in addition to the camshafts used in the standard models, there exist others for production racing and high performance. The only way to be certain of what you have is to check the timing it gives with the specified gaps for this work.

In general it is best to run what is listed for your model and set it to its correct timing. The exception is the use of the tuftrided camshaft which came along late in the life of the Commando. This has an even brownish-grey colour as a result of the process which gives hardness while retaining toughness. This camshaft would normally be of the last pattern so will only suit engines having points driven from the shaft end.

The original camshaft was changed for what was called the 'Daytona' cam around 1956, and this went into all 99 models and the 88 from that year. It was further amended for 1959 when it gained quietening ramps. This type may be marked QR on the shaft. Next came the first SS cam which was used by the SS models, the 650 and the Atlas. It was marked X1 or X2 and also went into the first Commando engines.

In 1969 a change was made to the points cam and rev-counter drives using the same cam form. This continued until it was joined in 1972 by another SS cam for the Combat engines. However, the latter was quickly dropped for 1973, so the 1969 part continued until renumbered for 1975.

The small twins stuck to one pair of camshafts for the 250 and another which served both the 350 and the 400. They are stamped on the end remote from the

driving gear, the Jubilee inlet being marked I7 and the exhaust E7. Larger models have the inlet marked I5N and the exhaust E5N.

Camshaft bushes

These did not change in the big twins until 1972 with the removal of the timed breather at the end of the camshaft. With the new arrangement came rolled camshaft bushes, which were steel with a bronze facing and oil grooves or scrolling, plus two thrust washers with location tags and the hardened steel thrust washer that had gone in for 1969. Up to then it had been part of the camshaft but it had to be separated to allow the rev-counter drive skew gear to be cut. The tags of the thrust washers are known to break off and get in the oil pump, so they should be removed.

The same bushes with just one tagged washer went into the 750 engines for 1973, but the 850 units had their own bushes while keeping the original washer. The bushes only were revised again for 1974. In all cases it is permissible to use scrolled bushes with scrolled shafts, or any scrolled part with any plain, but not plain on plain as the oil cannot get to where it is needed.

The small twins began with two pairs of bushes: a

flanged version on each timing-side end of the camshaft and a plain one on the other. For 1960 the design was revised to add a thrust plug, plate and spring at the left-hand end of both shafts, while the timing-side bushes were modified. This design continued for all models and years.

Timing-side drive

In the big twins this area is unusual for it employs both gear and chain drives to the camshaft, magneto, distributor and dynamo. For 1958 the dynamo was replaced by an alternator so its drive was revised, and from the same year some models began to use a distributor in the old magneto position. From 1969 the points moved into the timing cover so the distributor drive went.

Despite these changes the basic design altered little from start to finish, and some parts are common to all engines even though listed under different part numbers. The crankshaft pinion and its key changed for 1975 but the washer stayed the same throughout. The intermediate gear and sprocket assembly lost the ignition sprocket in 1969 and, at the same time, the bush, spindle, camshaft sprocket and cam-chain tensioner were altered to suit. The camshaft sprocket was also altered for 1958, when it no longer had to

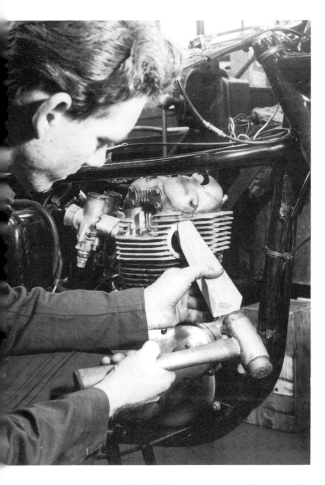

ABOVE *Removing the head of a 1962 650SS using a wooden block against the exhaust port roof*

ABOVE LEFT *Checking the timing chain with the slave cover in place and a spanner to hold the tension as needed; a 650SS, again 1962*

drive the dynamo, as were the gear and its bush for 1975. The spindle circlip remained the same for all years and the gear washer went when the distributor drive did. In 1961 a gear to suit a manual magneto, as fitted to the 88SS, was brought in.

The camshaft sprocket key was the same part as that used to secure the crankshaft pinion, and its original nut was joined by one able to drive a rev-counter gearbox in 1959. From 1969 it was back to a plain nut as the rev-counter drive was by skew gearing on the camshaft.

The cam drive chain was the same on all models but its tensioner changed in 1969 and 1974. The tensioner plates went from a pair to thick and thin in 1957 and back to a pair in 1975. The studs they were fitted to altered for 1972 along with their nuts, which had washers under them from 1959 onwards.

The dynamo was driven via a slipping clutch and gear on the back of the camshaft sprocket. This gear meshed with the dynamo gear, the dynamo itself being clamped to the front of the crankcase. The magneto went behind the cylinders where it was chain driven; the same chain drove a distributor as an alternative from 1958 to 1969. The magneto sprocket included an auto-advance unit, which was replaced by a peg-located sprocket for the distributor in 1958. A similar sprocket, without auto-advance, was also used on the manually-controlled magneto fitted to the 88SS for 1962.

The small twins had two gear-driven camshafts with a large idler gear to link them to the crankshaft pinion. All but a circlip were special and differed from the big twins. However, the same set of details served all models and years.

All these parts need to be cleaned and inspected for wear and, before removal, the timing marks need to be established. Use the correct pullers when necessary as they are always cheaper than damaged parts. Remember that if a gear is worn, the one it meshes with will also be damaged and a full set will be needed. If just one gear is changed, the existing gears will soon wear it to the same state as themselves.

Timing cover

This needs to be inspected for damage, flatness, clear oilways and good thread condition. Most owners polish it to a high degree as well. Check for cracks and the condition of the oil seal which runs on the crankshaft, controlling the oil supply, hence its importance. The first covers carried an oval nameplate, and although this was supposed to change to an engraved 'Norton' for 1957 this was only seen in the preview photos. The oval badge continued until 1956 when it was changed to a round plastic one set in the cover to match the tank badge. For 1958 the cover was altered to move the pressure-relief valve inside, but this valve was to remain on the lists for models with a rev-counter.

In 1959 a second cover was listed without badge but able to carry a rev-counter drive gearbox. A blanking plate was also listed to cover the hole if this facility was not fitted. This was modified in 1965 when it was joined by a similar item for the G15 and P11 models.

A revised cover went on to the first Commando engines, and the earlier types cannot be used. It changed in 1969 to incorporate the points and again in 1975. The points cover remained the same from 1969 but you could find you have some other type to suit a change to electronic ignition, or one with cooling fins or some other styling feature.

The points were driven from the inlet camshaft on the small twins, so the timing cover carried the contact assembly and a cover. Both covers were the same for all models and years.

Crankcase

The case halves will need cleaning well and checking for damage, cracks, poor threads and obstructed oilways. To remove or refit main bearings the case around them should be evenly heated, after which they should drop out. If you have to knock the case against a wooden block, first check for dowels to make sure you don't drive them into the case. The usual method of checking the case temperature is to spit on the bearing housing. If it spits back it's ready. A temperature of around 200 degrees Celsius (Gas Mark 5 or 6) is usually needed, and the drive side might have to get hotter still before the bearing will drop out. Don't use an oxy-acetylene torch or drill punch holes in the cases.

A ball or roller race must be completely cleaned

The 1958 Norton twin 99 engine with distributor and splayed carbs. This was the first year with an alternator

before checking, and if in doubt renew it. In fact, expect to renew bearings on a restoration as the cost is small compared to the trauma of changing them later.

The main bearings may benefit if held in place by Loctite, and replacements must be wiped clean before being dropped into place in the hot case. Don't forget any washers, shields or circlips that go with the mains.

Crankcase types

The original cases were changed in 1953, when the pivoted-fork frame was adopted, and again in 1958 when an alternator was fitted. This removed the dynamo and its seating from the front of the timing-side case and added the stator to the drive side.

This pair of cases was joined by another timing-side case in 1961 for the 650 engine, and by 1964 a new pair of cases was used for all except the 750. This had its own pair, the breather outlet being in line with the camshaft end and not further to the rear as on older engines. At the same time a variant for the drive side of the G15 models appeared.

In 1966 the timing side of the 650 case was amended and both sides of the 750 changed. New cases appeared for the Commando in 1968, and the timing side was altered in 1969 to suit the removal of the distributor and again in 1970 when both sides changed.

The whole assembly was altered for 1972 when the breather went to the base of the cases and internal webs were added. At the same time the threads changed to the Unified form. For the 750, in 1973, the distributor-drive hole was filled in, the blanking plate and fixing holes being deleted. The 850 case also appeared. This had tapped holes for the block bolts in its top surface, a breather pipe set in the top rear corner of the timing chest, breather holes through the timing-side case wall and no breather at the base of the cases. In addition, the sump filter made a welcome reappearance. There was a further change for 1975 when a timing plug appeared in the right case under the timing chest forward of the oil pump area.

Note that the 750 block can be fitted to the 850 cases but not the other way round as the bore spigot holes would not be large enough.

The small twins had a different crankcase for each engine size. Both smaller pairs of cases were altered in 1964 at engine 106838 when they adopted the gearbox from the 400.

Main bearings

These became a major problem on the early Commando, but up to that point all big-twin engines had the same arrangement of a roller on the drive side and a ball race on the timing side. Both were 30 × 72 × 19 mm. An oil seal was fitted outboard of the drive bearing and an oil sealing disc outside the timing race. These last two items were common to all models and years, even if both had three part numbers during that

The 646 cc Norton Manxman was first seen in 1961 in a US style but soon came on to the home market built as the other models

time. There may be shims between the bearings on the crankshaft. These were not really used to control endfloat as the crankshaft located on to the timing-side race. However, they limit any tendency for the bearing to move in its housing and keep the rods centralized in the cylinder bores.

In 1972 the Commando was fitted with new crankcase halves having roller bearings in both. These continued in the same size as before and required that the endfloat was correctly shimmed. The combination of stiffer cases, a high engine speed, over-advance of the timing and a flexible crankshaft led to rapid mains wear, the bearings already having become known for a short life. The increase in wear rate came from the roller shoulders digging into the bearing track as the shaft flexed. The solution was barrel-shaped rollers and what became known as 'Superblend' mains.

The first of these was listed as Norton part 063906 and is an RHP (was R&M) type 6MRJA30. The figure '6' is etched on and often hard to read but the rest of the number is stamped. With the advent of the 850 the bearings changed to Norton part 064118, which is FAG-type NJ306E. The 'E' at the end of the code is important as the NJ306 is not so strong and should not be used. From 1975 a circlip was added outboard of the drive-side oil seal.

For owners who are not keen on the idea of the crankshaft floating between two roller bearings there is an alternative. This is to fit a heavy-duty ball race on the timing side, an example being RHP-type M306 which has ten ball bearings instead of the usual seven or eight.

The small twins had the same arrangements as the original Dominator, the same parts going into all models and years. The bearings were the same 30 × 72 × 19 mm size as the big twins, with a roller on the drive side and a ball race on the timing. However, the part numbers were not the same, with a 28MJ30 on the timing side and an MRJA30 on the drive side. The reason for the difference is that the small-twin bearings have a large radius on the bore of the inner race to match the big radius ground on the crankshaft. Thus it is imperative that the correct bearings are used and that they are the right way round. The small-twin bearings will fit into the big twins although this may not be a good idea. As with the big twins, the small ones had an oil seal on the drive side and an oil sealing disc on the timing side. These items were the same parts as used in the larger engines.

Stator housing

This part was used from 1958, when the alternator was

first fitted, but did not appear on the Commando until 1975. Then it served to hold the stator clear of the starter-motor gear train and to support one end of a gear shaft. On other Commandos the stator locates to the inner chaincase.

The housing should be inspected for damage, a check being made for distortion as the part has to hold the stator concentric to the rotor to a close tolerance.

Assembly

In general this should be done as set out in the manual, with any amendments to allow for the use of modern sealants and fitting compounds. The sequence of locking up the major nuts may also be varied as long as none are left loose.

Slow and steady is the guiding rule, so make sure everything is as it should be on completing each stage and before moving on to the next.

Begin by laying out the first parts to be assembled and check that your tools are nice and clean. Put the

crankshaft together and fit the mains. Make quite sure there is nothing trapped behind the outer race when you do this or the bearing may tilt and the crankshaft fail to rotate freely.

Fit the crankshaft, camshaft and breather valve to the crankcase. If in any doubt, fit the other case half, bolt up and check that all is well. If it is, undo and proceed; if it is not then find out why. The case joint is prone to 'shuffling', that is slight movement when the engine is running, which may be detected by grey areas on the joint face. A silicone-rubber jointing compound is needed to deal with this but must be kept out of the wrong places, so don't use too much. Clamp up the case with bolts in all holes while the compound sets.

Fit the timing gears, chains and sprockets, and set the valve timing. Do up the nuts with the crank locked but do *not* hammer the nut on the end of the camshaft. The blows travel down the chain to the intermediate gear assembly, the spindle of which is only half supported—unless you are using a slave, cutaway timing case. A steady pull should do the trick.

Fit the oil pump, then the warm pistons followed by the block. You must remember to start all the block nuts on their studs before any are run down as usually it is necessary to lift the block a trifle to fit some of them in place. Fit the head gasket, the right way up where this is applicable, and then the head, making sure the valve gear is as it should be.

Install and time the magneto or distributor and then fit the timing cover, provided you are happy with the tension of the two chains. Be careful not to damage the crankshaft oil seal. On engines with points in the cover fit this using a tapered sleeve on the camshaft end to prevent it damaging the cover's oil seal. Then fit the advance unit and points.

Complete the assembly by adjusting the tappets and fitting the covers. During assembly you should have lubricated the parts as you went along and charged the crankshaft with oil. This should look after the bearing surfaces while you deal with the rest of the machine. Don't seal it completely if you have to store it for any length of time, and do turn it over occasionally.

The above applies mainly to the big twins but the small ones assemble with much the same techniques. Differences apply to the crankshaft and timing gear but the same slow, careful assembly using clean tools will ensure that the parts fit as they should. When assembling the crankcase halves make sure that they will go together without being strained. If they won't go, do not attempt to pull them up without checking first that you have put in the mains the right way round. It has been known for cases to be broken due to this error if the screws are forced to draw the halves together! A gasket was used originally between the cases, but a thin coat of a good sealant will do the job if the faces are in reasonable condition.

The new cylinder head of the 99 as adopted in 1960 with increased fin area and other alterations

4 Transmission

This covers all the mechanical parts from the engine crankshaft to the rear wheel sprocket, so it takes in two chains, four sprockets, a clutch and a set of gears. Included with the gears is the kickstart mechanism, and ancillary to them are the gearchange mechanism, clutch lift and gearbox shell.

Attention

Articles on the restoration of a machine often state that the owner has not stripped the gearbox but is using it as found. In many cases it is apparent that the box history is not known and this practice must be condemned.

Unless you check, you cannot be certain that a gear tooth is not about to fail or an errant part about to jam the gears. In the timescale of a restoration the period spent on inspecting the gears is minimal, and even on a straight rebuild the time will be well spent if, as a result, you make sure the box is not going to lock up on you.

Norton transmission

All twins had a four-speed gearbox with footchange, and on all but the Mk III Commando both this pedal and the kickstart lever went on the right. On the Mk III only, a left gear pedal was fitted. All the big twins had a separate gearbox and all the small twins had the assembly fitted into the crankcase to provide unit construction.

Both primary and final drives were by chain, with the early big twins having a single-strand primary and the Commandos a triplex chain. The small twins used a duplex version. All models had a multi-plate clutch but the Commando used a single diaphragm spring to clamp its plates, while the other models kept to the more usual arrangement of a number of small compression springs.

The Commando alone does not have a shock absorber built into the clutch body. It lacked this feature at first but an attempt to remedy the situation was made by incorporating one in the rear wheel hub from 1971.

Engine sprocket

All the twins have this item keyed to the crankshaft and held in place by a nut. Models fitted with an alternator have the rotor clamped in place by the same nut. Single, duplex and triplex sprockets were used on different series of machines. All need to be checked for their fit to the crankshaft and key and for the condition of their teeth. If healthy, continue to use the sprocket, but if there is any doubt change it along with the chain.

With all the early big twins adjustment of solo gearing was by changing the engine sprocket, and a range from 17 to 23 teeth was available from 1958 on. For sidecar use it was factory practice to change the gearbox sprocket, otherwise it remained the same throughout. Commando and small twins had a single engine sprocket size for all models and years respectively.

Of the actual parts used, one sprocket key was common to all big twins and another to the small ones. The early, single-row sprockets were all common in form, while the Commando had one part until 1975 when it was revised to suit the electric starter drive. The small twins used the same part throughout.

Primary chain

Expect to change this unless you find it in perfect condition. The early twins had chain of 0.5 in. pitch × 0.335 in. roller diameter × 0.305 in. between inner plates, more commonly known as $\frac{1}{2} \times \frac{5}{16}$ in. Commando machines all had $\frac{3}{8}$ in. triplex chain with dimensions of 0.375 × 0.25 × 0.225 in. The small twins had a duplex chain of the same dimensions.

The number of links was 92 for the Commando and 66 for the small twins, but it varied for the early big twins. The Dominator and Featherbed models ranged from 75 to 77 links, but the AMC hybrids such as the G15 series, P11 and N15 had 68 links.

Primary-chain tensioner

This is only found in the small twins and the Mk III Commando as all the other twins set the tension by moving the gearbox. The small twins used a slipper tensioner held in place by a pair of nuts, being

An early, 1954 model 88 Featherbed, with the larger front brake adopted that year

changed from a somewhat noisy metal slipper to a nylon one for 1961. The latter melts quickly if there is no oil in the chaincase, so watch this point.

The Mk III Commando had to have a tensioner as its primary-chain centres were fixed, unlike the preceding models. The design featured two spring-loaded plungers, each with a wear pad, which worked against the two chain runs. Oil in the chaincase helped in damping their movement. If left for a long time the oil may drain away but the tensioner will usually reprime itself. If not, this has to be done by removing the outer case, oiling the tensioner and moving the pistons by hand.

Clutch

Essentially, all Commando models have one type of clutch and the rest another, many parts being common to both big and small twins. While there were detail changes and variations in the number of plates, the two clutch designs did not vary much and the design of the older one could be traced back to that first used in 1934. Its one major change came with the AMC gearbox in 1956.

All the clutch parts should be cleaned and examined for wear or damage. Normal areas of wear are the tongues of the plates and the slots in the drum, the hub rollers or bearing and the springs which may lose their tension. Plates should be checked for flatness and the clutch nuts for the locking nib under the head.

For most parts renewal is the normal course of action and do this with hub rollers if necessary. Fit a new lock washer where applicable and new

LEFT *The driving transmission side of a 1957 model 88 which stayed much like this for many years*

compression springs if they are much below their free length.

The clutch springs of mid-1956 models must be adjusted so that the pressure plate lifts squarely and turns truly. If it does not, the clutch will drag and spoil the gearchange. For the same reason, the plates must be able to slide sideways in the slots which, in turn, must be free of burrs or notches.

Note Sections on the clutch details will cover early big twins, small twins and Commandos, in that order, so that similar parts are dealt with together.

Clutch hub

This fits on to a spline on the gearbox mainshaft and contains a shock absorber. It is retained by the mainshaft nut and single washer on the early twins, with two washers on the small ones.

The hub changed for the AMC gearbox during 1956 but not again on the early models. The small twins used their own version of the design, having a shoulder on the inboard end of the hub's plate splines. This went in 1960 at engine 89811, and the design of the clutch centre was amended in 1963 to suit the new gearbox mainshaft. The parts were used in each model as it appeared.

The Commando hub was a single part without shock absorber and it only changed once, for 1973, when it was hardened to suit the use of bronze plates. That year a tab washer was added to lock its nut in place.

Clutch shock absorber

This was built into the clutch hub and comprised a spider with three vanes which lay inside the centre and its vanes. Between the metal parts went wide drive and narrow rebound rubbers, the assembly being boxed in by a backplate, which also acted as

BELOW *The 1957 model 77 with sidecar frame and other details much as on the single-cylinder models*

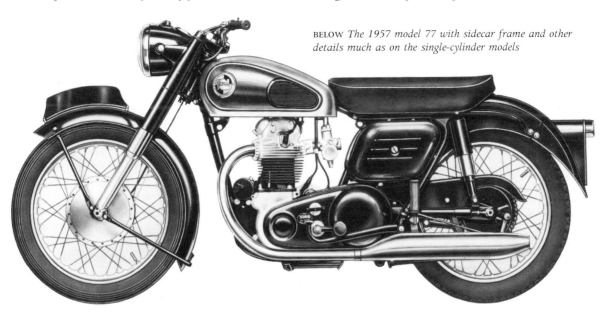

ABOVE *The chaincase of a 1960 model 99 de luxe with the rear enclosure panel removed. Alternator and coil ignition*

LEFT *The clamp nut for the primary chaincase must not be overtightened or the case will distort. The model here is a 1962 650SS*

part of the clutch bearing, and a front plate secured by three screws. The assembly should be checked and the rubbers changed if they seem at all soft or perished. Remove them by compressing the wide ones so the narrow sections can be picked out. Reverse this on assembly.

On the early twins most of the details, except the rubber buffers, were changed for the AMC gearbox. There was a further change to the front plate and its screws in 1961, and two further types of these were introduced for the 650 along with a 650 spider. These three items changed once more for 1964, and the screws were amended yet again for 1966.

The small twins had the centre and backplates changed for 1960, and the front plate and its screws for 1961, these items becoming common with the big twins. The spider was altered at the same time. All the

A 1962 650 joined to a sporting sidecar. Forks are special for this use and were developed after Eric Oliver's great ride in the TT with a standard outfit

parts were altered for 1963; again the front plate and its screws copied the larger models. The rubbers were common to both engine types for 1959 and from 1963, but between those years others were fitted.

Sprocket, drum and bearing

The sprocket and drum are formed into one item, and in the Commando the part also had the first clutch plate fixed to it. Wear is likely to be found on the sprocket teeth, in the housing slots or in the bearing it runs on. Commando clutch bearings may rumble when the clutch is operated, indicating that a change is likely to be needed.

The original Dominator had a sprocket and drum which also acted as a friction clutch plate, so it was pierced to take 20 inserts. This arrangement continued when the AMC gearbox came in during 1956, although a new part was used. It changed again for 1959 when the design was reversed so the clutch drum became a plain plate. Detail changes were made for 1964 and all forms of the sprocket and drum ran on 15 rollers carried in a cage, these parts being common to all models.

The same number of rollers was also used in the small twins, their cage being revised once for 1963. The drum, with its duplex sprocket, was altered for 1960 and 1963.

The Commando drum ran on a ball bearing which was positioned by a circlip in the drum bore, while the inner race was located by a circlip on the gearbox mainshaft. The bearing is a tight fit so needs to be pressed in or out if it needs changing.

The early Commandos had two small pins pressed into the inner drum surface to locate the first clutch plate. If these came loose it was very awkward to assemble the parts or to modify the arrangement due to the hardness of the drum. To overcome this, the design was modified for 1971 to attach the plate with three rivets. Experience has shown that, in fact, the pins or rivets can be left out as the plate won't come to any harm.

Springs, cups, studs and nuts

The early twins had a conventional design with three springs. These changed for 1956 along with the spring cups, studs, stud nuts and the spring screws which became special flanged nuts. In 1961 an alternative spring appeared for the 650 and with it another stud, both being revised further for 1964.

The small twins had their own springs and studs when introduced but used the same cups, spring nuts and stud nuts as the big twins. All remained the same for all models and years except the studs, which changed for 1960, 1961 and 1963.

Drive side of a 1964 Atlas

Diaphragm spring

This was used only in the Commando and comprises a conical disc with centre fingers that is held into the clutch drum by a large circlip. To remove the circlip the spring *must* be compressed with a suitable tool. Without this, it is highly dangerous to attempt to remove the circlip and just about impossible to replace it.

The same spring and circlip went into all versions of the Commando.

Plates

These come in various forms which can be reduced to friction, plain or pressure, although there may be more than one variety of one type in a clutch. The numbers of the first two depend on the power to be transmitted, and up to six are to be found. Early

clutches also had a band round the drum to keep oil off the plates, but with the AMC gearbox came new clutch inserts from Klinger that could cope with the oil so the band was no longer fitted. Any one plate is located by splines to either the clutch drum or the centre, but both plain and friction plates were used in either form, which calls for care when purchasing.

The 1949 Dominator had a clutch with five friction plates splined to the drum and six plain ones to the hub. In addition, the sprocket carried inserts, and a special plain plate went behind it. This clutch also went on to the first model 88, and when the AMC gearbox was adopted in 1956 the parts were changed but not the arrangement. The friction plates were still splined to the drum and the plain ones to the hub, but, thanks to the improved friction of the new inserts, the numbers of plates were reduced to four and five respectively. There was still a plain plate behind the clutch sprocket with its inserts.

All this changed for 1959 when a plain clutch drum was used and the splining arrangements were reversed. Thus, the four friction plates were splined to the hub and the four plain ones to the drum. In addition to these eight plates there were two more with inserts on one side only. One went behind the drum and was assembled to the hub and clutch race by the three spring studs. The other was the last plate to be assembled on to the hub and provided a face for the pressure plate to bear against as they revolved. Thus, both the single-sided friction plates turned with the hub, as did the main plates with bonded-on linings. At the same time, the plain plate material was altered to pin-planished steel, which was much less prone to distortion and which removed a cause of clutch drag.

For the 650 in 1961 the clutch had new friction plates although it kept to the existing plain ones, having five of each. Otherwise, the design was the same and for 1964 the parts were renumbered. Two years later the friction plates were modified except in the P11, which kept to the older type.

The small twins used some of the 1959 big-twin items but in smaller numbers, and there was no part-friction plate behind the clutch drum, only a plain disc to retain the drum on its rollers. The drum contained two friction and three plain plates, which all came from the big twins, plus two single-sided friction plates, one at each end of the assembly. Thus, one of these was the first to be fitted and the other the last, but they were not the same part, so care is needed.

The design became similar to that used by the big twins in 1960, with three friction, three plain and an outer single-sided friction plate. These were all 1959 parts and added to them were a single-sided friction plate behind the clutch drum and a shouldered plain version inside it as the first plate to go in. The drum was modified and the centre lost its shoulder. For 1963 the parts were renumbered, again using the same items as the big twins, and the centre spider changed

A 1969 Mercury with a rubber bung in the chaincase to give access to the clutch centre adjuster

to suit the new gearbox mainshaft.

The pressure plate of the first Dominator was a simple pressing, but the change to the AMC gearbox called for an adjuster in the plate. Thus, a new part with central tapped hole appeared along with an adjuster screw and locknut. It was joined by another without any flange in 1961 for the 650. The plate was amended in 1964, while the original served the small twins, and all models featured the same screw and locknut for all years. The flange of the pressure plate in three-plate clutches is about $\frac{5}{16}$ in. wide, and $\frac{3}{16}$ in. wide in four-plate assemblies.

The Commando had a plain plate held to the drum either by pins or, from 1971, by rivets. The other plates comprised three plain versions splined to the drum and four friction types splined to the hub. The first friction plates had many small pads bonded to them, but for 1971 a change was made to solid friction material. This changed again for 1973 when the friction plates became bronze and thinner, allowing five of them to be fitted along with four plain ones. The latter were still of the original type. At the same time the original pressure plate was altered and made thinner. Note that the clutch centre was hardened when the bronze plates came in, and this type must be used with them.

Clutch slip and drag

The early clutch works very well provided the plates are in a reasonable condition and the springs of comparable strengths. This is mainly due to the pushrod mushroom which is large enough to force the pressure plate to lift squarely, allowing the clutch plates to run free.

With the appearance of an adjuster screw in the pressure-plate centre in 1956, this excellent design feature was lost and it became necessary to adjust the springs until the clutch lifted cleanly. This is most important since poor adjustment is the main cause of clutch drag. It is well worth taking trouble over this, checking with either a wire pointer or, for the really fussy, a dial gauge.

The Commando has its own particular problems but at least the plates are very long wearing. Drag is often caused by the use of engine oil in the primary chaincase, and the remedy is to clean it all, refill the case with SAE 20 and ignore the service manual on this point in future. Another cause is the early steel plates notching the hub; a further reason is the pushrod bending and pumping gearbox oil along its length. This can be cured by splitting the rod into two with a ball bearing between the two halves, the ends of which would need to be hardened.

Commando clutch slip can occur if the plates are buckled or if the later, thin pressure plate is used on the early clutch with steel or solid friction plates. As an alternative to changing to the correct part, sometimes this condition may be corrected by fitting an extra plate. The solid friction plates slip when they become oil soaked and glazed, but this can be corrected by filing six radial grooves across each side. Avoid breathing the dust that results. The bronze plates also slip if too oily and may need periodic cleaning.

Part of the problem is that on all Commandos, except the Mk III, the oil-level screw in the chaincase is too high. The oil level should be checked with the machine on level ground and leant 10–15 degrees to the left when it should just appear in the threads of the level-screw hole.

Clutch mechanism

This is the system that connects the clutch-cable movement to the pressure plate. It lives under the outer gearbox cover and includes the clutch pushrod. Four designs were used, two in each twin size, but all come apart easily and should be checked over for wear or damage. The pushrod must be straight or the clutch will feel very heavy. Lubricate the load points of the mechanism on assembly so that the action is smooth and easy. Check all details for a smooth surface and polish, if necessary, so it will work more easily.

The first Dominator inherited the fast-thread, worm-and-nut design used by Norton from the early 1930s. For the twin the parts were enclosed within the gearbox cover. The lever is set and adjusted to give some play in the cable and to be at right angles to it when the clutch is lifted.

This design was replaced by a roller and shaped lever in the 1956 AMC gearbox which remained in use on all Commando models as well. The lever itself was revised for the Commando but all other details stayed the same for that period.

The mechanism is inclined to let the clutch in rather sharply, this being a function of the lever's cam form. The feel will be improved if this face of the lever is polished and if the ball bearing and roller it works against is replaced in the event of any dents or flats being found. If the clutch is heavy and the cable not sticking or kinked, the problem could be that the lever body is not in line with the cable which is pulling at an angle. Check before tightening the locking. Even more

One of the hybrids, in this case a 1967 Matchless G15

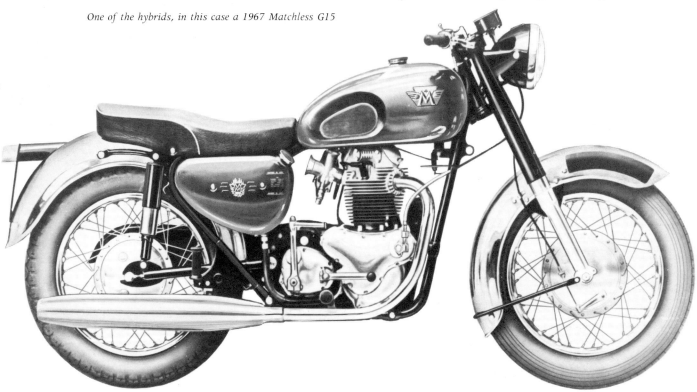

important is the clutch lever fitted to the handlebars. This should have its fulcrum screw and cable nipple centres only $\frac{7}{8}$ in. apart and no further. Levers with a greater centre distance are often fitted and make the clutch action much heavier than it need be.

The one other part in the system that varied was the pushrod. The early models had a two-part design with rod and mushroom. This was replaced by a single rod during 1956 which was used up to 1960, also appearing in the G15 models for 1964–65 and all Commandos. A second rod was used for the other big twins from 1961 to 1970.

The small twins used different systems, the first having a vertical rod with attached cable lever arm.

A model 33 AJS, also a hybrid and from 1967

The rod was partly cut away opposite the pushrod and there was a ball bearing between these two parts. These items were mounted in a housing in such a way that the movement of the lever was transmitted to the pushrod. When the gearbox was modified for the 400, and later adopted for the other models, another design was introduced. This featured a pair of discs with pressed-in ramps and a trio of ball bearings between them.

A 1964 Electra with its special chaincase and indicators at the ends of the handlebars

Chaincase types

These varied enough over the years to call for caution when obtaining spares. The first inner had a minor alteration for 1950 and another for 1953 and the pivoted-fork frame. This inner also went on to the 88 which had its own outer case, a little different from that used by all model 7 machines. The 88 inner was revised again for 1956 and once more for the AMC gearbox, although the outer stayed as it was. This outer also went on to the 77 which had its own inner.

The year 1958 brought the alternator with new inner and outer cases to suit. These were joined by another inner for the 650 in 1961 and, at the same time, a chrome-plated outer was listed as an option for all models. By 1964 the 650 inner was a common fit, while the plated outer went on to the Atlas and a painted one on to the SS models. The inner was revised in 1966, with a black outer on the 650SS and a chrome-plated version on the Atlas. Both had a hole pierced in the outer from late 1964 onwards. This was in line with the clutch centre to allow it to be adjusted without removing the outer case, as had been needed for the previous decade. A rubber bung sealed the hole.

The hybrids had their own series of cast-alloy cases, with one pair for the early G15 models, a second pair for the 1966-onwards machines and a third for the P11.

The Commando case differs from the above in that the seal is, in effect, a large O-ring set into the joint face of the inner and acting against the mating face of the outer. The latter was still held by a single nut and it carried screwed plugs to give access to the clutch centre, primary chain and ignition-timing strobe maker, plus a drain.

The outer case and the ignition indicator plate were changed for 1969 from the introduction of the S model, and the shape was altered to improve ground clearance. It changed again for 1972 when the inspection cap seals became O-rings. The final change came for 1975 to suit the left-hand gear pedal, electric start and chain tensioner, new inner and outer cases appearing along with ten screws to hold them together and a conventional gasket to seal the joint.

The small twins had a simple case design comprising inner and outer castings. These were common to the 250 and 350, but the inner changed for 1964 to suit the use of the 400 gearbox. The 400 itself had its own pair of extended cases to suit the electric starter and its drive.

Gearbox

All Norton twins had a four-speed gearbox with positive-stop gearchange and the kickstart lever on the right. All but the 1975-onwards Commando had a right-side gear pedal. The gearbox design dated back

Chaincase

Most Norton twins have a case based on the pressed-steel design first used in 1934, with a rubber-band seal between the two halves and a single, central fixing nut for the outer. The exceptions are the Commando from 1975, the small twins and the hybrids, which had cast-alloy cases held together by a number of small screws. All models have two case halves and none rely on the engine casting to form the inner one.

Whether cast or pressed, they need to be cleaned and inspected carefully for cracks, damage, poor threads, irregular joint faces or distortion. Be very careful to check on all the distance pieces that go behind the inner case, making sure they do their job without straining the case.

The case is prone to leaks, most being caused either by distortion of the inner, due to poor mounting, or distortion of the outer as a result of tightening its nut too much. In both cases, this can usually be rectified with some thought and a little panel beating. The rubber-band seal can be shortened as long as the join is at the top, and silicone-rubber sealant can be the solution to many ills. When assembling the pressed-steel case, remember that the footrest nut will push in the whole assembly as it is tightened and that this can cause distortion just as easily as an overtightened case nut.

to 1935 when Norton took over the earlier Sturmey Archer design, added a few improvements and had it made by Burman.

The gearchange mechanism was moved forward and down for the twins to give the 'laid-down' gearbox. It was further revised during 1956 when it became the AMC gearbox. This design, and most of the detail parts, continued on into the Commando series.

The small twins had their own gearbox and mechanism which came in two forms. The first was fitted on the 250 and 350 up to 1963, and the second went into the 400 and the other models from 1964 on. The change occurred at engine 106838.

In all cases, dismantling is straightforward and on big twins is best done with the box clamped in a vice by its bottom lug. Check the mesh between the camplate or drum as you go, and don't muddle the selector forks which may be identical but prefer to remain with the gears they have been run-in with. Be careful to keep the gears, washers, bushes and circlips in order, to ensure they go back where they came from, provided this is where they should go. During assembly all this needs to be watched, and the operation of the box and its gear selection must be checked out fully on the bench.

Gears

Inspect these carefully for any signs of wear or damage to the teeth and the driving dogs and splines. Replacement is usually the only answer if things are bad, although it is possible to build up the dogs and machine or grind them back to original if they are worn. Not easy to get right and very specialized.

The gears have changed over the years, so if parts are needed it is most important that they match. It is good practice to replace them in pairs as an old gear can easily wear out a new one. Consult the parts lists and check the numbers of teeth on the existing gears before shopping. Also note the form of the gear to guide you to the part you need.

All the 1949 gears came from the single-cylinder machines, but the sleeve gear was modified in 1950 which affected both its sprocket and bushes. A new set of parts, giving different ratios, went into the AMC gearbox for 1956 and gave a lower third but higher first. The sleeve-gear pair, the mainshaft second and layshaft third were changed in 1960. This returned the third-gear ratio to its earlier value and raised both first and second a touch. At the same time the layshaft top and mainshaft second gears were given new part numbers while remaining the same physical shape and interchanging with the earlier items.

The Commando kept to the same ratios on its appearance in 1968 but had revised sleeve- and first-gear pairs plus an amended layshaft second gear. For 1970 the third-gear pair were made in a stronger material, and in 1971 the first-gear pair and layshaft second gear reverted to the 1956 parts. In 1974 the second-gear ratio was raised by fitting a mainshaft gear with one more tooth and modifying the layshaft gear to suit. That year the sleeve gear was amended and gained a circlip to locate its bushes, but a popular remedy to stop them moving is to fit three, thus filling the available space. The sleeve gear was modified a little more for 1975.

A 1968 Commando with cast-alloy chaincase and odd seat

The small twins have two distinct gear sets. The first type had the mainshaft third and layshaft first and second modified for 1961 along with the sleeve gear. The second type was used initially in the 400 and then went into the smaller models, and it included a change of the three intermediate ratios. The very earliest sleeve gear had recesses to locate the third-gear dogs. The dog was in the form of a peg but this was changed to dogs on each gear which locked into one another.

Shafts

These need to be inspected for damaged splines, poor threads and the condition of the bearing surfaces. Replacement is the normal procedure if all is not well and, as with the gears, care is needed to make sure the correct part is obtained and that it will work with the other items.

On the big twins the mainshaft and layshaft changed for the AMC gearbox in 1956, and the first changed again in 1968 for the Commando. In this application it gained a groove for a circlip, against which the clutch located. Check the overall length of any new shaft against the original as the racing version differs from the road models. The layshaft first adopted for the 1956 AMC box remained in use for the Commando.

The small twins had two designs of shaft. The first had a shoulder for the clutch hub to locate against. This was dispensed with for 1961 and the 350, so the original is only to be found on the 250. There were no other variations.

Bushes and bearings

Ball races need to be cleaned completely before they are checked, and if there is any doubt about their condition they should be renewed. Some play is normal for ball races but there must be no rough spots. Bushes were used both for the layshaft and in the gears, and if worn can be renewed.

Norton were consistent with their big-twin bearing sizes, the sleeve gear turning in a ball race of $1\frac{1}{4} \times 2\frac{1}{2} \times \frac{5}{8}$ in. for all models. The ball race at the right end of the mainshaft was $\frac{5}{8} \times 1\frac{9}{16} \times \frac{7}{16}$ in. and that for the left end of the layshaft $17 \times 40 \times 12$ mm. Note that some early gearboxes may have a roller race for the layshaft, this being a feature of the 1935 design that was cheapened post-war.

The larger machines, especially the 850 Commando, benefited from a change back to the roller bearing. The one to use is type NJ203 with a C3 fit as used in the Commando from 1975. If the original ball race has failed it is usually essential to renew the other layshaft bearing in the kickstart axle.

The sleeve-gear bearing was protected by shim washers at first which must be kept in the right order. An oil seal was adopted for the AMC gearbox and served all the big twins from then on. A further change was to the sleeve-gear bearings for the mainshaft. At first there were two bushes, modified for 1950, and 13 rollers set in the gear end of the part. A retaining washer went next to them. Between the washer and the third-gear spline was a bronze thrust washer, the grooved side of which went against the sleeve gear. The washer takes the clutch thrust and if worn should be replaced. An indication that this is needed may be a tendency to jump out of gear.

The sleeve-gear rollers disappeared with the appearance of the AMC box, and a new pair of bushes served until a modification for 1975. There were other bushes within the free-running gears which changed in part number for the AMC box, while the layshaft bush in the kickstart axle did the same thing. It was modified for 1964 and returned to its 1957 form for 1966, but the 1964 type was fitted in the Commando.

The kickstart axle turned in a single bush in the inner cover at first, with a different bush for the model 88. The AMC box was amended to provide bushes in both inner and outer covers, and these were both altered in 1962 but then continued right through the Commando range.

The small twins went their own way with one set of

parts for the early machines and another for the 400 box. The latter used the oil seal and mainshaft right bearing from the big twins; its two kickstart bushes remained common to all models and years. The only gear to be bushed was the layshaft first, effective from 1961 on, with a second bush type for the 400 box. The layshaft bushes, especially on the sleeve-gear side, *must* be tight. If they turn the casting may be damaged, and on one side this is the crankcase.

Shell and covers

All models have an inner and outer cover with an access cover for the clutch cable. The gearbox shell of the big twins remained much the same for all years but for the small twins was part of the crankcase halves. All parts need to be checked, as with any other alloy casting, for cracks, damaged threads and distorted joint faces.

The original Dominator shell was joined by a second to suit the model 88 installation. In the main, the changes concerned the mounting lugs, but the inner cover was also changed to suit the Featherbed frame and its engine plates.

There was a new set of parts for the 1956 AMC box, and the shell continued in this form to the end of that

LEFT *Commando S chaincase in 1970 showing exposed stoplight switch along with brake and footrest details*

BELOW *The 1971 Fastback Mk III still with its special seat and tail*

LEFT *The 1972 745 cc Interstate showing the front Isolastic mounting and the ignition-switch location*

RIGHT *The 829 cc Interstate of 1973 which shows the different barrel used on the larger Commando engine*

model style, as did its access plate. The inner and outer covers were changed further, with variations to both in 1961 and 1962 to suit the kickstart-axle bushes. Both changed again for 1964 and the outer was also modified for 1965, although in 1966 it went back to and stayed with the 1964 part. When part hunting, remember that a special shell was brought in for the G15 series and amended in 1966. Norton shells are marked N or NA; AMC ones have an M.

The only part retained for the Commando was the inner cover, as the shell, outer and access plates were all new. The shell changed for 1973 and again for 1975 when a neutral light-switch hole was provided under the selector-cam hole. The inner changed for 1974, when a breather tube was inserted into its top face, and again for 1975. That year brought the left-mounted gear pedal, and the pedal shaft was extended to reach it through the inner cover in the area ahead of the shell. Thus, what had been a blind hole with bush became a through-hole.

The outer cover also changed for 1975 as it lost its gear-pedal shaft hole. The access cover changed for 1974 when its breather hole went, this function being taken over by the hole in the inner cover.

The small twins had two inner and outer covers, one pair to suit the early gearbox and the other for the 400 box and the later models that used it.

Gearchange mechanism

This starts with the rubber on the gear pedal and runs through to the selector forks which move the gears.

There are several wear points that need to be checked, the fork sides being one possible area for attention. The various springs need to be changed if tired, and the whole mechanism must operate smoothly.

The big twins began with their version of the pre-war design revised to suit the 'laid-down' configuration. This was amended for the AMC box in 1956 which continued with little change on to the Commando up to 1974. There were detail alterations to the index plunger spring, pawl carrier spring and gear lever in 1961 and to the stop plate in 1973, but most of the 1974 Commando items were as those in the first AMC box in 1956.

The camplate for the G15CSR of 1966–67 was special to that model, and the standard plate was altered for 1971 and in 1975 when it gained a detent for the neutral switch. The gear pedal for the G15CSR was special to that model but also went on the 1969 Commando in place of the original. It was listed as available in chrome or dull. For 1972 it gained a new number and was replaced by the left pedal in 1975. The latter had its clamp slot under the spindle hole and not behind it as before. A rear-set, racing-type lever and linkage were available as an option for 1961–65, and a rear-facing pedal went on the JPR in 1974. The same pedal rubber went on all the standard models with the AMC gearbox, but the racing lever had its own rubber.

A poor gearchange is often caused by the pawl spring having a slight bias, which prevents the pawl from sitting square to the ratchet when at rest. A small

set in the appropriate leg should cure this, otherwise it may call for the spare spring most owners always carry.

The small twins had their own arrangements even though all used the same pedal rubber as their big brothers. Virtually all the other parts were special and none of the early ones continued into the later 400 box. The first design had a camplate of sector form moved round by a big-twin-style, positive-stop mechanism. There were changes to the stop plate and camplate plunger for 1960 and to the pedal return spring for 1961.

The 400 box featured a barrel-cam design with the two selector forks running on the barrel. This was meshed with a quadrant which was moved by a positive-stop mechanism having a face-cam form of pawl and ratchet. There were changes to the gear indicator and camplate plunger for 1964 but nothing else.

Kickstarter

All the big twins and the 400 cc small twin used the same system of a spring-loaded pawl engaging with ratchet teeth cut internally in a recess in the layshaft first gear. In all cases the parts need to be cleaned and examined for wear, replacement being the normal remedy for trouble.

The 1949 design used many parts from the 1946 single-cylinder gearbox and was joined by an alternative axle and spring cover for the 88. All was revised for the AMC box in 1956, and this was joined by a folding-crank option the next year. The axle and return spring were revised for 1962 and the axle bush changed in 1964, but it went back to its 1957 form for 1966.

Most of the mechanism, including many 1957 parts, went into the Commando in 1968, but the kickstart crank itself was new and of the folding type. For 1969 it was listed as chrome or dull to match the gear pedal and was joined by a longer version for the 850 in 1974. This was revised for 1975 with a spring-loaded ball to keep the crank in its selected position. At the same time an oil seal was fitted between the axle and case instead of the O-ring used previously. The latter was prone to leak as it was being used in the wrong application.

The kickstart pawl was changed to a tougher material for 1971 but some have been known to break. If it does, the pieces can jam the mechanism so the crank lever goes down and digs into the road. Thus, any odd misbehaviour of the kickstart needs to be investigated at once, even if this means a strip-down by the roadside. Later pawls have an M on the side and are steel castings which should be hard, but check a new one in case it is still soft.

Also beware of pattern kickstart cranks that may foul the exhaust pipe. If the machine is in pieces a check can be made by placing a new and old crank side by side with their inner faces on a flat surface. It should then be possible to see if they are the same.

The 400 small-twin gearbox used a similar system to the big twins but different parts. The only change was to the axle oil seal for 1964. The early small twins kept to their face ratchet design with minor detail changes in 1960 and 1961 plus a new crank and pedal in the latter year.

Gearbox sprocket

Expect to renew this. Check for worn or damaged teeth, tired splines that don't fit the sleeve gear well and a rough oil-seal surface. Fit a new oil seal unless the existing one is perfect, which I doubt. One type served all big twins with the AMC box (1956–77) and the 400 small-twin box. The early small twins used another.

The first big twin had a 19-tooth sprocket when used solo and a 17-tooth version when fitted with a sidecar. The sprocket was modified for 1950 and revised for the AMC box but the concept remained the same up to the Commando. The one important change came in 1965 when the rear chain width was altered from $\frac{1}{4}$ to $\frac{3}{8}$ in.

At first the Commando list included both 19- and 21-tooth sprockets, and up to 1972 the 19-tooth one was the usual fit. For 1973 it was changed to 21 teeth as part of the factory corrections for the many

A 1966 Atlas fitted out for police use with special seat, mirrors and blue lamp

mechanical troubles being experienced, and for 1974 moved on to 22 teeth The UK models kept to this, but in the US it was back to 20 teeth for 1975. For those who wish to differ, a range of sprockets from 19 to 24 teeth was listed for the Commando for 1972–75, and there are also versions with 16 or 17 teeth.

The small twins have a 17-tooth sprocket on the 250 and a 19-tooth one on the two larger machines. However, there are two versions of each to suit the two gearbox types, and the correct one is essential as it has to match the sleeve-gear spline.

The sprocket nut, its lockwasher and the washer locking screw were the same for 1956–77 in the AMC box and were on the same lines as all Nortons from pre-war days. When the AMC box was introduced a spacer was fitted behind the sprocket. The small twins used a nut and lockwasher, with one pair of parts for the early models and another for the 400 box. Both had their own type of spacer, and none of the parts were common to the big twins.

Rear chain

Bound to need renewal on any rebuild. The big twins began with 0.625 in. pitch × 0.4 in. roller diameter × 0.255 in. between inner plates (better known as $\frac{5}{8}$ × $\frac{1}{4}$ in.). For 1965 onwards the width changed to 0.38 in. and the size name to $\frac{5}{8}$ × $\frac{3}{8}$ in. Chain lengths vary from 90 links for the first model 7 to 100 for the P11 and Mk III Commando. Except for the models 7 and 77, all fall in the range 97 to 100 links. The small twins used chain of 0.5 × 0.335 × 0.305 in. dimensions, with 121 links for the 250 and 120 for the other two.

Assembly

This is a straightforward job but the details need to be checked as you go along. Bearings should be held in place with Loctite for added security and joint faces can be sealed with the traditional gasket or a silicone-rubber compound. As always, use the latter sparingly.

Work to the manual and check each stage for correct operation. Make certain you have the selector forks in the correct position and engaged in the proper cam track. Double-check the gear selection as a mistake can be traumatic on the road. Do make sure you have the gears with small shoulders the correct way round so the shoulder is against the adjacent bearing, giving a working clearance between the teeth and the bearing outer race. If you leave the main nuts until you have the machine assembled so you can use the brake to hold the shaft, make sure you cannot forget to do them up by some means or other.

Remember to fill the gearbox and primary chaincase with oil before using the machine. With the small twins you must make sure you have enough oil as the first pint will not even reach the gears due to the shape of the box. Thus, they would run dry and soon wear if the full amount is not used. A label tied on the filler or the gear pedal will act as a reminder.

5 Carburettor and exhaust

These are two areas that can give the restorer considerable problems unless the parts are simply replaced with new examples. The difficulties arise because the first wears and the second corrodes all the time the machine is in use, so their condition changes continuously. Both affect the performance of the machine, especially the carburettor, and both are important to the final appearance of the machine.

All Norton twins had Amal carburettors, and the standard models used type 6 versions to 1954, Monoblocs from 1955 to 1966, and Concentrics from 1967. Twin racing GPs were offered for the Clubman's 88 in 1955–56.

A variety of exhaust systems was fitted to the twins over the years, the most common being a separate exhaust pipe and silencer mounted low down on each side. In the early 1960s siamezed pipes were used for a year or two with the silencer low on the right, while the mid-1960s brought more variety for the hybrids. Balance pipes did not appear until 1973 and then on the 850 Commando only.

The Amal number system

Amal stamped all carburettor bodies with a number sequence that was their method of stock control. This was the build standard, and up to the late Concentrics was related directly to the internal settings of the instrument. Thus, if *any* setting was changed the assembly received a new part number and was stored accordingly. In this manner they could ensure that they delivered the correct unit to their many customers who, in turn, could readily check them on to the correct machines.

The type 6 carburettors were stamped with the basic type number followed by two letters, an oblique line and a further three-digit mark. The type number is 275 for units up to $\frac{7}{8}$ in. bore, 76 or 276 for those of $\frac{15}{16}$ in. to $1\frac{1}{16}$ in., and 289 for $1\frac{1}{8}$ in. or over. The two letters give the build standard of the settings, while the final series indicates the float chamber which goes with the unit.

Monobloc carburettors have no need for the last mark and are stamped with the type number followed by a two- or three-digit, build-standard number. The first can be 375, 376 or 389, with the same size limits as the type 6. The Monobloc also exists in pairs, with one float-chamber body removed, for use in some twin-carburettor installations where the unmodified unit provides the chamber for both instruments. The two are connected by a short piece of flexible pipe.

The Concentric carburettor uses the same system for the 600 and 900 series, the units being lettered R or L for right- or left-hand, followed by a 6 or 9 plus the bore in mm (to give 626 or 928 for example) with the build standard to finish. The effect of this system can be seen in the carburettor-settings list.

A perfectionist would seek to fit a carburettor with the correct number stamped on it but otherwise there is no obstacle to just changing the settings to the correct ones for the machine in question. Note that the Commando lists given are from Amal data and sometimes are at variance with the parts list and other published information. A carburation check to confirm the settings is always a good idea once everything else has been set correctly.

Amal restoration

The instrument has to be taken apart and checked over. New fibre washers, float needle and seating are normal practice, and a new needle and jet may not come amiss. Checking the mounting flange for flatness, its holes for clearance and all the internal passages for obstructions is also usual with any rebuild. Pilot-screw damage is common.

The problems arise from body and slide wear plus doubtful threads, especially the one for the top ring. Most of the other threads can be repaired or reclaimed with an insert, even in some cases by a thread change with a new mating part made from scratch. The top ring, or mixing chamber cap, is more tricky and often the chamber thread will be found to be damaged or worn away to a taper. It is possible to cut it deeper and make a new ring, but this is a skilled engineering job needing good equipment.

The wear problem can be dealt with by sleeving the body, but again this is a difficult job that must be done to a high level of precision. As with all carburettor work, it must be tackled with a delicate touch as the

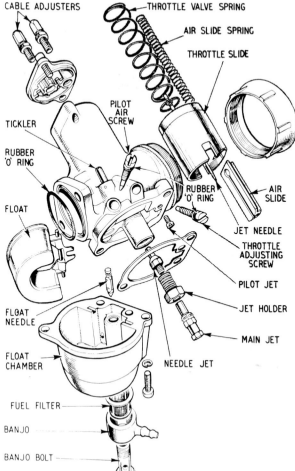

ABOVE *The Phoenix conversion for the Commando using an SU carburettor*

LEFT *Exploded view of the Amal Concentric carburettor*

parts are fragile and easily broken.

If you can find replacement parts it will be easier than repairing an old carburettor, and the notes about Amal numbering should help. The units were handed, so you must check that you have the correct item for your model; also note the positions of throttle stop and air screw.

Chambers and their floats require normal inspection, but usually only the needle and its seating wear. Make sure the float in a Monobloc can move freely on its pivot as a tight spot can cause confusion. Check all floats for leaks.

Assemble the instrument with care, making sure the petrol-feed area is as it should be. It is well worth connecting this up to a tank and checking that it holds a level and without flooding. Better to find out before it goes back on to the machine and drips all over the magneto.

Earlier Amal bodies were finished in a silver-grey paint specially developed to resist petrol. This is no longer available as no one is prepared to order the large quantity required by the makers, so a problem exists. Do not be tempted to use any other paint without a trial first; it may react with the fuel to produce a dreadful mess that is more a sludge than anything and then a full clean-out will be needed. Better to go for bead blasting which gives a similar appearance, but do check every passage afterwards in case the carburettor was not correctly masked.

Petrol pipes

The twins used flexible pipes from the start, and although the detail arrangements varied over the years, the general design comprised a length of pipe swaged on to short lengths of rigid tube carrying the end fittings. Nuts on these secured the assembly to the taps and float chamber.

The early types of armoured hose or transparent plastic need to be treated with suspicion as both may leak with age. Replacement is essential on safety grounds. The pipe and its end fittings need to be inspected regardless of type or age: the pipe for cracks or wear spots, and the fittings for the way they seat and seal plus the condition of the nut threads. Old pipes can take a set and be very stiff so they pull on the tap or carburettor, while the nuts may distort or stretch so they don't spin on as they should.

If new pipes are needed and total originality is not required, modern black neoprene is to be recommended as it has a long life and holds on to the fittings well, even without clips. It also remains very flexible in cold weather which is a good point. When making up pipes ensure they are long enough not to pull at the ends or kink, that they lie naturally and that there are no vertical loops which can cause air locks.

Air filter

The element should be cleaned, renewed or washed, dried and re-oiled according to type, while the body needs to be repaired and finished as any other sheet-steel component. The hose connecting the filter to the carburettor must be checked carefully for cracks which could cause air leaks. Removing the filter will weaken the mixture, so a carburation check is essential.

For many years the filter was an optional fitting and went between the oil tank and the battery. It was listed as early as 1953 and was usually to be seen on touring models rather than sports machines. It was also an option for the small twins, and this situation continued up to the Commando.

The Commando had an air filter from the start, the same design serving up to 1974 and the Mk IIA. The original had a front plate with connections to the carburettors, a rear plate, an element and a perforated surround. The front plate was chromed for 1969, and both front and rear changed for 1971, 1972 and 1973.

In 1974 the element size increased and the rear plate was modified, while the Mk IIA was introduced with a plastic housing for an oiled element. This could be washed and reused if in good condition. The same design continued on to the Mk III.

Exhaust system

This comprises the pipes and silencers plus the clips, brackets and stays which hold them to the machine. The parts are chrome-plated steel, and the finish often suffers from both heat and corrosion which detracts greatly from the machine's appearance.

Fortunately replacement with pattern parts is possible for these popular models, and it is worth paying a sensible price for the items rather than looking for the cheapest. The pipes and silencers are an important facet of the looks of the machine so are well worth getting right for the sake of a little extra money. Quality parts will also fit better and last longer.

If the pipes, clips and brackets are in good order it may be feasible to clean and polish them for further use. Before the final polish they should be checked for their fit to the machine mounting points and to the cylinder head. On most models the pipes are clamped with nuts screwed into the exhaust ports, but the small twins have push-in pipes. For them you may need to swell the pipe to ensure it is a snug fit in the port; heat plus a wooden wedge may be needed to do this. In all other cases, the pipe must fit squarely into the port and the nut must run true into the threads without damaging them. If any parts are distorted, real care may be needed to get everything back into line.

The brackets and clips should be easy to repair and refinish, if this is needed, as most are simple parts. The correct nuts, bolts and washers, plus any special parts

Special inlet tract used by Paul Dunstall in 1965 on a 650

used with the clips, should be checked and refurbished as necessary. Heat shields were fitted on some models, and these need similar treatment.

The silencer body is much more of a problem if it is in poor condition and you wish to reuse it. Often the thin outer shell will have corroded from the inside, which makes repair a skilled metal-working job. A further problem is the plating, for firms that undertake such work will not want to put a dirty silencer in their tanks, and it is just about impossible to clean it fully.

Thus, the existing silencer can only really be used if in good order, and the practical alternative has to be a pattern part unless you are lucky enough to locate an unused original.

Exhaust-pipe types

There are a good few variations and it is important to get the correct one or you may have problems in fit and alignment. The early pair were changed in 1953 to suit the pivoted-fork frame and were joined by a pair for the 88. Another pair went on both the 88 and 99 for 1956 when the light-alloy head first appeared.

The year 1957 brought three pairs of pipes for the 77, 88 and 99, while the last two changed again for 1960. These continued in 1961 on the basic models but with three other pipe pairs, two of the siameze pattern. One of these went on to the 88SS and 99SS, the other being an option for the 650. As standard, this had its own pair of pipes on the lines of the smaller models.

There were further changes for 1962, with the 88SS adopting the standard 650 pipes. These also went on to the 650SS, which ran better with the twin system than with the siamezed version. The 99SS stayed siamezed, and this system was available as an option for any model.

The arrangement continued for both the 88 and 650 models, and the SS system also went on to the Atlas for the home market. For the USA, the Atlas and 650 had a pair of larger-bore pipes, and this arrangement continued for the Featherbed models.

The hybrids made their own arrangements, most G15 models using the same system but not the CSR, which had nice swept-back pipes until 1968 when it took the common pair. The G15CS, P11 and P11A all had their own special pair of pipes with attendant fixings.

The Commando began with a pair of low-level pipes which were also used on the R. They were joined by another set for the S in 1969. For that machine both pipes were taken on to the left side and run at waist level above the primary chaincase. The upper pipe came from the right exhaust port, and both pipes and silencers were fitted with a heat shield to protect the rider and passenger from burns.

For 1970 the original pipes were altered to include a bend just ahead of the silencers, which were tilted up

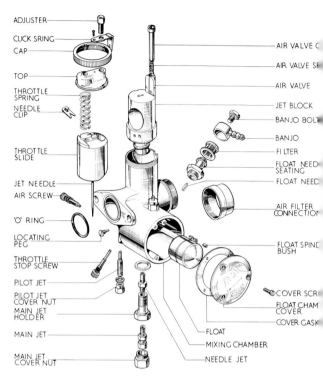

a little as a result. A pair of waist-level pipes for the Street Scrambler came in 1971, and in this case there was one on each side of the machine, again with a heat shield for protection. All the other models kept the basic 1970 pipes, but for 1972 there were two new pairs. One set continued the upswept-silencer theme and went on the Fastback, Roadster and Hi-Rider models, while the other had a kink near the silencer end of the pipe and went on the Interstate and police model Interpol.

The same two pairs of pipes went on the 750s for 1973, but there were two more sets for the 850s. These served the same models, other than the Fastback which was not built in 850 form, and were in the same style but with a balance tube near the exhaust ports. Both were modified for 1974, but kept the same balance tube, and were joined by another pair for the Mk IIA models. These alone continued into 1975 with a revised balance pipe. The JPR of 1974 had its own pair of pipes finished in matt black.

The small twins had a much simpler arrangement, with one pair of pipes for the 250 and another that served both the 350 and the 400.

The exhaust-pipe nut and gasket remained the same from 1949 to 1971. For 1972 a lockring was introduced and both nut and gasket altered, the nut so that the ring could lock into it and the gasket to become corrugated. Both were modified for 1973 but only went on the 750. The 850 used a different design with its own nut and gasket but kept the same lockring. In

LEFT *The Amal Monobloc carburettor shown in exploded form. Note the chamber side which must seal and the feed-pipe details*

RIGHT *Norton silencer without tailpipe as used for some years and seen here on a 1956 model 99*

BELOW *The twin pipes of the 1970 Commando S with shields to protect rider and passenger. Note incorrect wire locking of exhaust-pipe nut*

ABOVE *The 1970 Commando S showing off its special exhaust system*

BELOW *Black cap or 'bean can' silencer seen on a 1975 Mk III along with the disc rear brake*

*Another view of the black cap silencer here fitted on a 1974
Mk IIA 850*

addition, each pipe had a pair of split collets for the
nut to bear upon.

There were no changes until 1975 for the Mk III. On
this machine the gasket and split collet were replaced
by a spherical seating and one-piece collet ring. On the
small twins, the pipes simply pushed into the ports
with no other fastening.

Silencer types

The model 7 began with a pair of handed silencers,
much as those used on some other road models, with
tubular shape and offset inlet and tailpipe. A new pear
shape was introduced for the Featherbed model, the
silencers having a triangular outline and flattened
cross-section. These went on to the model 7 from 1953
and the pivoted-fork frame.

The shape changed again for 1956 when a pair of
tubular silencers was adopted once more, but this time

with no tailpipe at all. The inlet continued to be offset
and the outlet end was simply rounded to run the
metal into the exit hole. There were detail changes for
1957, but for 1960 a single new silencer was used for
both sides of the machine. This had a central inlet, and
the last section of the body tapered to give a different
shape to the 1956 version. There was still no tailpipe.

The same shape, but with an offset inlet, was used
in right and left forms for the 650 in 1961. The same
pair of silencers went on to the 88SS and 650SS for
1962, while the right silencer was used for the
siamezed exhaust-pipe systems in 1961–62.

While the standard and de luxe models continued
with two of the 1960-type silencers to the end, the
other models had the 1961 650 pair. In time these went
on to the Atlas and first Commandos. In addition, they
appeared on the G15CS and N15CS, but there was
another pair for the other G15 models and two more to
suit the P11 and P11A.

The Commando used the 1961 650 pair for 1968–70,
with another pair for the US machines in 1970. For
1969 a reverse-cone style with long megaphone and
short rear cone went on the S. This design, under a

91

The swept-back pipe of a Dunstall 650 from 1965 showing how to wire-lock the nut and other details of the café racer conversion

new part number, went on to all models for 1971. The part continued on the Fastback, Roadster and Hi-Rider for 1972–73 and was joined by another shape for the Interstate and Interpol models. For these, the front megaphone section was shorter and the reverse cone much longer, so the join between the two moved into the front half of the silencer. A mute became available for the older type but is not recommended and is best removed.

The same two silencers were used on the 850 models in 1973, but the mute in the first was not the same part as for the 750. This variation went in 1974 when a new and quieter silencer appeared with cylindrical body and black end cap. This is variously described as 'bean can' or 'black cap' and came with detail variances to suit the different models, including one in matt black for the JPR. Of the five types listed for 1974, only one ran on for 1975 with the end cap available as a spare although it had to be riveted into place.

The small twins did not have silencers of their own but used the current big-twin parts. Thus, the 250 was launched with the 1959 type with offset inlet and no tailpipe. The 400 took the 1960 type with centre inlet, no tailpipe and a tapered body end when it appeared in 1963. At the same time the silencer was used for the 250 and 350, the latter having had the 250 part up to then.

Don't forget that the whole system must fit the machine without stress or strain to avoid fracture or parts coming adrift. Be especially careful with the Commando and its rubber mountings between the silencers and the frame.

6 Lubrication

All Norton twins have a dry-sump system with a separate oil tank mounted on the right side of the machine beneath the saddle or front of the dualseat. A duplex-gear oil pump, driven by a worm on the crankshaft, went inside the timing cover which contained some of the oil galleries. A pressure gauge was fitted in the top of the petrol tank of the early model 7, but only for 1949–52 and, thus, on plunger-frame machines only.

A pressure-release valve went into the timing cover and a filter was provided on the feed line in the oil tank. From around 1953, another was fitted in the underside of the crankcase. From 1972 an external, cartridge filter was used in the return line. The rockers were lubricated with a pressure feed from the timing cover on the Atlas and Commando engines after number 116371 in 1966, but by a take-off from the return line on all other models, including the small twins.

Engine breathing on the big twins was via small radial holes in the camshaft, which was hollow. It drove a timed disc at its left end, and this arrangement was used up to 1971. For the 1972–73 750 a breather was taken from the back of the crankcase, and on the 850 it came from the back of the timing chest behind the block. The small twins simply had a breather pipe from the crankcase to the top of the oil tank.

Oil pump
This will run for a long time with little wear as it works in oil. When worn, it can usually be reclaimed by lapping the parts so the pump turns smoothly without end play. According to the factory, the pump did not let oil flow through it when the engine was not running, but this optimistic outlook was not reinforced by owners. Many found, and still do find, that some or all of the tank contents will find its way to the sump over a period of time. If not too much, the scavenge side will soon return it to the tank. Only on the Mk III engines from 1975 is there an anti-drain valve in the timing case, which was rather late in the day for most owners.

The pump itself was very similar to that of the singles; thus, its design dated from 1931. Many of the details were common but not all, so care is needed if a complete pump is sought. In 1961 a larger-capacity pump was introduced for the 650, and this is normally stamped with a letter S.

Up to then, the pump had been driven by a three-start worm which continued on the big twins until 1966. For that year a new pump was introduced along with a six-start worm and suitable mating gear. These items had been available for some time for competition use but were not advised for the 650-type S pump. The six-start worm was used first on the Electra and then on the 250 and 350 twins in 1963 from engine 106838.

The same pump and worm went into the first Commando. The pump was modified for 1972 and again for 1975 when a new sealing washer appeared along with the anti-drain valve piston and spring. The new sealing washer replaced the older one which had served for so long, often with shims to set it. For all earlier models, including the small twins, the conical rubber seal needs to have shims added behind it, so the cover will not quite go home until pressed. The Commando used the same worm and gear for all versions.

The small twins began with the same pump and gear as then in use for the big twins, but the worm that drove it differed to suit their crankshaft. These parts went on the 350, but the 400 had the six-start worm, and during 1963 this became the common part along with a revised pump.

Release valve and pressure gauge
The valve was a spring-loaded assembly that controlled the pressure of the oil reaching the engine. If the specified pressure was exceeded, excess oil was returned to the sump and from there to the oil tank. The assembly had its own gauze filter, which was fitted to keep dirt or grit away from the valve. More than one type was used and they need to be dismantled, cleaned and inspected. They seldom give trouble but check that the valve cuts off cleanly and look out for a tired pressure spring.

The big twins started and finished with an assembly that screwed into the rear of the timing

The need for lubrication demonstrated by Vic Willoughby flat out on a 1962 650SS

cover. For 1958 it was replaced by another design with a separate filter, situated in the rear of the timing cover, and a spring-loaded valve inside the cover which was only accessible by removing it. The early design remained in use when a timing cover with rev-counter drive was fitted. This became standard on the SS models so, in time, it outlasted the 1958 revamp which went after 1963. The original continued on to the Commando and was used on all variants of that model.

The small twins had their own design of spring-loaded plunger valve with filter which screwed into the inner face of the timing cover. The same assembly served all models and years.

The pressure gauge was only fitted for 1949–52 and went into the top of the petrol tank. It took its reading from a tapping in the rear of the timing cover just below the pressure-relief valve. When the gauge was no longer fitted the tapping was blanked off with a plug, and this point can be used by any owner who wishes to check the oil pressure. This does not apply to the timing cover introduced in 1958, but all models with the early-type, pressure-release valve have this facility.

A permanently-fitted gauge is not recommended as the reading obtained depends on so many factors, and any fault in the pipe or gauge means no oil pressure in the engine. More useful would be an oil-temperature gauge connected to the oil tank.

Filters

Essentially two from 1953 to 1971, one in the oil tank and the other in the engine sump. The former was also used on the 1949–52 models. They are made from a metal gauze or mesh, and need to be inspected for damage which could cause the oil not to be strained. The mesh is either soldered or silver-soldered in place so can be replaced or repaired with two provisos. First is not to restrict the oil flow and second is not to decrease the degree of filtration. Thus, do not replace a fine gauze with a wide mesh, or the reverse. Also check the parts for damage to the mechanical fixing and function.

The tank filter first changed for 1956 when a new style of oil tank was adopted, and this remained in use to 1965. For the next year another filter was fitted, with a further type for the G15 and N15 models. A new filter appeared for the Commando, being joined by a second type for the S in 1969. The latter filter became the standard for 1970 and following years. The small twins had the same filter as the big twins in 1956, and the one type was common to all models and years.

The sump filter was housed in a body which screwed into the underside of the crankcase, one assembly serving all the big twins from 1953 to 1971. For 1972 the filter was dispensed with and, in its place, there was a car-type cartridge filter tucked between the gearbox plates behind the engine. It was fitted in the return line to the oil tank and not in the feed as shown in the 1972–73 parts lists. It had a Jubilee clip round the element to clamp it to a bracket on the frame as a precaution against it coming undone. Don't overtighten the element or it will be very hard to remove 5000 miles later.

This arrangement was used on the 1973 750, but the 850 was fitted with the sump filter as well, and this continued on to the later versions of this model.

The small twins had a different sump filter comprising a plate, held to the base of the crankcase by four studs, and a gauze to match it. Oil drained through this on its way back to the pump. The plate used by the 250 was of pressed steel and also went on to the 350, while the 400 had its own cast in aluminium. This was adopted by the smaller models in 1964. They interchange.

Rocker-box oiling

For all models up to 650 cc this was arranged with a tee off the return oil pipe. In some cases this resulted in a rather marginal oil supply to the rockers, and one solution suggested by the factory in the 1960s was to place a finger over the return pipe, with the engine ticking over, to force more oil to the cylinder head. Be careful that the return pipe is not pushed off by the pressure, allowing oil to drop on the floor.

A rather more sophisticated approach was to fit a restrictor in the return line upstream of the tee which had the same effect. The part involved was the tank-return union adaptor, used as standard on the 250 de luxe as part 22148. This was featured on the small twins up to 1962.

From 1966 and engine 116372 the Atlas, and later the Commando, adopted another arrangement, the feed being taken from the pressure side of the system with a banjo-bolt connection in the rear of the timing chest. As pressure in this line can reach 70 psi, it must be secure and all joints made strong enough to withstand this.

The pipes themselves varied to suit the frame and oil tank, but in all cases they must not be allowed to chafe. The black plastic pipe used on the late Commando models is much better mechanically than the earlier rigid pipe, unless you are concerned with original appearance. More so where it holds oil at pump pressure rather than just from the return line.

The oil-tank cap had a dipstick on the 1959 Jubilee. Note also the seat fixing, tank bolt and tooltray

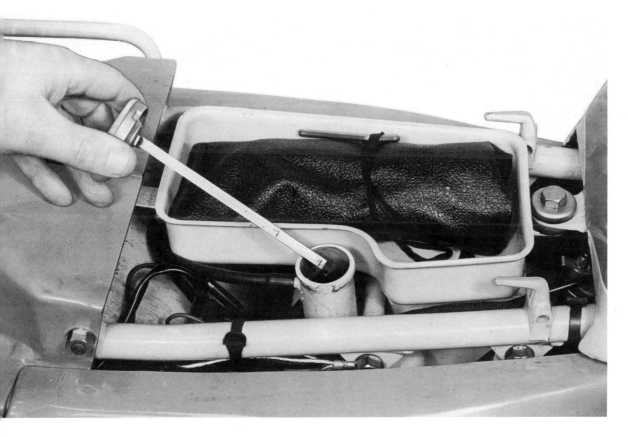

Pipes

The main ones were the feed and return that connected the oil tank to the engine, but there were also the rocker-box pipes, breathers and vent pipes. All need to be inspected for signs of cracks or leaks. Check carefully any flexible pipes as their material may deteriorate and swell up or break away. Either fault could block the pipe. Also check for any loose material that could flap about and stop the flow once this begins but which would make the pipe appear clear when inspected. A rare fault maybe, but confusing and expensive if it happens.

Breather system

This is an area that seems to give owners a headache if it presents any problems. Perhaps the snag is that it consists largely of holes and, as such, cannot appear on a parts list.

All Norton big twins up to 1971 have a timed rotary breather disc driven by the left end of the camshaft. It comprises a fixed disc with ports, a rotating disc with ears that fit into the camshaft and a spring that holds the two discs together.

Normally, the device is trouble free, but it can be jammed or broken on assembly. If this happens the engine either breathes all the time and loses oil rapidly, or it cannot breathe at all and the pressures generated force their way out elsewhere, causing leaks. The latter trouble will also occur if the breather pipe is blocked in any way.

The parts involved remained the same for 1949–71 except for the rotating disc, which changed for 1964 on. For 1972 this system was replaced by a simple tube run from the base of the crankcase at the rear to the oil tank. A separator was fitted in the body bolted to the case. This continued for 1973 on the 750, but on the 850 it was dispensed with in favour of a tube inserted in the top rear of the timing-chest area of the right crankcase. The other end of the tube was connected to a breather pipe, and this arrangement remained in use from then on. It proved to be the most successful system and can be adapted for earlier engines, provided the pipe is fitted at an angle so the oil tends to drain back into the engine and there are holes added through the timing-chest wall as on the 850.

The small twins avoided all this with a breather pipe run from the top of the crankcase to the oil tank. This appeared to be sufficient for these models as it was used on all of them. The early pipe sits just above the gearbox sprocket, and care must be taken to

ABOVE LEFT *Blocking the oil feed pipe on a 1956 model 99 after detaching the connection from the engine*

LEFT *The Norton oil pump and the feed seal which must press firmly against the timing cover using shims as needed*

The drive side of a 1967 Atlas showing chaincase, engine breather and magneto

ensure that it is not caught by the chain on the overrun. From engine 106838 the pipe exits from near the back of the gearbox, so there is no problem.

On all engines good breathing is as important as good joints in cutting out oil leaks, so it is vital that all the parts do their job correctly, including all the holes within the engine that contribute to the system.

Oil tank

This container always sits in the same place but comes in various shapes and sizes. Leaving aside the finish, which is covered later, the tank needs to be cleaned and inspected. On a running model the cleaning is, or should be, no problem, but an unknown tank can be full of horrors. Oil tanks seem able to harbour more dirt, sludge, spiders and unknown substances than even the underside of mudguards; maybe it's the confined atmosphere. Whatever it is, you have to get everything out. This may take every solvent and detergent you have, but clean the tank must be, both inside and out.

Only then can it be checked over. Look for cracks and split seams, which will need to be welded up. Oil tanks are prone to this due to the combination of heat and vibration. Thus, the mounting system and the actual fastenings need to be inspected to ensure they are not straining the tank or themselves. Make corrections as necessary. Also inspect all the pipe or union threads and any washer seating faces that may need cleaning up. If the latter has to be done, it is worth assembling the parts and checking that paraffin won't seep through the joint, even if you have to clean it out again. Better that than finding an oil leak later.

arrangement continued for these models.

In general, the 88SS and 650SS were both fitted with the standard 650 tank for 1962, but some had a modified tank with a froth tower at the top. With this arrangement, the engine breather was connected to the top of the tank and the tower was vented to feed any mist on to the rear chain. In time, the tank used on the SS also went on the Atlas, and a new part was common to all from 1964. These models continued in this way and were joined by others for the hybrids. In total, there were six extra tanks to suit these, with

LEFT *Oil-tank cap plus dipstick on a 1960 model 99 de luxe, the tank being special to suit the enclosure*

BELOW *The 1972 Commando 745 cc Production Racer with its special tank, seat and fairing*

Check the fit of the tank cap and its washer. Examine the breather, froth tower, rear chain feed or any other ancillary feature.

Oil-tank types

There were quite a number of these to suit the different frames and models over the years. The original went into the model 7 only and was joined by another for the 88. Both were changed for 1955 when a bayonet filler cap replaced the earlier wing-nut fastening, and for 1956 there was a single new tank with ribbed side to match the new battery enclosure. This was revised for 1957 when it was joined by another tank that was for the model 77 alone. This was shaped to fit into the angle of the rear subframe of that machine.

The tank was altered again for 1960 and the slim-line frame when it was joined by another with extended filler neck to suit the rear enclosure of de luxe models. Two more tanks came in 1961 to suit the 650 in standard and de luxe forms, and this

even the P11 and P11A having two different items.

The tanks had a hinged filler cap with wing nut at first, but from 1955 went over to a bayonet fixing. This cap was altered for 1956 and joined by another for de luxe models in 1960. For 1964 there was another cap which continued on these machines.

The small twins had two tanks and two caps. The first went on to the 250 and 350 de luxe models and had a dipstick, while the second went on to the standard versions including the 400. The caps were to suit, those used on the small de luxe machines being the same parts as fitted to the big twins.

The Commando ran through a whole range of tanks, effectively a new one for each year. The first was changed for 1969 and was joined by another for the S, the latter going on to the Roadster for 1970. From then on, there was just one tank for each year, but it was also changed each time although not to any great extent.

The Commando began with the 1964 filler cap but this changed for 1969, 1971 and 1974. More important is the mounting of the tank, which is a known trouble spot. Therefore, the rubbers need to be checked and fitted with care to avoid straining them or the tank. Failure of the rubbers allows the tank to move about enough to split, and the result can be exciting if it remains undetected.

Rear-chain lubrication
This was usually done by directing the oil-tank vent pipe at the chain, but this was not really much of a success. For town use, it required a higher-than-normal tank level to get much oil on to the chain at all, while at speed a lower level was required to prevent an excess of oil on the chain and the rest of the machine. The engine preferred matters the other way round, and the notion of a low oil level for high-speed motorway use is odd.

It is also possible to arrange for the engine breather pipe to vent on to the rear chain, but Norton came up with a regulator system for Commando owners, although this was not very successful. However, they persevered with it and, while it had a change or two, it remained on the machine up to 1974.

Engine-oil grade

An area of myths and folklore, over which owners argue well into the night. In the beginning there were straight oils that were thick or thin. They had no additives and did not last long. The grade of oil was classed by an SAE number (usually 20, 30, 40 or 50), the rider changing to a thinner grade for the winter and back to a thicker oil in the summer.

Then additives were put in the oil to prevent oxidation, inhibit rust, improve the load level and much more to give monogrades. These still needed to be changed to suit the season but lasted longer. They are especially suited to all ball-and-roller engines, and many motorcycle engines are just that.

Finally there came multigrades, which combined the merits of thick oil for hot running with thin oil for easy starting, even in winter. These had an unfortunate time when first introduced, but those days are long gone and modern quality multigrades are excellent for engines with plain bearings. Without them, cold starting would be very difficult indeed.

For many years Norton recommended SAE 40 in summer and SAE 30 in winter, and most owners prefer to keep to a monograde. Some go up to SAE 50 in summer; a filter and regular oil changes all help. A good 20/50 multigrade is better than a poor monograde, but the additives don't last so long in a high-temperature, high-specific-output engine, so the oil change periods must not be extended. The small twins can be run on 20/50.

Many readers may disagree with the above and, as always, the choice is theirs, but it does seem that a good monograde is to be preferred in these engines.

Transmission-oil grades

Monogrades are more usual in these areas, which are not subject to the same temperature range as the engine. SAE 20 goes in the primary chaincase, with an alternative of SAE 20 or 50 in the later machines.

The gearbox used an SAE 40 oil for many years, but as the power went up and heavier loads were generated on the gears it was changed to an EP90 gear oil. This has a similar viscosity to the earlier engine-oil grade but is able to cope better with the stresses involved and is to be recommended for all models. With their lower loadings, the small twins are happy with 20/50 in the gearbox and chaincase, which is convenient if nothing else.

The oil filter as adopted by the Commando in 1972 with Jubilee clip—shown on a 1973 Roadster

7 Electrics

This is an area that gives many owners considerable difficulties, and even some very skilled engine fitters will own that it is a big mystery to them. The problem occurs, in part, because you never see the substance, only its effects. Also, like an oil leak, it can spread all over the place without any obvious evidence as to where it came from.

If you intend to carry out a restoration, you have to accept that you must wrestle with the subject or it could defeat you. Fortunately, real electrical faults are rare, despite what you may think, as nearly all troubles are caused by mechanical failure of one form or another. Most can be cured by correct assembly and settings. Remember the need to comply with current, local legislation.

Helpful points to remember are as follows. The system has two sides, one dealing with charging and the other with use. Although they may connect in operation and control, they can be thought of as two distinct areas and dealt with accordingly. The most common fault is a poor earth, which is simply a poor connection for the return of the current rather than its supply. Also very common is a poor connection in the supply leads. Finally, buy the tools for the job, which means lighter spanners or wrenches, smaller screwdrivers, pliers, cutters, electrician's soldering iron and a small meter. The last does not have to be anything special as continuity checks will be its main job, but it will help a great deal. An old ammeter, preferably with centre zero and reading 15 amps or so, is also worth having to check current flow in and out of the battery. Even if the machine has its own, it is not always convenient to use, so a meter with leads can be better.

Norton electrical systems
Initially, Norton equipped their twins with the traditional magneto and dynamo with separate control unit, contriving to hang on to the former longer than most other firms. Their first use of coil ignition was in 1958, but it was not until 1967 that finally they had to concede that the magneto was no more and go to coil ignition. However, this had a capacitor emergency back-up system.

Long before then, in 1958, the charging side had been taken over by an alternator, which was used by all models from then on. With it came the first moves to coil ignition for the standard models, but the sports machines tended to keep to the magneto. Usually this was advanced automatically, but not always.

At first the coil-ignition points went into a distributor, which was fitted in the magneto position and driven by the same chain. However, from 1969 the Commando moved to timing-chest points driven from the end of the camshaft.

The system voltage was 6 volts until 1964 when a change was made to 12 volts, but the 400 was on 12 volts from its start in 1963. All the small twins had coil ignition and an alternator to provide the battery charge. The 6-volt systems used switch control to regulate the output, but with 12 volts came a zener diode, better control, more electric power and simpler wiring.

Magneto types
The model 7 began with a Lucas K2F with auto-advance built into its drive sprocket. This instrument was flange-mounted to the back of the timing chest where it was chain-driven from the camshaft intermediate gear-and-sprocket assembly. All magnetos rotated anti-clockwise when viewed from the driven end. There was mention of a BTH unit as an alternative in a 1949 road test, but elsewhere only the Lucas was listed.

This arrangement continued until 1958 when the alternator and coil ignition were adopted. In 1961 the magneto returned as an option for the 650, and in 1962 it came on the 650SS as standard. A magneto was also fitted as standard to the 88SS, but in this case a manual advance was specified. This situation continued into 1967, but from 1964 only the auto-advance magneto was listed. Only 175 of the 88SS models went out with manual advance; the rest had the automatic design. This also went on to the Atlas and later the hybrids which used the same engine.

Magneto service
This concerns the points gap, which is 0.012 in., and

ABOVE *Waterproofing the HT terminals of a twin magneto on a model 88*

BELOW *Exploded view of a twin-cylinder magneto showing the safety gap screws among the details*

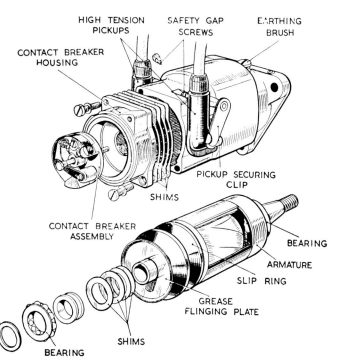

HIGH TENSION PICKUPS

SAFETY GAP SCREWS

EARTHING BRUSH

CONTACT BREAKER HOUSING

PICKUP SECURING CLIP

SHIMS

CONTACT BREAKER ASSEMBLY

BEARING

ARMATURE

SLIP RING

GREASE FLINGING PLATE

BEARING

SHIMS

the brushes. There are several of the latter for, in addition to the high-tension lead pick-ups in each side of the body, there is a brush in the rear of the points plate on face-cam magnetos and an earth brush. In many cases there is a brush in the cap for the earthing lead, and if the magneto fails to work this is one time when a connection to earth is not wanted, so disconnect it. In use, the low-tension side needs earthing to kill the magneto, and an intermittent fault in the line or the button can be a trial to deal with.

Lucas magnetos have safety gap screws and these *must* be removed before any real dismantling is done, otherwise the slip ring will be damaged. All brushes need to be examined for cracks and checked for free movement in their holders and their general condition. If worn, they should be replaced. Note that on occasion a brush or gap screw may be masked by a label, so care must always be exercised.

Magneto renovation

There is not a great deal more that can be done with a magneto, other than to clean it and possibly replace the bearings. Dismantling is straightforward, but mark parts first as they can often be reversed. Once apart, the details can be cleaned and inspected, especially for any cracks that could leak the high-tension current to earth.

Replacing and setting up magneto bearings is a fairly skilled job, and it is even more tricky to change a condenser or rewind an armature. Unless you are really competent in this work, it should be sent to a specialist. This is particularly true if the magneto has lost some of its magnetism and is sparking poorly, if at all. Magnetizing equipment is complex and expensive, so it is not really a practical proposition for any other than the professional.

Grease the bearings on assembly, which should give no problems. Do make sure all the little insulating washers and bushes are in the right place. More ignition systems fail to work after a rebuild for this reason than any other. Fit the leads, clamp the magneto in the vice, earth the plugs to it and give it a spin (anti-clockwise, of course). Check that the earthing connection does its job.

Dynamo type and drive

Only Lucas dynamos were fitted and only the type E3L. This went on to all model 7s, the 88 and 99 up to 1957 and the 77 for 1957–58. All were clamped to the front of the crankcase, with further fixings to the rear surface of the front end of the timing chest.

The dynamo was gear-driven from the camshaft, and a slipping clutch was incorporated within the sprocket and gear. The clutch was similar in design to that of the conventional mag-dyno, so the drive gear could slip in relation to the camshaft sprocket under shock loads. The dynamo armature carried a mating pinion.

Thus, it was easy enough to remove the dynamo and, if desired for competition purposes, to blank off the resulting hole with a small plate.

Dynamo testing

This can begin on the machine by disconnecting the leads to the dynamo. Join the two terminals, D and F, and connect a voltmeter from the join to the dynamo body. Run the machine so the dynamo speed is up to 1000 rpm and look for the voltage reading to rise smoothly and quickly to 10 volts. Don't run the dynamo faster in an attempt to push the voltage value up. If there is no reading at all look to the brush gear; if the reading is about 0.5 volts the field winding is suspect; and if between 1.5 and 2 volts the armature winding is the likely culprit.

The dynamo will need to be dismantled for any further work.

Dynamo service

Mark parts before taking them apart and proceed with delicacy as some items are rather brittle. Clean all the connections to reduce contact resistance, checking that all wires are in good order and not frayed in any way. Examine the brushes and replace them if worn down to about $\frac{5}{16}$ in. Make sure the brushes, whether old or new, move freely in their boxes and that the brush springs are strong enough to hold them in contact with the commutator.

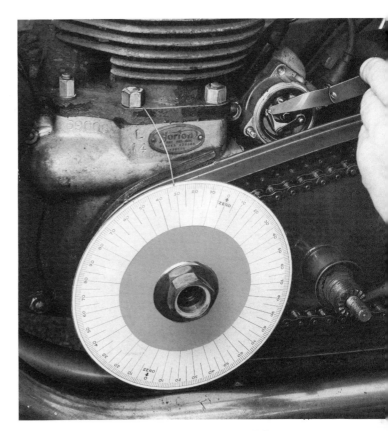

Setting the ignition timing using a degree disc and feelers to detect when the points open. The machine is a 1956 99

The commutator will need cleaning, and if burnt may need machining to restore it to a truly round profile. Should this be needed, remove only the minimum of material and be prepared to undercut the commutator segments. Also examine the wire connections to the segments for any signs of overheating, which may indicate problems in the armature. Clean out all the carbon dust as it can short out the insulated wires.

Armature rewinds and field-coil replacement are best left to specialists. The former requires special equipment, but the latter can be attempted with fewer facilities. There are two problems to overcome: first is the single fixing screw, which must be tight, and second is ensuring the new coil is really home in the body. Service departments use a special driver for the first problem and an expander for the second, but both can be overcome in the home workshop.

Grease the two ball races but not too much or it will be all over the commutator. Reassemble with care to ensure everything goes back where it came from.

The finished dynamo can be tested off the engine by connecting it to a battery so that it becomes an electric motor. This is done by joining the F and D terminals and connecting the join and the dynamo body to a 6-volt battery. The body connection is to the

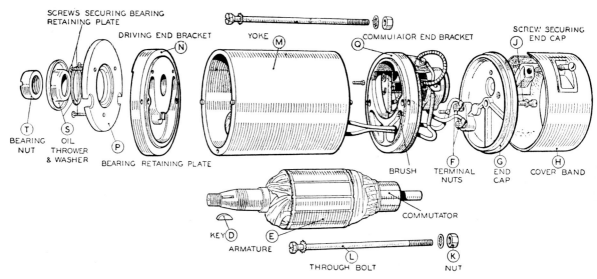

SCREWS SECURING BEARING RETAINING PLATE
DRIVING END BRACKET
YOKE (M)
COMMUTATOR END BRACKET (Q)
SCREW SECURING END CAP (J)
(N)
BEARING NUT (T)
OIL THROWER & WASHER (S)
BEARING RETAINING PLATE (P)
BRUSH (F)
TERMINAL NUTS
END CAP (G)
COVER BAND (H)
KEY (D)
ARMATURE (E)
COMMUTATOR
THROUGH BOLT (L)
NUT (K)

POLE SHOE RETAINING SCREW
FIELD COIL
POLE SHOE

ABOVE *The Lucas E3H dynamo shown exploded*

LEFT *Using an expander tool to set the field coil into a dynamo body. The retaining screw needs to be very tight*

terminal that is earthed normally, and if all is well the armature will revolve. This is not as good a test as with a voltmeter, but it is useful if the engine has been taken apart and may not be available for some while.

Regulator unit

This is also known as the compensated voltage control unit or cvc and may be referred to as the automatic voltage control or avc. This should not be confused with the later cvc used for cars. Here, the initials stand for current voltage control, and the unit has three coils in its assembly under the cover.

The motorcycle cvc is simpler, with just one control coil plus the cut-out under its lid. It has fewer connections than most cars, just four terminals in a row, and these are usually connected to wires which plug in and are held by a strip secured by two screws. The wires are positioned by this strip, and the screws are of different sizes to prevent a reversal of the connections.

All the twins had the MCR2 regulator up to 1956, and it differed from the older MCR1 in that the control

resistor became a carbon disc fitted to the main frame behind the coils. It can be recognized by a swelling put in the back of the cover to clear the resistor. On these two models the terminals were labelled FADE, but for 1957 the unit was changed to an RB107 which had its connections in the order FAED.

The cvc is a delicate, electro-mechanical assembly and must be treated as such. It can be set up and adjusted by the owner, but this must be done precisely or the system will not work as it should. Really no different to valve clearances or ignition timing.

Regulator function

Two jobs are done by the cvc unit. The regulator side switches a resistor into series with the field coil to reduce the field current and the generated output. It is in a state of vibration while doing this. The cut-out is simply a switch that disconnects the dynamo from the battery when needed to prevent the latter trying to motor the former, which would discharge the battery.

Confusion with the unit usually arises because the theoretical circuit diagram, practical wiring diagram and the unit itself all look completely different. Further confusion arises because the internal frame is used as part of the electric circuit but is not an earth. In truth, it connects via the cut-out points to the battery supply line, so it is insulated from the mounting frame.

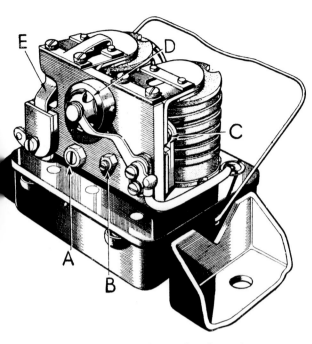

The Lucas MCR2 cvc with its carbon disc resistor

Regulator service

If you decide to work on the cvc, trace out the electrical circuit first so you know where each part fits into the scheme of things. Then it will be much easier to check each item for continuity or open circuit using your meter. In most cases the only problem will be the mechanical aspects of the contacts, their cleanliness and their adjustment. With those taken care of, all the circuits are likely to function as they should.

Looking at the coils, the one on the left with a few turns of heavy gauge wire about its middle is the regulator. The first adjustment is by moving the

The RB107 cvc as used by Norton twins from 1957

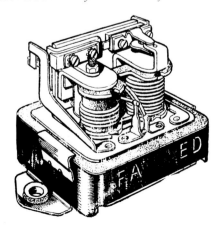

armature, which is the bent steel part pulled by the coil magnetism and carrying one of the contacts. The next adjustment is made by bending the fixed contact on the MCR units. Finally, an adjuster screw at the rear needs setting.

Air gaps are required between the vertical leg of the armature that carries the contact and the frame, and between the horizontal leg and the bobbin core on the MCR2. Both should be 0.02 in., but the second has a tolerance of minus 0.008 in. The points gap on the MCR2 should be between 0.006 and 0.017 in., with the armature held against the bobbin core.

The RB107 has a different method of adjustment. The armature screws are undone, a feeler gauge of 0.021 in. put between the armature and the bobbin and the screws done up. Then the contacts are adjusted so they just touch with the feeler gauge still in place.

The remaining adjustments are made with the cvc wired to the machine. Put card between the cut-out points and disconnect the lead from terminal A. Connect a voltmeter between terminals D and E, and run the dynamo at about 3000 rpm. At 20 degrees Celsius the reading should be 8.0 to 8.4 volts, and it can be adjusted with the screw at the rear. If the temperature rises deduct 0.2 volts for every 10 degrees Celsius, and if it falls add it. Then run the dynamo at about 4500 rpm when the reading should not exceed 8.9 volts. Do all this quickly or errors will occur. If in doubt do it in steps.

Cut-out setting

For the MCR2 the armature-to-frame air gap should be 0.014 in. and to the bobbin core 0.011 to 0.015 in. With these two gaps held correctly by gauges, press the armature down on them and check that the gap between the armature and stop-plate arm is 0.03 to 0.034 in. Bend the arm if adjustment is necessary. Then place a 0.025 in. gauge between the armature shim and core face, checking that the contact gap is between 0.002 and 0.006 in. Bend the fixed contact bracket to adjust.

The RB107 is set by pressing the armature down to the core face and checking the gap between its stop arm and its tongue. This should be 0.025 to 0.04 in. Bend the stop arm to adjust. Then adjust the fixed contact blade to give a blade deflection of 0.01 to 0.02 in. when the armature is pressed firmly down on the core face.

Cut-out checking

This is done on the machine, and a full test covers both cut-in and cut-out. For the first, connect an ammeter in the lead from dynamo terminal D to cvc terminal D and a voltmeter between there and terminal E. Gradually bring the engine speed up and watch for the voltmeter pointer to flick back as the points close. This should occur at 6.3 to 6.7 volts and is adjusted by the screw, which increases the setting when turned clockwise. The ammeter should show a charge when the points close. When the engine stops, the ammeter discharge reading is taken and should be between 3 and 5 amps when the contacts open.

The cut-out check is done by detaching lead A from the cvc and connecting a voltmeter between terminals A and E. Run up the dynamo to 3000 rpm, then let its speed die away slowly. The voltage should be between 4.8 and 5.5 volts when the contacts open and the reading drops to zero.

Regulator oddments

The resistance used in the cvc, which is placed in the field circuit, can be measured if you have a good meter. The value for a carbon type is 36–45 ohms, while with the wire-wound type of the MCR1 it is 27–33 ohms.

If your machine has the short E3 dynamo fitted in error, it ought to have an MCR1 cvc. If this is not available, the MCR2 listed under part number 37144A should be used.

You can use the machine without the battery as long as the cvc is working correctly. In some cases this may not be fully legal, but it can be useful in an emergency. However, if the battery is in circuit it must be kept topped up, otherwise the control is fooled into providing excess current which can ruin the battery, dynamo and cvc.

The contact points do get dirty and may need cleaning. If they do they will need resetting for sure.

Should the dynamo polarity have reversed itself, which does happen, just hold the cut-out points together for a second or two and then pull them apart.

Do make sure that dynamo terminal D is connected to cvc terminal D, and F to F. Although the dynamo leads are held by a kidney-shaped plate and the cvc plate is non-reversible, they could have been switched at some time. Detach the leads and check by meter as they often run out of sight on the machine.

Modern regulators

By using modern electronic components, the problems of the electro-mechanical cvc can be removed with solid-state devices. This is electronic engineering, quite outside most people's knowledge, but specialist suppliers make it easy for the rest of us.

A unit is available to replace the cvc and comprises a waterproof box that does the same job and enables the machine to be converted to 12 volts. Battery and bulbs also need changing but not the horn, and since the change boosts output better lights can be fitted. The new assembly is small enough to tuck out of sight, so the alteration is not at all obvious for owners who wish to keep up appearances.

While this change departs from total originality, it is to be recommended for any machine used on a regular basis in modern traffic where good lights are

ABOVE *Checking the air gap of an alternator which must be done all the way round. This one is on a Commando*

RIGHT *The alternator and distributor as on a 1963 model 88*

essential. The move to 12 volts not only greatly improves the electrical efficiency of the system but also allows halogen lights to be used as a further bonus.

Alternator

Norton adopted the alternator on the twins for 1958, and with it came the advantages of no touching parts to wear and other delights. Unfortunately these included control problems and boiled batteries, so all was not quite as good as it might have been. In time, the zener diode came along and with it arrived better control and 12-volt systems.

The 1958 machines were fitted with a Lucas RM15 unit which was changed to an RM19 for 1962. The year 1967 saw a further change to the RM21 with encapsulated windings, and this went on to the Commando as well. For 1975 and the Mk III, the even more powerful RM23 was fitted. If desired this can be used on older Commandos. There is also the RM24, which has a higher output at low speed, but as this is a three-phase design it needs a different rectifier and zener diodes. It was never a factory fitment but became available from specialists.

The small twins differed in that while all had an alternator, it was supplied by Wico-Pacey and not Lucas. The same 50-watt item went on all 250 and 350 engines, with another 12-volt type for the 400.

Alternator checking

There is not a great deal that can be done other than cleaning and inspection. Check that the rotor has been running clear of the coil poles and look at the wiring for any damage. Use a meter to check continuity and insulation, establishing which coils are connected together and how the wires attach to them. Compare this with your wiring diagram and keep notes on this aspect, which may help a good deal when sorting out the connections to the rectifier.

Make sure the rotor is a good fit on the crankshaft. If not, it may be machined to locate on a made-up spacer against the engine sprocket. With care and ingenuity, it is possible to achieve a better design than the original. This will also overcome a damaged crankshaft end by providing some other means of holding the rotor true.

It is possible for the rotor centre to become loose within the assembly which may give rise to a nasty knocking noise in the engine. A cure is to machine away enough of the alloy side to allow the core to be removed and then to refit it using a Loctite gap filler.

Rectifier

Early alternators had their output turned into direct current by massive selenium-plate rectifiers. The original boxes soon became a smaller set of four plates on a single central bolt and, in time, this assembly was replaced by a similar silicon-diode rectifier.

All the four-plate types give full wave rectification, and the central stud is one of the direct-current connections and must be treated as such. It connects to the earthed side of the battery. The three plate connections have the second direct-current line in the middle flanked by the two alternating-current connections. These last two may be connected either way round as reversal will not affect the rectifier operation at all.

The rectifier can be cleaned and its electrical function checked for the correct working of each diode. These must pass current one way but not the other, and a meter or battery and bulb will act as a tester. Do not move the central clamping nut or the device will fail. The nut tension controls the efficiency of the unit and must be left alone. Therefore, care is needed when fixing the device to the machine.

Alternator control

On the face of it, the stator coils connect to the rectifier, which connects to the battery to complete the circuit. Unfortunately, there are complications. First, the output needs to be controlled to suit the load, and second, it would be nice to be able to start even with a flat battery. Coping with these problems introduces complications in the switches and wiring, and the result can be confusion.

On big twins the control is provided for 6-volt systems by stator coil switching. The basic control is that two coils are permanently connected, and with the lights off the remaining four are short-circuited to reduce the output of the two in use. With the pilot light on, the four are open circuit so they don't affect the other two, and with the headlight on all six are connected. This means that the light switch has to be joined electrically to the charging circuit.

The 250 and 350 twins used a different system with two sets of three coils in the alternator. When running with no lights three coils were connected and the current was sent down a resistance wire to balance the load. With the pilot light on, the resistance wire was switched out of circuit, and with the headlamp on all six coils were connected.

Problem two is overcome on the big twins by switching four coils to supply the ignition circuit direct, leaving two to assist the battery on an emergency basis. All six coils are used for ignition on the 250 and 350.

On the big twins, where a 12-volt system was in use, a zener diode was employed for control. The same part

The ignition switch, distributor, battery and capacitor on a 1968 Commando Fastback

was fitted from 1964 onwards, two being used on the Mk III Commandos built from 1975 on. The 650 and Atlas models have a heat sink to dissipate the excess energy of the alternator, but the Commando models use the right footrest plate, or both of them in the case of the Mk III. One of the plate bolts is also used for the zener earth lead. Thus, it is longer than appears necessary at first sight.

The 400 differed from the big twins in that, although it had a 12-volt system, the alternator output was controlled by a relay-type voltage regulator similar to a dynamo cvc. The stator had six coils, two of which were permanently connected, while the other four were brought into circuit by the regulator when the battery was low.

If the connections are not as they should be or the switch contacts are dirty, all manner of charging problems will arise. The situation is confused further by variations that were available over the years and which may have been incorporated in a system. Generally, the mechanical components are interchangeable, and on the electrical side it is just a question of joining wires, so anything is possible.

To add to the problem, Lucas also changed the wire colours on the early alternators as the originals tended to become indistinguishable. First they were light, mid and dark green. Then light green, green and yellow, and dark green. Finally green and white, green and yellow, and green and black. If you don't have an original stator, rectifier and harness you could have variations.

The Wipac alternator used white, light green and orange, white being common to both sets of coils. The 250 and 350 had equal outputs on the orange and light green wires, but for the 400 light green gave low output and orange twice as much.

Further complications arise in that, where the machine has magneto ignition, the above applies with two coils always in circuit. For models with coil ignition it was common to have four in use and the mid and dark green connections reversed. The lead from rectifier to light switch, usually light green, may be disconnected and taped up as this has a further trimming effect on the output. The connections were often reversed for winter riding, especially if a sidecar was fitted, and changed back for summer to avoid a boiled battery.

To sort out what you have and how to connect it you need to work out the alternator leads and circuit, the rectifier leads and the switch circuits. Then use the wiring diagram for the model to trace what happens at each switch position. Not easy, I know, as normally the diagrams don't give the switch circuits, and without those it is difficult. Hence the need to check the switch itself with a meter, writing down the results.

Alternator voltage conversion

This popular way of getting more out of the system is easily carried out. It simplifies the wiring as all six alternator coils are connected permanently to the rectifier, which has the zener diode fitted between its supply terminal and earth. The actual details vary according to the machine circuit but can be sorted out using the wiring diagram and the information already established for the switches.

When first introduced the zeners could not cope with controlling the full output when there was no headlight load, so the switched connection was still needed. This had two coils which were on permanently for machines fitted with a magneto and four where coil ignition was used. Modern zeners can cope.

Battery, ignition coils, bulbs, and possibly rectifier and ignition condenser will need changing. The horn is not essential, but any ancillaries need to be remembered.

The battery installation on a 1959 Jubilee was tucked in behind the oil tank

Coil ignition

This was first used in 1958 and continued for the standard models when the SS versions reverted to a magneto. During 1967 all changed over to coil ignition, but with the back-up of a capacitor system. This was fired by the points and acted as an emergency circuit, or the main circuit if no battery was fitted.

The same arrangement went on to the Commando models, but all the small twins kept to a simple coil-ignition system with the points in the timing cover and their cam driven by the inlet camshaft. The big twins had a distributor from 1958 to 1963, but when they reverted to coil ignition in 1967 they used a twin-points assembly in the distributor position. This was used by the Commando up to 1969 and the first Commando S model. From then on the big twins had their points in the timing cover.

Distributor and points

Essentially you clean and inspect. Replace the points, oil the advance mechanism and make sure there are no cracks in the cap or the rotor arm. See if the bearings are in good order and that the spindle turns freely. Attend to anything in trouble and rebuild.

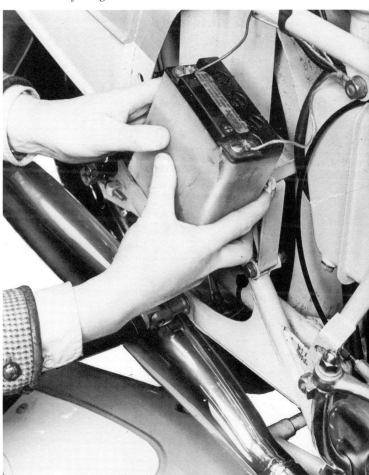

Do make sure the points wire connection is the correct side of its insulating washers and check it with the meter.

Inspect the small pivot points in the advance mechanism and repair or replace as necessary. Replace the advance springs if these are tired and check you have the correct type of advance unit installed.

Timing-cover points and advance

The points plate on the Commando came in various forms, but generally what is wanted is one that allows each contact set to be timed by itself following renewal. Some of the clamping screws are small and delicate, so care is advised. The advance mechanism was part of the Combat engine saga, so any early one should be changed for the later design or problems will arise.

The small twins had their own design but make sure the correct advance unit is used. The overhaul procedure is the same as for the distributor system. It is essential to lubricate the advance mechanism.

Energy transfer and AC ignition

In these designs some of the alternator windings are connected directly to a special ignition coil. This allows the machine to run without battery in the same manner as one fitted with a magneto, but the ignition timing is critical. Points cam and advance unit are specially designed for the job and the right parts must

ABOVE *The distributor with two sets of points on a 1969 Mercury*

RIGHT *Checking the points gap of a 1959 Jubilee which had them set in the timing cover*

be used for it to operate effectively. The distributor range is limited and essential to the operation. Otherwise it is checked over as the others.

Ignition timing

This is often a source of great concern to owners. In one sense it is important, but on the other hand the actual figure used may be less so. What is often forgotten is that the engine may be 20 or more years old, worn in various ways and running on a different blend of fuel to that available when it was new.

So while the original figure makes a good starting point it is not sacrosanct. The old-fashioned technique of advancing the setting until the engine pinks on a rising road and then backing it off a little still works, even if it is awkward to carry out on some models.

Check the timing you decide to use on full advance and on both cylinders. The retard figure is much less important so may be ignored, although the more particular among us will check it to be sure. It is not uncommon for a variation to arise between the cylinders, and this should be removed if possible as the engine will run more smoothly. Beware of slack in the drive when checking, and of slack in distributor bearings which can give a false reading. Recheck if in any doubt.

By 1964 the battery of the Jubilee had moved to the left side of the machine and sat under a cover

Electronic ignition

A worthwhile modification for late-type machines, being available in various forms to replace magneto or coil ignition. It is also possible to adapt a system to existing parts and retain the original drive.

The installation instructions supplied with the kit should be followed carefully, especially regarding the timing. Electronic advance is normal, so the mechanical device must be discarded or locked, and the timing will have to be checked with a strobe. Therefore, a timing mark will be needed. This must be checked with a timing disc before the ignition is set up.

In addition to the electronic-ignition kits, a further option takes the form of capacitor ignition using the alternator as a power source, a 12-volt zener diode control, a storage capacitor and the original points and advance mechanism. Effectively this is a variation of the earlier energy-transfer system but is much better in use and is, in essence, the same as that installed from mid-1967 onwards.

Sparking plug, cap and lead

The plugs should be replaced by a modern equivalent, although many owners do like to keep the originals if they are to hand. Some refit them for a concours, but for normal use a new pair of plugs should be fitted. Check that the plug top is tight as it can cause a misfire if loose. Grades are listed in Appendix 7.

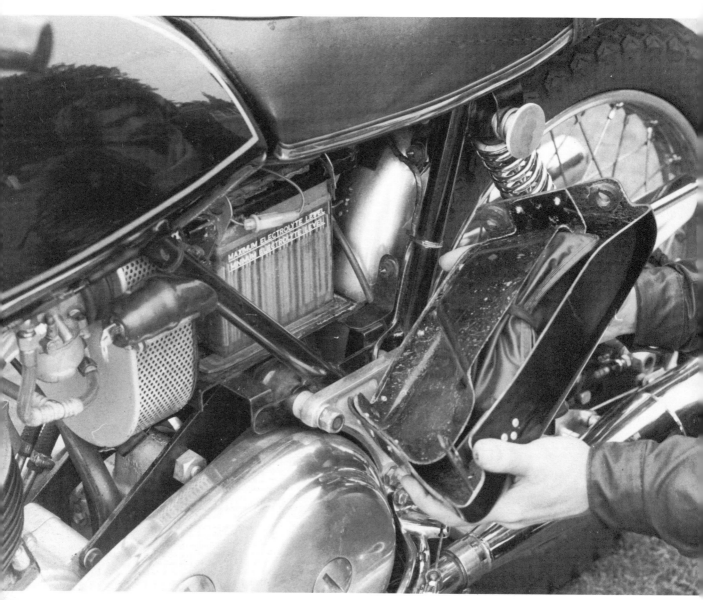

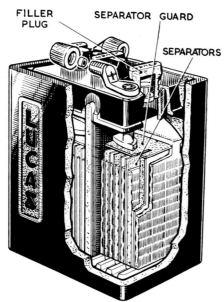

FILLER PLUG   SEPARATOR GUARD

SEPARATORS

ABOVE *The battery and its cover complete with toolkit on a 1972 Interstate*

LEFT *A typical 6-volt battery—this is a Lucas PU7E/11*

RIGHT *A 1975 Mk III Interstate with electric start and left-side gearchange*

The caps should contain suppressors, and the leads must be in good condition. Make sure the ends are clean and make a good connection or an odd misfire may occur.

Starter

Just two Norton twin models were fitted with an electric starter: the Electra and the Mk III Commando. Both had the motor mounted behind the cylinders where it drove the left crankshaft end, but in other respects they differed.

The Electra had a Lucas M3 motor with an epicyclic reduction gear in its end housing. A chain-drive linked this with a sprocket and sprag assembly mounted on the crankshaft inside the primary chaincase. It worked well. The Commando had a Prestolite motor and a train of gears to its roller sprag clutch. It was expected to do more than its size or gearing really allowed and became known as an 'assister', or just as 'one of the biggest space wasters ever'.

In both cases, the electric wiring and brushes are heavy-duty to cope with the currents involved. The parts need stripping, cleaning, checking and assembling as usual, with replacement or repair as required.

Check the solenoid for correct operation, all wiring and connections which must be good and tight, the kill switch on the Commando in case it has corroded, and the sprag-clutch assembly in both applications.

Lighting

Renovation of the lights is mainly by replacement as most of the parts are fragile and are either complete and working or in pieces. The bulb containers may need repairing and finishing, which should be done in the same way as for any other item.

The current legal requirements need to be considered for any machine being used on the road as some of the earlier fittings do not comply with them. In particular, rear lamps have increased in size— necessary to cope with modern traffic conditions.

Norton twins used a variety of lighting systems over the years, but most changes were brought about by alterations to the electrical system or by revised styling.

Headlamp and switch types

Originally, the Norton twin was built with a traditional arrangement and had a separate headlamp shell with a small panel set in it. This carried the

ammeter with the light switch behind it. Right at the start an 8 in. lamp was specified but soon this became a 7 in. version. The model 7 had its speedometer mounted in a small panel fixed between the tops of the fork legs.

This panel was enlarged for the 88 so it could also carry the ammeter, which went on the right, and the light switch on the left. Thus, a simple headlamp shell was used, but this did have an underslung pilot lamp as a pre-focus light unit was fitted. This had its bulb dropped in from the rear and offered a much better light output, but at that time a separate pilot had to be provided.

The same light unit and underslung pilot went on to the model 7 for 1953, but the switch and ammeter remained as they were. The next change came for 1956, by which time the technical problem of mounting the pilot bulb in the pre-focus light unit had

been solved. Thus, the underslung pilot went and a longer shell was fitted. This had a small, detachable panel to carry the speedometer, with the ammeter and light switch still to right and left respectively.

For 1957 these items were fitted directly into the headlamp shell rather than on a separate panel, except for the model 77 which kept to the 1956 design. A further change for the models that adopted the alternator and coil ignition came in 1958, a three-position switch appearing in the centre of the lighting unit. It gave on, off and emergency-start ignition.

This layout continued on the big twins with coil ignition until the Commando appeared. Where a magneto was fitted, as on the SS models, the combined switch was replaced by a simple lighting switch.

A new light switch came in with the move to a 12-volt system in 1964 as the wiring and connections were simplified. The basic positions stayed as they

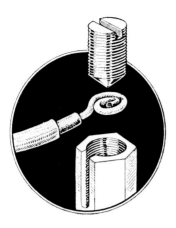

ABOVE *Early post and screw connection showing how the wire should be rolled into a ball. Solder with care, if at all*

LEFT *The ignition coil and switch on a 1968 P11A, all rather tucked away*

RIGHT *The separate switch panel used on a 1956 model 99 and the large knob to help the rider wearing winter gloves*

were but some machines were being built in a more sporting style. Instead of only having the rev-counter on a fork top bracket these had both instruments on brackets, which made access to the switch awkward. To deal with this the switch was mounted between the instruments, and the shell was altered to suit. From 1967 this became the standard arrangement until the Mercury of 1969, which had just a light switch and speedometer on the bracket.

The Commando was laid out a little differently with the ignition switch just in front of the left side panel. For the S and Roadster of 1969–70 it moved to the top front corner of the left side panel. The headlamp shell still carried an ammeter along with a three-position light switch and a main-beam warning light.

This layout was altered for 1971 when the ignition switch changed from a simple two-position on/off type to one with four positions. At the same time the ammeter went and the headlamp shell carried just a two-position light switch behind a line of three warning lights. These were green, red and amber from left to right, and the two outer ones had small shields round them. They showed the use of main beam, ignition on and turn indicators in use respectively.

The JPR used a similar arrangement but with the parts mounted in the fairing. The light switch went below and between the instruments, while the warning lights were ahead and in a cluster. The left was red and the right green, both having shields, while the amber went in the middle.

The parts stayed where they were until 1975 and the Mk III. For that model the main switch was moved

on to the fork crown and surrounded by four warning lights in a small housing. These were coloured red for ignition, blue for main beam, green for neutral and amber for turn indicators.

The small twins had a 6 in. headlamp with the speedometer mounted in the rear of the shell. An ammeter went ahead of it and was flanked by a light switch on the left and an ignition switch on the right. From 1961 all small twins changed to a 7 in. light and shell.

The bulb types and ratings should be as specified by the parts list for all machines if a standard build is sought, but for those riders seeking an improvement there are replacement light units available. If you have a 12-volt system a halogen lamp can be used. This is well worth fitting if you seek the best in lighting.

Stop and tail light

At first the twins only had a tail light, the round Lucas MT211, but for 1953 this was changed to a rectangular stop and tail light with moulded, red-plastic lens. In 1955 a separate reflector appeared beneath the rear number plate, and in 1957 the type 564 rear light was fitted. This had an integral reflector.

The 564 remained in use for a decade and was joined in 1966 by the 679, which went on the N15, P11 and the G15 models except the G15CSR. In time, this took over and went on to the Commando as well, but it was altered slightly for 1972 when it gained a gasket. The lamp changed more drastically for 1973 when it became much larger with a square format. This stayed in use from then on.

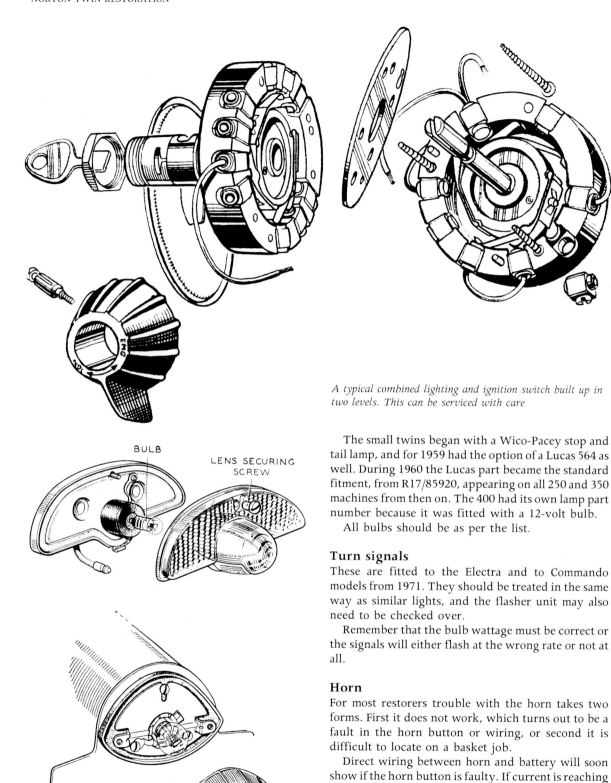

A typical combined lighting and ignition switch built up in two levels. This can be serviced with care

BULB

LENS SECURING SCREW

The small twins began with a Wico-Pacey stop and tail lamp, and for 1959 had the option of a Lucas 564 as well. During 1960 the Lucas part became the standard fitment, from R17/85920, appearing on all 250 and 350 machines from then on. The 400 had its own lamp part number because it was fitted with a 12-volt bulb.

All bulbs should be as per the list.

Turn signals

These are fitted to the Electra and to Commando models from 1971. They should be treated in the same way as similar lights, and the flasher unit may also need to be checked over.

Remember that the bulb wattage must be correct or the signals will either flash at the wrong rate or not at all.

Horn

For most restorers trouble with the horn takes two forms. First it does not work, which turns out to be a fault in the horn button or wiring, or second it is difficult to locate on a basket job.

Direct wiring between horn and battery will soon show if the horn button is faulty. If current is reaching the horn and nothing is happening, it may need adjustment. This might be by a screw in the back or a

Lucas rear lamps with model 590 at the top and 529 below

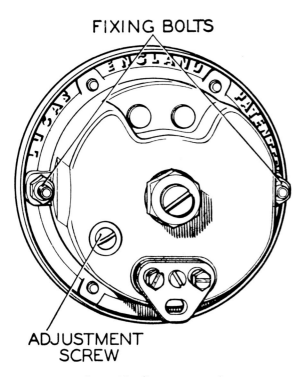

FIXING BOLTS

ADJUSTMENT
SCREW

Lucas HF1234 horn with adjustment screw in rear

Battery

The problem on some models is appearance. While the battery lived outside enclosing panels, its looks were an important aspect of the left side of the machine. It is possible to obtain facsimiles of the early black-bodied, 6-volt battery, which is one solution. Another is to adapt an old battery by cutting out the interior and fitting a modern one inside it.

For the rest, keep it clean, check the specific gravity and smear protective jelly on the terminals to prevent corrosion. If the battery has been removed from the machine, keep it working by running it down with a 3-watt bulb and then recharging it. This will prevent it from collapsing when asked to do some real work.

Up to 1963 the big twins had a 6-volt system, but from 1964 all changed to 12 volts. This was done by fitting twin 6-volt batteries except on the P11, which had a single 12-volt version. The Commando models all had a single 12-volt battery. The 250 and 350 small twins had a 6-volt Exide on the right of all de luxe models and on the left on the standard machines. A second battery was added under the seat of the 400 to provide the 12-volt system. This was a feature on that model from its inception in 1963.

nut under a cover. However, some horns may have no adjustment facility at all. Where provided, the adjuster should be moved no more than one or two notches at a time. On a scale of 24 notches this equals one full turn of the screw. Six notches from just not sounding should be about right, but the current flow should also be monitored; anything over 5 amps indicates a need for specialist attention.

Don't move the centre screw as this controls the basic points adjustment and needs special equipment to set. Given this and care, the horn may be stripped and the case renovated in the same way as any other part.

Horn position

The horn was hung from the left saddle-spring lug on model 7 plunger-frame machines. With the advent of the pivoted-fork frame in 1953, the horn was moved to a position in the right subframe angle just aft of the oil tank, where it stayed.

The Featherbed-frame models all had the horn tucked under the petrol tank, where it was hung from the head steady. The horn type also changed from the HF1235 to the HF1441. It altered in 1962 but stayed in the same place over the years. On the Commando it was moved to a point under the battery box, where it stayed. At first, the small twins had their horn set in the front fork apron just beneath the headlamp, but it moved to beneath the tank in 1961. They had a Lucas 5H horn at first, but from 1962 used an 8H.

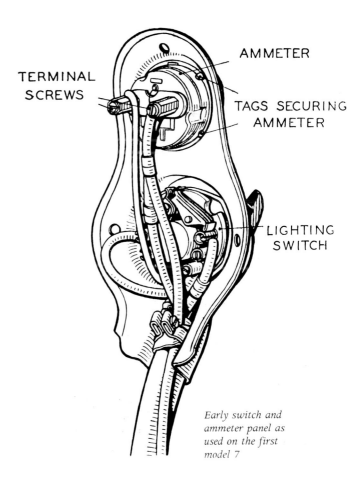

TERMINAL
SCREWS

AMMETER

TAGS SECURING
AMMETER

LIGHTING
SWITCH

Early switch and ammeter panel as used on the first model 7

Ammeter

There is not much one can do to repair one of these, so either you have one working or it just acts as a dummy to give an original appearance. In this situation, one terminal can be used as a junction point, but if the insulation of the case is in any doubt it is best to keep the wiring away from it altogether.

Wiring

The prime source of electrical troubles, with poor connections, poor earths and intermittent leaks to earth being the major problems. Switches can also cause many headaches if the contacts are not clean and making good connections.

If you intend to use the existing harness it must be checked over carefully for signs of damage or chafing. These must be repaired. All wires must be checked for continuity, a wiring diagram being most useful for this. Most of those given in manuals are really circuits and are very hard to use in practice, so it is well worth drawing your own. You can lay it out as on the machine and add the internal switch connections, making it easy to see where the current is supposed to flow.

FITTING A "LUCAR" SERVICE CONNECTOR

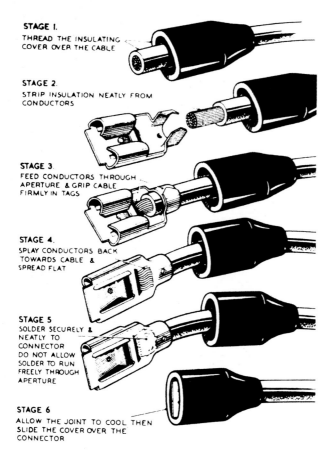

STAGE 1.
THREAD THE INSULATING COVER OVER THE CABLE

STAGE 2.
STRIP INSULATION NEATLY FROM CONDUCTORS

STAGE 3.
FEED CONDUCTORS THROUGH APERTURE & GRIP CABLE FIRMLY IN TAGS

STAGE 4.
SPLAY CONDUCTORS BACK TOWARDS CABLE & SPREAD FLAT

STAGE 5
SOLDER SECURELY & NEATLY TO CONNECTOR DO NOT ALLOW SOLDER TO RUN FREELY THROUGH APERTURE

STAGE 6
ALLOW THE JOINT TO COOL THEN SLIDE THE COVER OVER THE CONNECTOR

You will find that one section of the wiring is concerned with charging the battery and connects generator and control. The other covers the consumption side and all flows from one point. An item using current may be connected directly, as is the horn, via the ignition switch to the coil, or via the light switch. Total isolation of the battery from the system did not come until later. The horn current is not taken through the ammeter, so the lead to this comes before the instrument, and the same applies to some stop lamps.

If you have any rewiring to do, first sort out the wiring diagram and then decide on the wire type and gauge you will use. Early models usually had black rubber-covered wire, possibly with a coloured or numbered sleeve at the end. This form of insulation perishes and is used no longer. Modern wires are colour-coded to ensure correct connections. The wire gauge depends on the current carried, and it is as well to err on the fat side to keep voltage drop to a minimum.

A new harness is best built up on the machine, ensuring it fits well. Tape it into place as you go and then remove it as one assembly, binding the wires into a bundle to keep the weather at bay. Tape or heat-shrink tubing can be used for this provided the finished harness will accommodate the necessary movement in the headstock area. Elsewhere, it must be held firmly so it cannot fray and is not trapped or pinched at any point.

Joints and connections need careful attention. Joins in the wires are best made with modern connectors, each wire being crimped or soldered to its terminal. Avoid nicking the wire when stripping the insulation, although this is not easy, and don't use an excess of solder. In avionics work, individual strands are counted to make sure none are missing and inspected for marks, and you can expect to see each one just outlined by its solder shroud. Achieve even half that standard and you won't have any problems.

Crimp-on connectors normally call for special tools, but a serviceable connection can be made using pliers of one sort or another plus common sense. Make sure the wire is held firmly and not at all loose. If the wires are soldered in place don't let the solder run back into the wire or its rigidity will cause it to fracture under vibration. When dealing with older types of switches with terminal posts just roll the wire into a ball under the fixing screw. If you do use solder play safe by clamping the wire securely a short distance from the terminal. Electrical strapping will look neater than tape on the final assembly.

Fitting a push-on connector of the type which became common for many makes and models

Switches

These must be checked for correct operation with a meter. The older type can be taken apart for cleaning, but watch for rollers with springs behind them that may fly out and roll all over the floor. Recheck the operation after assembly. Draw the connections on your wiring diagram so you can see how the components connect up in each switch position.

In addition to the more complex light and ignition switches, check out the dip-switch, horn button, stop-light switch and cut-out for correct operation. As you connect them into the circuit check each, in turn, to ensure correct operation without any errant connections.

Earthing

All the older machines rely on the cycle parts to do this job, which is why they often have problems.

An Interpol on show at Brighton in 1969 with Neale Shilton in attendance with notice

Having carefully restored the protective paintwork of frame, forks, mudguards and panels, it is rather a shame to damage this finish to complete the earth return.

The answer is to run an earth wire from each item back to the battery or to a convenient junction point. The wires must be of a suitable gauge for carrying the current from all items to which they are connected and are best earthed, both to the frame and the engine, at one point. Don't forget that the ignition system must have a complete circuit for both high- and low-tension loops and that the Commando engine is suspended on rubber.

Fuses

These were not fitted to early machines but are a good insurance for all. At the very least, a single 35-amp fuse in the main battery line can save the day in the event of a short circuit, while for more sophistication a modern fuse box with several fuses and spares can be wired into the circuits. Separate protection for the lights and ignition makes sense, but this can be extended to a fuse for each circuit.

8 The finish

This is the process that produces the final appearance, whether that is polished, plated or painted, and always the result depends on preparation. The final top coat is the easy stage, but the work necessary to bring the surface to the required standard for that coat takes time and effort.

The production finishes used by Norton were to polish castings or leave them as cast, to plate certain major items and the details with either chromium or cadmium, and to paint the steel parts that made up the bulk of the cycle side along with certain cast-iron items using the stove-enamelling process.

Petrol tanks and wheel rims were both chrome-plated and painted on the earlier models, while the plastic and rubber items were as moulded. Transfers were added as a final touch at certain points.

Cleaning the parts

Right at the start you will have removed the outer dirt from the machine, but now each part needs further attention. The process used depends on the part, its job, its material and the required finish. For concealed items cleaning is most likely all that is needed, but the visible parts require more effort.

Cleaning can be done mechanically or chemically depending on the surface finish desired and the shape and area in question. Some of the chemicals are not readily available in the small quantities needed by the amateur, and all must be treated with caution; always wear protective clothing. Read the instructions carefully, including the warning notes and what to do if you splash yourself.

Detergents

A normal household washing powder is most useful for cleaning castings. They are best done in a heated saucepan, and before immersion all steel items must be removed. Don't leave the parts in for longer than is necessary as many of these products are acidic in nature and will attack the castings. When the parts are clean, wash them with hot water to remove all traces of detergent and then dry the castings.

Often this is all that will be needed to restore an engine or gearbox casting that is simply dirty with ingrained oil, but do make sure all the detergent is removed.

Mechanical

At its simplest, this involves scraping away the finish, usually paint, with a knife or some similar tool. This is slow, tiring and tedious but will get down to the bare metal in time. It can also damage the surface if you are not careful to prevent the knife digging in.

More usually, it means some form of blasting process, where small particles are blown at the item to be cleaned so they knock the finish off. The speed, severity, substrate damage and visual finish depend on the abrasive material used.

For removing rust, paint and corrosion, aluminous-oxide grit blasting is suitable for motorcycle parts. Iron grit or shot are not. They would damage castings badly and blow holes in sheet metal, so avoid them. A less common and more delicate process is vapour blasting, where the abrasive medium is carried in water, but the most popular method for smaller items is bead blasting.

This uses glass beads and so does not blow material away. It is also used on castings that have been grit-blasted as that process tends to open the metal pores. The beads close them up again, flatten the surface out and give it a polish that can range from matt to gloss.

All parts should be cleaned thoroughly, and oil, grease and loose rust removed before they are taken for blasting. Threads, cylinder bores, close-tolerance holes, headstock bearings, oilways and tapped holes will need protecting, not so much from damage but to make sure nothing is trapped which could cause damage later. It is too easy to block an essential oilway with beads, leading to a wrecked engine in minutes.

Blanking off these vulnerable areas can be done with nuts, bolts, pieces of tube, several layers of masking tape or even Blu-Tack. This last is excellent in recesses as it just absorbs the beads, which come

Rather strange racer pictured in 1961 in the USA. Lots of work had gone into this machine

A 1975 Interstate Mk III

away with it afterwards. Items such as headstocks in frames can be sealed with a length of studding, two metal discs and rubber discs cut from an old inner tube. Don't forget a screw for the grease-nipple hole or your work will have been wasted.

The alternative to blasting is to remove paint, rust and, inevitably, some metal using emery. The manual method involves cloth strips, which can be useful on frame tubes, but for most items powered assistance is essential. This takes the form of an electric drill and an emery flap wheel which is used to remove deep scratches from the metal and to blend the damaged area into the rest. For the best results, as with the blasters, you should let the tool do the work without forcing it. Don't use a sanding disc as it will take off too much and most likely score the surface.

An extension of this work is to finer and finer grades of abrasive, so that you finish up with a polished surface. This is normally applied to the timing cover, gearbox end cover and outer primary chaincase, but is often extended by owners to many more of the light-alloy castings. However, this will reduce the metal's ability to dissipate heat and may not be as original.

Polishing can be done by hand, with mops or by a combination of the two. Industrial polishers use large mops driven at high speed by good-sized electric motors, for they take a lot of power. They can also round off edges and draw out drilled holes in a very short time, so if you have access to such equipment practise on some scrap before beginning on your Norton parts.

Small mops can be used in an electric drill and must be kept charged with mop soap. Proceed with care, especially where there are sharp edges you wish to keep. Before polishing the easy areas, you should deal with the awkward crevices. It is very tempting to do the job the other way round but not advisable.

The manual method of polishing involves using wet-and-dry emery-cloth in paraffin. You need a medium-grade cloth followed by two grades of fine, and it is a tedious, dirty job. The recesses can be done with an emery-stick, which may be driven by a drill, and the major areas can be polished with a Loyblox. This is a block of rubber impregnated with emery-grit which can be used wet or dry.

The final touch is a polish with Solvol Autosol applied with a soft cloth.

Chemical

There are chemical cleaners available for light-alloy parts and, as with detergent, after use they must be washed away well. Most are acidic in nature, so care is necessary when using them and the instructions must be followed.

More usually, chemical cleaning means a paint stripper. This is another messy operation but one that is quick and effective. Wear protective clothing and avoid contact with the fluid by wearing gloves and eyeshields. It is a nasty substance.

Spread out plenty of newspaper, put out the parts for stripping and paint on the liquid. After a while the paint will start to bubble up and often comes away in sheets. A scraper may be needed to help it along, and all the old paint must come away. Then get rid of the old paint and paper, remembering that it is now an industrial hazard. Burning is a good method, but it will smell and must be done out of doors.

The parts will need to be cleaned with water, if the stripper was so based, or thinners and wire wool. You *must* make sure that all the old paint and stripper are removed or the new coat will lift within days of application.

At this point you may find patches of filler from some previous repair under the paint. All of these will have to come away so you can get down to bare metal and check on the exact damage. Don't be tempted to leave them as, having been disturbed by what you have done so far, they will be close to falling out anyway.

Rust

Now the steel parts will be in an ideal state for them to rust. However they have been cleaned, they will begin to oxidize immediately, and any handling will make matters worse due to the acids of the skin. So proceed to the next stage quickly.

If there is a delay and surface rust forms, it will have to be removed again before the finishing process is continued. There are a number of products available to do this, most having a phosphoric-acid base. Many

Cutaway standard Navigator of the form that is often seen at shows

will also act as a primer for painting, but if the part has to be plated, wax or oil would be a better protection as they can be removed by degreasing.

Parts that are due to be painted should be given one coat of etch primer as soon as possible after the blasting or stripping process. This will keep the rust at bay while you draw breath.

Restoring the surface

If the part is to be plated, a metallic surface is essential and defects cannot be resin-filled as for painted items. Thus, it may be necessary to weld or braze the part, depending on the material, in order to obtain the required surface.

This technique will work for castings and the heavier steel parts, but sheet-steel components in general, and the petrol tank in particular, need sheet-metal skills. If you have these you will possess the hammers and dollies to do the work; if you don't, you

had best farm out all but the simplest tasks.

Even professional restorers often send petrol tanks to a specialist, as a repair usually entails cutting out the bottom to give access for panel beating and then welding it back in again. A skilled job and not one to be attempted, unless you really know what you are doing.

During preparation, it is well worth rounding off the sharp edges of items such as engine plates and frame lugs. This will reduce any tendency to chipping and will improve appearance in the long term.

Filling

Steel or iron parts, which have been left for years, are likely to have a pitted surface, and it is not practical to fill the pits with braze or cut back the surface to remove them. The former would take forever and the latter weaken the part far too much.

One answer is a resin filler, which may come as a

FAR LEFT *1969 Commando S with camshaft points and new rev-counter drive*

BELOW *Navigator de luxe of 1961 fitted with panniers, screen and legshields*

brushed-on liquid or a two-part, resin-and-hardener kit. Several coats will be needed to give body to the surface and ensure all traces of pitting have gone. Once this is done, the part will need to be left for several days for the filler to harden fully.

An alternative is lead filling as used for cars. The area to be treated has to be tinned first, which is done using a flux containing powdered lead. This is brushed on and warmed with a blowlamp. Do not use a welding torch as the heat will be too high and too local.

Continue by adding the lead, which comes as an alloy of lead and tin in sticks. The blowlamp will allow the lead to be kept movable without it running, and a hardwood spatula will let you push it about. Wear a mask, try not to put too much on at once, remember you can always add more if needed, and finally dress down with a file and flattening paper.

Once the damage has been filled, the surface has to be rubbed down with 320-grade, wet-and-dry emery, used wet. It is a tedious job as the aim is a smooth, even surface that blends in with the rest of the part without bumps or hollows. This is not easy to get right first time, but hollows can always be given another coat of filler, so you have another chance.

Pinholes in the surface are dealt with using stopper in a similar way.

When you are quite certain that the entire surface of the part is perfect, you can move on, but don't delude yourself. Any mark or imperfection will shine through, no matter how many coats of paint you put on.

Painting

The traditional method of applying paint is by a number of brushed-on coats, the surface being rubbed down between each. This was far too slow for mass-produced machines, so the job was speeded up using

ABOVE *Party with the 1958 model 99 Nomad during a press try-out*

RIGHT *Shining up a 1964 650SS ready for a customer*

spray or dip techniques and stove-enamelling paint. This gave a hard finish with a deep gloss that stood up to knocks well.

In contrast, a brushed finish either took a great deal of time to apply or looked poor and was easily damaged. Fortunately, this is no longer the case, although time and care are still needed if a really good finish is wanted. Using synthetic enamel, it is easy to obtain good coverage, a deep gloss and a hard surface that won't chip readily, and even if it is damaged it can be touched in without much trouble.

Therefore, most restorers use this finish. The most common make is Tekaloid, which is favoured by many professionals. Others simply shop at a high-street store and produce very good results using the enamel as it comes or as a two-part product. The second component is a hardener which reduces drying time. It is also possible to low-temperature bake the finish.

A short drying time is characteristic of cellulose, which is normally used for spraying. It must be mixed with thinners, is volatile and flammable, and must be handled with care as it can be dangerous medically.

Fast drying is desirable as it helps to combat the home restorer's greatest enemies when painting: dust and midges. For this reason, some do use a cellulose, but in the end the finish depends far more on the preparation, clean atmosphere and operator care than the paint type.

To achieve this situation there are certain guide lines to follow. Paint after rain has washed dust from the atmosphere. Choose a warm, still day and damp down the working area. Wear clothes that do not harbour dust, so avoid wool. Work in an area free from draughts and don't open the door once you have begun. However, don't forget that you do need air to breathe! Hang the parts from wire, not string, with the least important face pointing upwards. Use a tack rag on the surface immediately before you start. Don't breathe on the work, and leave the working area as soon as you have finished painting.

If the paint is to be applied by brush, the name Hamilton comes up most often. A 1 in. wide brush will cover most items but a $\frac{1}{2}$ in. version may be needed for details and a 2 in. one for mudguards or the rear panels. Run-in the brushes on something unimportant, washing out dirt with clean paraffin in several stages until it is really clean. Tap the handle against a piece of wood to shake out the surplus; do not finger the bristles or wipe them with a rag. After use, clean the brush in paraffin, wash it in warm soapy water followed by clear water and leave to dry.

When painting pour a little paint into a clean cup and load the brush from that. Do not put the brush in the paint tin. Apply the paint with long flowing strokes, allowing the brush to run down the part under its own weight to avoid brush marks. A light touch will give a lovely finish.

Two or three coats are usual, and between each the surface must be rubbed down with 500-grade wet-and-dry, used wet. This gives a smooth surface and allows you to see where the next coat has to go, not always easy with a dark, glossy finish.

There are two areas where this type of finish will not work so well. One is where there is heat, so brake drums and cylinder barrels are better stove-enamelled. This means masking off and filling damaged areas with materials that will cope with the baking temperature. The other is the petrol tank where the problem is resistance to petrol and staining. It's fine if you never spill anything when refuelling and the cap seal does its job, but otherwise consider

going to an expert.

Some restorers give the tank a coat of polyurethane lacquer, but this is not advisable as it will react with any spilt petrol and act as a paint stripper.

Paint colour

Black is black for most of us, but colours seem to come in so many shades and suffer from fading, which leads to matching problems.

Also remember that all paints are not the same, and while you can spray synthetic on to cellulose, it won't work the other way round. Using a sealer or isolator may work but don't expect too much. Better to take it back to the basic surface.

Keep to one type of paint for all stages and colours, including any lining.

Paint colours are given in Appendix 4 and in greater detail than in *Norton Twins*, so the information given should take precedence over that volume. Matching is another matter, and an area of original paint that has been shielded from the light will act as the best guide. The inside of the toolbox or the underside of a clip are possible sources, but if your machine has been repainted fully at some time, this matching is lost.

It may be possible to judge what you are after from a brochure or a contemporary magazine advertisement, otherwise you will have to find a machine to study. Museums, shows and meetings are all possible sources. Or you may be lucky to find a part in the right colour and still in its wrapper. Worth buying whether you need it or not just for the match.

Once you know what colour you need, you have to get the paint shop to mix it for you. Start from the British Standard Colour Chart as this should get you near, but expect to experiment a little. Persevere on

ABOVE *The model 7 in 1955 with plastic tank badge and pivoted-fork frame*

BELOW *A 1967 hybrid in the form of an AJS model 33CSR*

ABOVE *Norton café racer with all the goodies of the time*   BELOW *Model 99 of 1957 with classic Norton finish*

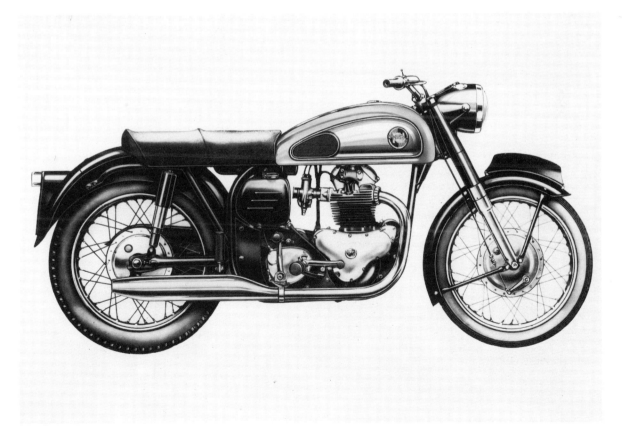

odd parts until you are satisfied it is correct or the shade you want.

Spraying

This takes more cash to get the equipment and tends to be expensive in paint as much misses the work and ends up on the walls. The technique has been described often but, as with the brush, practice, preparation and no dust are the keys to success.

Investigate spray-paint types as some give off a lethal vapour and are not for the amateur at all. Learn how to operate the spray gun, the effects of your techniques and changes to them. Practise first.

Observe all safety precautions, which are more stringent for spraying due to the fire risk and the fumes. Keep a fire extinguisher of the correct type to hand. Make sure ventilation is good, remove naked flames, gas heaters or open radiant fires, and check your electrics in case anything can spark. Wear a mask when working.

Coatings

An alternative to painting is plastic coating or powder coating. This will not give the gloss required by the perfectionist, but the coats are tough. There are limitations on colour choice, and filler cannot be used as it won't stand the process temperature. Also plastic coating may peel off if rust gets under the surface at any point.

ABOVE *Norton Commando on an ISDT trip in 1968*

RIGHT *Roadster Mk III in 1975 showing the tank finish in white with broad blue stripe*

Again, preparation is important and will reflect in the final appearance. Dip-coating can be done at home on items such as stands, the main requirements being a means to heat the part up to around 300 degrees Celsius and a container for the powder into which the part is dipped. An old, clean oil can will do for a start.

Plating

Plating, like painting, depends on preparation for a good result. This means cleaning the surface and polishing it without damaging it. Once more the files, emery and elbow grease are needed, but with some of the small parts the biggest problem is holding them.

You can pay the plater to do this initial surface preparation, but it is a labour-intensive job and will be costly. The more you can do yourself, the better. Some parts cannot be replated as no one will allow them in their chroming bath. The two common ones are silencers and wheel rims as they would contaminate the bath solution.

After preparation, the trick is to find a good plater who is interested in your motorcycle work, and the

best way is through recommendations from fellow enthusiasts. Whether you are aiming for a concours job or not, expect to pay for good workmanship. In the long run, this is always less expensive than a cheap job.

The major plated parts are finished with chromium but other plating processes are needed as well. Normally, nuts and bolts that are not chromed are either cadmium- or zinc-plated. Bright nickel may be found on the spoke nipples.

Aluminium castings may be plated, although this does nothing for heat dispersion, or they can be anodized. This improves their corrosion resistance, and the film formed on the surface can be dyed in a

ABOVE *Commando S on test at Brands Hatch in 1969*

RIGHT *The Atlas of 1966 built to police specification*

range of colours, with matt black helping heat dissipation and looking very smart. Note that the process acts as an insulator, so don't forget that your electrics need a path for the current.

Lining and transfers

Signwriters do this freehand, and one solution used by many restorers is to farm out the job. Alternatives include plastic tapes that are simply laid on and either left at that or varnished. Masking with pvc tape will give the outline required or, for straighter lines, car lining tape may be used. This has a centre strip that is removed to leave two outers parallel to each other. Application is tricky but not as much as trying to do it freehand. Don't forget that lining paint must be the same type as the overall finish or you will have trouble. Remove the tape before the paint has dried fully to prevent any lifting of the edges. Gold lining will need a clear coat to protect it, and yacht varnish is often favoured.

Transfers are the final touch for a machine and should be applied with care according to their directions. Make sure they go in the correct place and, when dry, protect with a thin coat of clear varnish.

Stainless steel

An alternative for many steel parts that are normally chrome-plated is stainless steel. Many owners refuse to use parts made of it, but in the right application and correct grade it will banish corrosion problems forever.

There are a good number of stainless steels, some magnetic and suitable for hardening, some not fully corrosion-resistant, and so on, as with other metals. With the correct specification all will be well, provided the part is correctly machined.

Fibreglass

This material was used for the petrol tank and side covers of some Commando models, and it poses its own set of problems for finishing. In addition, the use of the material for petrol tanks was always suspect and was banned in the UK during 1973. From that date tanks were legally required to be made in metal, but some authorities think this always applied and was retrospective.

The change arose because many early fibreglass tanks were made by home workers, and in far too many cases their quality standards were not good enough. The result was leaks, shortly followed by fires. There were also cases of tanks breaking up in accidents with the consequent fire hazard.

Current EEC regulations allow the use of non-metal tanks, but at the time of writing this does not apply to the UK.

Which leaves certain Norton owners in a quandary if they want to use their machines on the road. There does not appear to be any easy answer if the original appearance is to be kept. Possible solutions are to remake the tank in metal or to bond a metal tank into the original fibreglass shell. A change to another Norton tank in metal loses originality but is likely to be the easiest solution. However, check clearance underneath to make sure all will be well.

Commando built up by Challenge Motors of Barcelona around 1972

The repair and finishing of fibreglass is different to parts made in metal. So different, in fact, that they are really not the same jobs at all. Metal is hard and unaffected by paint stripper or paint solvents. Fibreglass is a mixture of glass strands and resin, and the latter can be attacked all too easily. Being soft, it is easily marked and scores can be produced readily.

When the material was first introduced we were told that repairs would be easy, which is true if you simply want to join up a crack or fill a hole. If you also want a smooth surface for your final paint, the job takes much longer. Tissue layers have to be used to build up the surface before it is shaped, smoothed and rubbed down.

Painting also takes much longer as each coat must be left for a week, sometimes two, to make sure any interaction is complete. If this is not done the result will look nice for a month but then all the repairs will show through.

Practise your technique on a scrap part, allowing as much time as you can between steps to make sure all the chemicals have done their job and stopped reacting. This is golden rule one when dealing with any fibreglass part. Making sure you use the correct materials has to be rule two, and reading the instructions *first* is number three.

9 Frame and stands

With these items you have something solid to work on, so most minor repairs are easy to do. Bent brackets can be heated and returned to their correct position, and cracks around them welded. Holes may need welding and redrilling if elongated, or tapping out if their threads are damaged.

However, the real work on the frame is to check its alignment. This can be done with string and straight edges but does take a good eye to spot areas where there is a problem. A straightforward bend due to a crash is easy to see, but the twist that five years of sidecar work may induce is less obvious.

Setting the frame straight again is a specialized job which should be farmed out. Before this is done, check it over for cracks that will need welding, for the fit of the head races in the headstock, and the rear fork pivot. Attention to any of these areas will involve heat which could cause distortion. Best to get all the minor work out of the way so that once straight the frame can be painted.

The stands need similar attention and are often distorted due to misuse. Expect to find damaged pivot holes needing attention, and check that the spring attachment is in good order and will hold the spring as the stand moves. Inspect the stand feet as these do wear and may need to be built up again to ensure the machine stands correctly when parked.

Plunger frame

The first model 7 used the standard Norton plunger frame of the era, suitably modified to accept the twin engine and laid-down gearbox, and it remained in use up to 1952. The plungers must be kept well greased to avoid wear in the bushes.

The plungers are simple to work on, but care must be exercised when extracting them from between the frame fork ends. If they are simply levered out the springs will fly apart and could cause injury, so a rod should be used to hold the parts together. This is inserted by moving the assembly partially to one side to expose the centre hole. Fit the rod plus nuts and washers to take the load, reversing the procedure on refitting.

Featherbed frame

This was first seen on the works racing Nortons in 1950 and went on to the model 88 for 1952. It set a standard against which other machines were measured for many years. Attention is as for the plunger frame plus the pivot for the rear fork.

The rear fork also needs to be inspected, and its bushes may need to be changed. It should be easy to remove the fork provided the long stud that holds it has not corroded and seized to the bushes. If it has, a press or heat may be needed to move it. In extreme cases it may have to be cut. Proper maintenance will ensure that it does not happen again.

The bushes were of the Silentbloc type and may well need replacement due to old age. If heat has been applied they will need renewal, but their removal can be awkward. New ones press into place. When the fork is refitted it should be positioned at mid-travel before it is clamped. This holds the bearings in a position from which they will suffer minimal strain as the fork moves.

The original frame had its subframe bolted into place, but for 1955 the subframe was welded on. In 1956 the detail was amended to suit the new oil tank and battery cover. There was a change in 1957 to add a gusset plate outboard of the right-side, pivoted-fork support plate, which tidied this area up. The next change came for 1960 when the de luxe models were introduced with rear enclosure. To suit this, and to allow the rider to tuck in his legs more, the frame was pulled in around the dualseat nose area, the duplex tubes being closer together. This frame was quickly given the name 'slim-line'. Thus, by definition, the earlier one became the 'wide-line'.

Two frames were introduced at that point, one for standard machines and the other for the de luxe versions. Both were amended for 1961 with a new seat location, and both were also used by the two versions of the 650. A further change came in for 1963, by which time only the standard-frame type remained, going on to the two SS models and the Atlas. It had the front engine mounts reversed, so the tails of the lugs were turned up instead of down. There were further small changes for 1966 and 1968.

The rear fork also had its share of alterations, needing to accommodate the full-width hub in 1955 and revised wheel adjusters the following year. For 1959 it had to be able to take the optional full chaincase, and in 1960 was revised to suit the 'slim-line' frame. It ran on in this form to 1970.

Pivoted-fork frame

This is the frame type used by the 7, 77, hybrids and small twins, that is, the models without Featherbed or Commando frames.

The first came in 1953 for the 7 and was adapted from the plunger frame. A rear fork was fitted along with a brace between the pivot housing and the tail end of the rear engine plates. This frame remained in use to 1955.

In 1957 it came back in a revised and simpler form for the 77 sidecar model, which was only listed for two seasons. Then a similar frame appeared for the Nomad models.

The next appearance of this type of frame was for the Atlas scrambler in late 1963, but in this case an

ABOVE *Vic Willoughby testing a 1956 model 99 in the Isle of Man*

ABOVE RIGHT *The Eric Oliver outfit on test in 1958. It has the Daytona kit, twin GPs, raised compression ratio, large inlet valves, megaphones and is aligned to a Watsonian Monaco chair with 9 in. of lead*

AMC-type CSR frame was used. The same basis was employed for the G15 and 33 variants plus the N15. Finally came the P11 which led on to the Ranger. This used the Matchless G85CS frame.

The small twins went their own way with a built-up construction using a single downtube formed from sheet metal, a centre channel section and two loops with side bracing stays. This design was kept for all models, but with detail variations to suit the standard versions without the rear enclosure. The rear fork stayed the same for the 250 and 350, but the 400 had an extra lug to accept a torque arm from the larger rear brake. In the de luxe version the side bracing stays were bolted on, while the standard-frame types were

welded. The de luxe frame also had extra lugs welded to its right rear side to take the battery holder.

Commando frame

This is unique due to the Isolastic principle where the engine, gearbox and pivoted fork are assembled as one unit and rubber-mounted to the frame. This looks like many others, with a single top tube and duplex engine rails, but lacks the usual pivoted-fork mountings. The frame needs to be checked over just as any other.

The Commando frame changed in most years for one reason or another, the first alteration being made for the good reason that the original broke around the headstock area. The 1968 frame had a gusset wrapped round to link the spine and headstock, but this failed to spread the load enough and fractures occurred in the spine at the join. To cure this the 1969 frame had a bracing tube added beneath the spine, running back from the base of the headstock to the seat nose area.

For 1970 the centre-stand tube was strengthened, while 1971 saw the centre stand pivoted in the gearbox plates rather than from the frame. At the same time the prop-stand pivot became part of the frame and the leg was held in place by a circlip. This was none too successful, so for 1972 a lug was welded to the frame and the leg held by a pivot bolt with nut and washer.

Two frames were listed in 1973, one for the 750 and another for the 850, which had a change in the head angle. The next year brought larger gussets between the rear loop and the seat tube to prevent the loop bending. The gussets concerned were the inner ones that also supported the tops of the rear units. An epoxy paint finish appeared in 1975 together with a clip on the right side of the rear loop to act as a caliper support when needed.

Commando rear fork

The fork itself was quite conventional, with a pair of pressed-in bronze bushes to act as bearings. The pivot pin was a simple ground pin held in a tube which was welded into the rear engine-plate assembly. Less usual were the lubrication methods adopted. These were to supply the surfaces with EP140 oil, if possible, or

EP90 if the thick grade was not available.

The oil was contained by sealed end caps held by a long 5BA bolt and fed via small holes to the working surfaces. It was added via a grease nipple, and problems arose because many owners used grease instead of oil and blocked the small holes. This either led to wear or seizure, the latter producing a worn spindle and tube. An oversize spindle was listed under part number 064077 and is 0.005 in. larger, so the tube needs to be reamed out.

The spindle was held by a single bolt at first, but for the Mk III in 1975 this changed to a pair of cotter bolts which was much better. The owners club suggests that an improvement can be made to the original, once the spindle matches the tube, by fitting exhaust-pipe, U-bolt clamps on to the tube.

The fork was changed twice over the years, first for 1973 when it had gussets added between the arms and the cross-tube, and second for 1975. With the latter came fittings for the rear disc brake, revised rear wheel adjusters and shorter bushes with a wick oil-feed system.

Finally, remember that all Commando rear forks should be lubricated with *oil*.

Commando engine mountings

There were three of these: the head steady, front mounting and rear gearbox mounting. Their purpose was to allow the mechanics and chassis to move relative to one another in a single plane without any tilt.

A 1969 Mercury in a 1967 frame—sales were slow by then. The capacitor is for ignition

The standard model Jubilee of 1961 minus enclosure but plus centre panel and right-side oil tank

BELOW *David Dixon testing a 1962 Atlas on the TT circuit and here seen at Bedstead corner*

LEFT *A 1967 model on show with high-rise bars*

RIGHT *Another hybrid in the form of a 1966 model 33 AJS*

The original head-steady stay was a pressing with a form that was overstrained in manufacture and, thus, prone to fracturing. As its presence prevents the engine, and hence the rear wheel, from tilting relative to the frame, it is an important item and best up-dated. This can be done by fitting the box-section type introduced in 1973 under part number 064179, and revised for 1974 as 065459. A further option is to fit the Norvil head steady listed by Fair Spares under CZ48-B10. This is claimed to improve high-speed stability. Never weld a broken head steady—always replace it with the up-dated part. In all cases check that the rubber mounts are in good order and securely fitted to the frame.

The front and rear mountings differ in detail but share the same design basis. Both have a large tube bolted rigidly to the engine and gearbox assembly, the tube centre coinciding with the fixing hole centres in the frame. A rod passes through these holes and the centre of the tube, and between them are the rubber discs which provide the isolating function.

The front tube had twin plates welded to it which were bolted to the front of the crankcase. At the rear, the tube was welded to the two plates which surrounded the gearbox, bolted to the back of the crankcase and carried the pivoted-fork spindle. It also carried the centre stand from 1971 on.

There were four rubbers in each mounting assembly plus distance tubes and protective gaiters. Among these items, the 1973-onwards, bronze-impregnated, PTFE washers are to be preferred to the earlier polyurethane types. The circlip location introduced at the same time stops the buffers from moving over. This last problem can be dealt with by adding a further distance piece to locate them, and the owners club suggests garden hose or a turn or two of tape as a solution. The gaiters also changed at that time, and the later rubber ones are preferred to the earlier, shiny, pvc type. Lubricate all parts with rubber or silicone grease rather than normal grease. If it must be used, a thin, sticky type is the best choice.

The heart of the Isolastic system is the adjustment which controls side play of one part in relation to the other. This was adjusted with shims up to 1974, and the factory setting was 0.01 in. Rider experience indicates that this can be reduced to 0.005 in. or less, but there must be some clearance or the frame and/or head steady will break. Use the minimum number of shims to make up the thickness needed, for example fit one of 0.03 in. rather than three of 0.01 in., or one each of 0.01 in. and 0.02 in.

For 1975 the mounting design was altered to

provide a threaded adjustment, so the shims were
needed no longer. The setting remained the same but
adjusting this became simpler, with one part to turn to
set the gap and another to lock the first. These Mk III
adjustable mountings can be fitted to earlier machines,
but while the rear assembly fits directly with no
modification the front one needs the centre tube to be
shortened.

Head races

Expect to renew these on a restoration, unless they are
in perfect condition. Even if they are, change the ball
bearings of a cup-and-cone design. The model 7 and 77
both had this form of head race with 34 balls split
equally between the two bearings. However, not all
the detail parts were the same.

The Featherbed-frame models used a pair of angular

RIGHT *The Commando frame with the extra tube added for 1969 as the original was inclined to break*

BELOW *The first Commando frame with a gusset wrapped round the headstock*

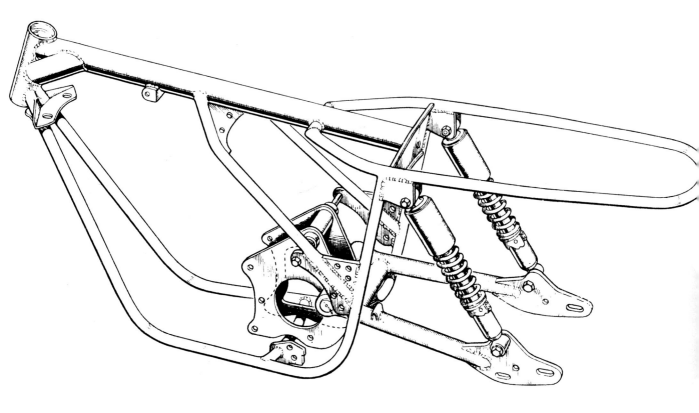

ABOVE *The 1973 Roadster Mk V with the 745 cc engine*

A 1971 Roadster Mk II which had a more traditional style than the first Commando models

contact ball bearings of 25 × 52 × 15 mm up to 1963, after which they changed to the cup-and-cone type, this time with 36 balls. The P11 models had their own set of parts, using a total of 56 balls to carry the forks. A favourite and worthwhile modification is to convert to taper roller bearings for the head races on all models.

The Commando began with the same set of parts as the late Featherbeds, but from 1971 changed to a pair of sealed ball races. The lightweights used cup-and-cone bearings, with 36 balls of $\frac{1}{4}$ in. diameter on the 250. The same number and size of balls went on to the 350 and 400, but in their case another set of cups and cones was used to accept the Roadholder forks.

In all cases, the fitting and adjusting instructions should be followed carefully and closely.

Centre stand

The model 7 inherited its stand from the ES2 and continued with this until a change was needed to suit the pivoted-fork frame introduced in 1953. This stand also went on the model 77 during its short life.

The 88 had its own stand to suit the Featherbed frame, and this went on to all models except the Atlas and the export 650. These had their own part. The hybrids used various stands to suit their special build-up.

The Commando stand began life attached to the frame and was strengthened for 1969. In 1971 it was made to pivot from the rear engine plates and amended for 1972 to add a gusset between the leg and the toe peg. A new stand of strengthened design was introduced for the 850 in 1973 and was used from then on. In addition to its extended bracing, it also had improved pivots, and for owners of 1971–73 750s a kit was available (as part 064874) to enable them to fit the more robust assembly.

The small twins had just one stand for the 250 and 350 models, and another for the 400. This differed by having an extension to provide extra leverage for the foot. It was never installed on the 250/350 frame, but will fit straight on and makes for easier parking.

Prop-stand

This was introduced for the model 7 and the singles during 1949, so it does not appear until the 1950 lists. For these machines the assembly bolted to the left front engine plate, so it was well positioned and folded

ABOVE *Commando Fastback and S models with a Mercury*

ABOVE LEFT *Racing Commando with non-racing tyres at Snetterton in 1969*

well out of the way. This arrangement continued on to the pivoted-fork version in 1953, but the 77 had the stand leg attached to a frame lug.

The Featherbed frame models used a clamped-on assembly, which remained in use for all models and years except the Atlas and some late export 650s. These had their own stand leg, which was changed for 1966 and went on to the P11 the next year. It was modified for 1968 when it continued on both the Atlas and the P11A, while the G15 series had their own leg and spring.

The Commando began with a clamped-on prop-stand, but for 1971 this was changed to one where the leg was pivoted on a pin welded to the frame and retained by a circlip. The latter was prone to falling off. For 1972 the leg was bolted to a frame lug and gained a peg for a stop rubber. It was changed in detail for 1974 and 1975. The original spring was changed for 1971 and 1972, after which it continued unchanged.

All the small twins used the same stand leg, but the 400 had a different spring and mounting lug. In each case, the stand was attached to the bottom of the main frame downtube on the left side, and was always listed as optional equipment.

10 Suspension

All models had telescopic-fork front suspension which, except for the 250, was based on the famous Roadholder forks. The first models used the original 'long' type, but the 88 was fitted with the 'short' Manx version. The Commando continued with the Roadholder forks, at first with gaiters and later without them on some models. Of the small twins, the 250 began with a pair of lightweight AMC forks with hydraulic damping. The 350 and 400 models had Roadholders with an internal spring change.

At the rear, the model 7 had plunger suspension for 1949–52, otherwise all models had a pivoted-rear-fork system with two spring-and-damper units.

Telescopic forks
Most of these are similar in design, and restoration follows common lines. Strip the forks, following the procedure given in the manual, and examine the parts

Matchless G15CSR of 1967 with Norton engine set off by the swept-back pipes

*A Commando
Mk IIA 829 cc
Roadster from 1974*

*A 1959 Jubilee
with its full
enclosure*

*Roadster Mk I
from 1973 with
829 cc engine*

for wear. Check each leg for worn bushes or sliders, which may call for repair or replacement.

Bent fork legs are common, and rolling them on a flat surface will reveal this. Wear can be overcome by hard chroming and grinding to size if new parts cannot be found. This will also deal with any pitting of the surface, but if the pitting is minor it can be filled with epoxy resin and rubbed down when hard.

Expect to renew fork bushes and seals, but most of the other internal parts operate in oil and seldom wear. Check the springs for tiredness and shortening. If this has happened, try to find new springs of the correct rate. Packing can be and is done, but it will affect the rate and may restrict fork movement. It can also give rise to crashing sounds if things have gone against you.

All threads need to be checked carefully and repaired as required. As they hold the forks together or the front wheel in, they do have a bearing on your well-being. Check the lower legs with care for any signs of damage.

If the fork tubes have been bent, it is most likely that the crowns will also be bent or distorted. Sometimes this manifests itself as the head races being tight at one point but slack at another. The crowns must be true to the forks, and the frame and their threads checked.

Assemble to the book, making sure the head races are adjusted correctly and that the fork legs are

ABOVE *The Jubilee standard model in 1964 with a few detail changes*

RIGHT *The 1974 829 cc Roadster Mk IA*

parallel so they will move freely without binding. Fill with the correct grade of oil, trying to put the same amount in each leg.

Telescopic-fork types

The long type fitted to the models 7 and 77 has external springs and a taper rod damper held to the bottom of the fork leg. There were few changes, and those that did occur were mainly to suit the deeper headlamp shell of the 77. This meant new upper shrouds and a couple of minor details.

The short forks fitted to the 88 had internal springs and a shuttle damper attached to the top and bottom of the forks. The upper shrouds changed for 1956, the legs for 1957, and the oil damper tube for 1959. Otherwise the forks continued, in solo form, as they were until 1964 when they were made wider, which affected quite a number of the detail parts. The main visible difference was the addition of a steering lock on the fork crown. From 1959, sidecar forks with different crowns and stronger springs were also available.

In the main, hybrids used Norton forks, with detail changes to the main tube length and to allow fitting to the AMC frame. The exception to this was the P11 model which had Matchless forks.

The Commando began with its own version of the Roadholder fork, and for 1969 introduced a slightly altered type without gaiters for the S model. This style was adopted for all models in 1971 when the upper shrouds, which carried the headlamp-shell supports, were made shorter and of a smaller diameter to promote the slim-line look then in vogue. At the same time, the head races became sealed ball bearings without adjustment.

For 1972 there were two fork types, one unchanged to suit the drum brake and the other with a new right leg having lugs for the disc-brake caliper. Both continued in the lists to 1974, but the legs were reversed for the Mk III in 1975. This put the caliper on the left and in front of the leg instead of behind it as before.

The reason for the move was that the original arrangement caused the machines to pull to the left and the switch-round cured the problem, even if the reasons were obscure. Because of this, there are a good number of Commandos that have had the fork legs swapped over, so a left-side caliper is no guarantee that the machine is a Mk III. Fortunately, there are several other major features unique to this model that aid identification.

On the small twins the light AMC forks went on to the 1959 250, the ends being slotted to accept sleeve nuts on the ends of the front wheel spindle. For 1960 this was changed to a long spindle, which could be withdrawn to allow wheel removal in the usual fashion, the fork ends being modified to suit although the spindle was still held by a sleeve nut.

With the standard version in 1961 came a change to the upper shrouds which were joined originally by a pressing that carried the horn. This went, so the shrouds became two separate items and the horn was positioned under the tank. At the same time the top-crown pressing was modified. For 1963 the legs were altered so the mudguard stays fitted into them below the wheel spindle instead of above it. The spindle was lengthened and retained by a conventional nut.

The 350 and 400 models used the forks from the big twins of their year with just the springs changed. There were changes in 1964 and these reflected the alterations made to the big-twin forks.

Steering-crown types

These may also be called fork yokes or the top one may be referred to as the head clip, and the lower as the crown and column. The first pair served the model 7 and another the 77. On the Featherbed models there was a change to the top for 1956 when the fork-top instrument panel went, otherwise they ran on until 1964 when the forks became wider. The new pair

ABOVE *A 1953 model 88 being raced by Ronald Scriwardana who missed a first due to the silencer coming off*

LEFT *The P11 of 1967 with short seat and other off-road fittings*

FAR RIGHT *Adjusting the preload on a Girling rear unit. The machine is a 1960 model 99*

served most models prior to the Commando, the exceptions being the P11 model and the lower crown and stem on the hybrid G15CS and N15CS.

The original Commando crowns were joined by a second pair in 1969 for the S model, and these were used for all 1970 models. The design was changed for 1971 so that the stem became part of the top crown and this new pair was used on all 750 machines from then on. The 850 had its own pair to suit its revised head angle. In all cases, the crowns must be kept as a pair although it is possible to fit the 750 crowns to an 850 frame. For 1975 and the Mk III a new pair was introduced.

The 250 had a pressed-steel top crown which was changed for 1961 when the shrouds were altered. The lower crown was an assembly of crown, stem and top fork tubes that was used for all years. The 350 and 400 models fitted the Roadholder parts from the big twins and, like them, went to wider forks for 1964.

Steering damper
This was only listed for 1959–68 as an option on the big twins, but it existed in solo and sidecar forms plus another for the P11 right at the end. The two main types differ, the sidecar version having two friction discs that work on a large-diameter boss on the underside of the lower sidecar crown. The parts will not fit the solo crown for which there was a second kit with a single friction disc of a different size.

In all cases, the condition of screw threads, discs and detail parts needs to be checked, with renovation as required.

Plunger frame
This was used only by the model 7 for 1949–52, and the precautions to be taken when working on the plunger units have been described in the previous chapter. They concern the need to restrain the springs to prevent them flying about during removal or replacement.

Check that the covers can move up and down without scraping on one another as this will ruin them very quickly.

Rear suspension units
Norton fitted sealed rear units on their machines, and these offer limited scope to the restorer. In all cases, the outer covers and springs can be removed, but the actual damper unit is sealed. The rubber mounting bushes can be renewed, but repair of the unit requires that it is dismantled which, for most people, is not possible.

Given machining equipment, it is feasible to strip, repair and rebuild units, but it is a specialized business. If replacement units cannot be found, alternatives will have to be fitted. These are available, and it should be possible to find one with similar closed and open lengths, end fixings and spring. In

many cases, these new units have improved (and sometimes adjustable) damping, and can be stripped for repair when needed.

In all cases check that the eyes at the ends of the unit and the frame attachments are in good order and will carry the loads they are called upon to support.

The original Featherbed units of 1952 were quite special for the time. They were joined by another pair, from Armstrong, for the model 7 in 1953. In 1957 a change was made to Girling units although some Armstrongs may have been used. These are easily recognized by the knurled band round the centre of the unit.

The Girlings were revised for 1960 when both solo and sidecar spring rates were listed, and there was a further revision in 1962. Three other units appeared during the middle and late 1960s to suit the hybrids.

The Commando had its own rear units which, at first, had top covers, so only the lower part of the suspension spring was exposed. For 1971 these changed to a type without covers, and this practice was continued from then on although it had an adverse effect on the life of the dampers. It is well worth fitting covers or gaiters to keep road dirt off the damper rods and away from the unit seals.

11 Painted parts and plated details

This chapter covers the mass of major parts and minor fittings that are mostly steel pressings and nearly all painted. A few are forged or die-cast and some plated with chromium or cadmium.

The steel pressings need to be checked over for repair. This may entail a simple bending job to straighten a bracket or a complex panel-beating job for such items as the rear enclosure or mudguard. Often the parts will need to be welded, either to mend cracks or to rejoin sections that have come apart. Unwanted holes will need to be filled and the external signs of all this work removed before the finish is applied.

The problems in this area arise not so much with the repairs, which are usually straightforward, but with collecting all the parts and ensuring that what you have gathered up is correct for your model. In all too many cases, production changes did not affect fit, and if they did the parts could be modified to suit. Thus, machines built up from parts can often include cycle details from many models, and worst of all can be the basket jobs.

The latter need very careful checking over from the first. It is easy to see that you have a pair of mudguards, although less so to be sure they are the correct pair, but much more difficult to be sure you have a full set of engine plates or torque stays. Therefore, the following sections are not concerned with the repair of the parts, which follows standard procedures, but with their correct identification.

Knowledge, part numbers and changes will all help ensure that the cycle spares bought from dealer or autojumble will be correct for your project.

Engine and gearbox plates

The first model 7 adopted the arrangements of the existing singles, with a pair of engine plates in front of the crankcase and two more at left and right to the rear. These assemblies included the footrest tube, and for 1950 the left one was modified.

For the pivoted-fork frame in 1953 the same four plates were used together with a support bridge. This was attached to the aft end of the rear plates, behind the top gearbox mounting, and to the pivoted-fork

lugs where it also supported the rear mudguard. The model 77 used a similar arrangement with the same front plates for 1957–58.

The Featherbed frame carried the engine and gearbox as an assembly, with a pair of small plates at the front and a second, much larger pair at the rear. The latter ran above and below the gearbox to link to the frame and also supported the battery and oil tank. The front plates were a pair on all models and years.

The rear plates always differed in minor ways and were altered for 1956 and the AMC gearbox. The left-hand plate was changed again for 1958 when the alternator appeared. From then on these two remained in use. For 1956 a cover was added on top of the rear plates to improve their appearance, and for 1958 it was revised to suit the distributor, being joined by a front cover to fill the gap left by the departure of the dynamo. The original rear cover later reappeared on the SS models fitted with a magneto. Thus, it remained in use longer than the 1958 type.

In addition to these plates, there were others made to suit the various hybrids and the frames fitted with the Atlas engine.

The Commando lacked engine plates in the normal sense due to its unique design. Instead it had a front and, much larger, rear mounting. Each of these was a welded assembly which incorporated a tube to hold the isolating rubbers. The front unit was altered for 1971 and changed for 1975 to suit the adjustable mounting design. At the rear there was an alteration for 1971 and more changes for the following two years. Finally, for 1975 there was the new adjustable system plus a change to cotter-bolt clamping for the rear-fork pivot pin.

On the small twins there were no engine plates as the unit was bolted directly into the frame channel members.

Engine steady

This links the top of the engine to the frame, and on the Commando is one of the rubber mountings covered in an earlier chapter. A variety of parts was used for the other models, but in all cases they need to fit properly and without strain.

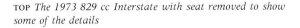

TOP *The 1973 829 cc Interstate with seat removed to show some of the details*

ABOVE *Side panel as fitted to the above model*

ABOVE RIGHT *Rear end detail of the Interstate for 1973*

The models 7 and 77 used similar types of steady but the Featherbed differed. For that model the detail part was altered for 1961 and again for 1962, but only in respect of the horn mounting holes. In other ways they interchange and were joined later by other designs on the hybrids.

The small twins had their own steadies, one for the 250 and another for the two larger models. In addition, from 1959 to 1963, the 250 had two head clamping plates under the four central head studs.

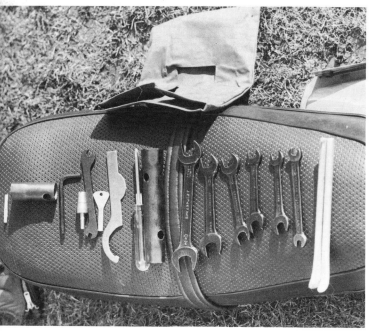

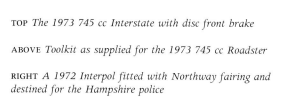

TOP *The 1973 745 cc Interstate with disc front brake*

ABOVE *Toolkit as supplied for the 1973 745 cc Roadster*

RIGHT *A 1972 Interpol fitted with Northway fairing and destined for the Hampshire police*

Exhaust-pipe and silencer brackets

The first of these was not used on 'real' Nortons but did appear on some G15 models. Silencer brackets appeared first in 1956, being left- and right-handed, and the following year the left-hand version was altered. Two of a new type were listed for the 77.

New left and right brackets came in 1960 for the slim-line frame, and these continued in use until replaced by two new parts in 1966. For 1961 there was one bracket for the SS models, which remained listed in 1962 for the 99SS only. In addition, the 1956 right bracket reappeared for 1961–62 for use on the 650 when this was fitted with an optional exhaust system.

The Commando models had a rubber mounting for the exhaust systems, allowing them to be fixed rigidly to the engine and move relative to the frame. Each mounting comprised plates to suit the silencers, frame plates and rubbers, while the assembly also supported the pillion footrests in most cases.

The small twins had a pair of silencer brackets for the 250 which went, in time, on to the 350. A new pair was introduced for the 400, and by 1964 was also in use on the two smaller machines.

Undershield

This item did not appear until the P11 in 1967 and was seen next in 1971 on the Commando Street Scrambler. It was simply a plate shaped to fit between the frame tubes and curved under the engine, being held by clips.

From 1972 it was listed as a spare for any model but always as an option.

Fork shrouds

These cover the fork tubes between the two crowns, and in most cases have a bracket welded to them to support the headlamp. Only on the 250 do they extend down the fork to the lower leg, and in this case their fit needs to be checked when they and the headlamp are bolted up. They must run clear of the leg because if they scrape they will damage themselves and continue to wear away both parts.

The original shrouds, left and right, came from the single-cylinder machines and were used by all model 7 machines. A second pair went on the model 77 and a third on the 88. These last were changed for 1956 when a deeper headlamp shell was fitted, and again for 1964 when the forks were widened.

For 1966 they were given slots in place of holes for the shell bolts, and the same parts went on to the Commando up to 1970. They were joined by a second pair for 1969 for the S model. These differed only in having a chrome-plated finish in place of the black-painted one. For 1971 a new, slimmer pair was brought in and remained in use from then on.

The small twins had two distinct fork types, and the light one used for the 250 began with an apron that included the shrouds as an assembly. This was

Side panel of the 1970 model S removed to show air filter, oil tank and battery all neatly tucked in

arranged so the tubes reached down to the fork legs, which were amended for 1960 in relation to the wheel fixing. For 1961 the 250 changed to a pair of shrouds which remained in use from then on, while the legs only changed with respect to the mudguard-stay fixing point.

The 350 and 400 used the shrouds that came with the big-twin forks and, thus, were changed for 1964 when the forks were widened.

Fork cover tubes

These went below the bottom crown and extended down to the lower leg or the seal holder to cover the springs and tubes. As with the 250 shrouds, they must run true and not scrape, otherwise the parts will be damaged and worn very rapidly.

The 1970 Roadster, an S with Fastback exhausts

The models 7 and 77 used the same parts for all years, having a top and lower tube on each fork leg. The 88 had a top tube only, as the lower one was really the seal housing. The top one was changed for 1956, and the seal housing was altered for 1964. The G15 had its own pair of tubes which had an alternative top for 1966.

The Commando began with fork gaiters which were attached to an extension tube on the seal housing. These were dispensed with for the model S in 1969, as they were for all models from 1971 on.

The shrouds did this job on the 250 small twin, while the 350 and 400 used the parts from the big-twin forks. As for them, the seal housing was altered for 1964.

Headlamp shell

All of these are very similar as they carry the same light unit in most cases, but there were some variations. The shell is none too easy to repair but examples from other models can often be used if necessary. Threads, general shape and condition need to be checked. The finish may be paint or chrome-plate.

The first model 7 had a shell that carried a small panel with light switch and ammeter. For 1953 it was modified to accept the underslung pilot lamp. The model 88 began with this feature, otherwise its shell was plain.

In 1956 it was made deeper, having a separate panel for the instruments and switch. For 1957 these were mounted directly in the shell except on the model 77, which used the 1956 arrangement. The shell was revised a little for 1958 when coil ignition was adopted along with the alternator, and this layout continued with a new switch type in 1964. From this time some machines had the switch moved, and for 1967 it was fitted elsewhere.

The Commando shell began with an ammeter, light switch and one warning light. For 1971 the ammeter went but there were three warning lights, and for 1975 the shell was plain, with the controls and lamps fitted elsewhere.

The small twins had a smaller shell in which was mounted the speedometer, an ammeter, and light and ignition switches. For 1961 the size increased to 7 in. Thus, a new shell was fitted, appearing on all models and years from then on.

Mudguards, their stays and front stand

All these parts are associated, and as there were a good few changes over the years some care is needed to ensure that all the correct parts are to hand. If they are not, the mudguards may be fabricated from others or from stock parts. The stays and supports can also be made from strip or tube as called for. When flattening the ends of a tube, before drilling the mounting hole, add a piece of flat stock inside the tube. This will give it more body and stop the walls from cracking.

Above all else, do make sure the mudguards are properly secured and cannot revolve round the wheel. Check that they sit correctly with a good line to the tyres and that all the stays and supports line up and bolt down without strain. Only when you are satisfied fully with the mechanical aspects should you move on and complete the finishing.

Front mudguard

The model 7 began with a conventional guard supported by a bridge between the fork legs, a pair of simple front stays and a one-piece rear stay that doubled as a front stand. In 1950 the bridge was listed as a separate item and the front stays were amended.

Four of these stays were used by the 88, which lacked a front stand and had its own slimmer mudguard with a bridge to suit. The model 7 guard was altered in 1953 to suit a reduction in wheel diameter, and a similar style went on to the 77 in 1957. This had its own stays, but used the 7's front stand.

With the introduction of the 99 in 1956, both Featherbed models had a revised mudguard with a more pointed nose and a tail that extended further round the wheel. This moved the rear stays further down from the horizontal and, at the same time, new stays were introduced with a different end angle and a new bridge.

For 1957 the 77 made its brief appearance, and for 1959 the mudguards and stays became available with a chrome-plated finish as an option. For 1960 and the de

First version Commando with Isolastic mountings and other shiny items on this show model

luxe models there came a mudguard with a greater valance area, while the next year saw that item listed with a chrome finish for export versions of the 650.

The next change was for 1964 when the forks were widened and various mudguards listed. There was a painted version for the 88SS and 650SS with its bridge and stays; another, chrome-plated, type was listed for the export 650 and the Atlas, with the same bridge but chrome-plated stays; and there were three more for the hybrids, having their own detail parts. Some of these hybrid parts changed for 1966, and the P11 had its own set of items.

The Commando set off much as the models that preceded it, with a simple mudguard blade held by an integral bridge and stays. Unlike the older model, these ran from the fork to the guard and back in U-form, so there were only two of them instead of four as in the past.

For 1969 chrome-plated versions appeared for the S model, and for 1970 these went on to the Roadster as well. All models, other than the police Interpol, had chrome-plated mudguards for 1971, with a special unit having rubber mountings for the Street Scrambler. Unlike the others, this was mounted to the underside of the bottom fork crown and was without stays.

A stainless-steel mudguard for the Interstate arrived in 1972, but the stay shape was the same for all models. This guard became the standard fitment for 1973, and for 1974 it was fitted with a mud flap. For 1975 it kept the flap but was altered to have a rear stay only. The JPR had its own guard which was bolted to the fork legs without any stays.

The 250 began with a massive front mudguard in keeping with its enclosed style. This had a deep valance and a single pair of rear stays. It remained on the de luxe Jubilee, but when the Navigator appeared it had a smaller valance as both standard and de luxe versions of the machine used the mudguard from the de luxe big twins. A chrome-plated version was listed as standard for the export 400 and as an option for the home market. The standard 250 used the valanced, big-twin mudguard but with one stay only. For 1963 its stays were altered to run beneath the wheel spindle, and the 400 took the chrome-plated part as standard. There was a revised mudguard for the 350 to allow for the wider forks.

Rear mudguard

The plunger-frame model 7 had a two-part mudguard with side stays that also served as lifting handles. When the pivoted-fork frame arrived in 1953 new parts were needed, but the two-section arrangement remained to allow the tail to be removed and let the rear wheel roll out. The mudguard was amended for 1955 when it became a little longer, but the stays were unchanged.

The 88 began with a simple blade mudguard bolted to the subframe loop. For 1955 it was changed to a two-part type of deeper section with valances and a detachable tail. In addition it adopted the support stays from the model 7. Both parts of the mudguard and the stays were amended to improve the line for 1956, and the tail section was used by the 77 for 1957. The mudguard front and stays were special to this model, the stays coming from the ES2. For 1959 a chrome-plated finish was listed as an option.

The next change came in 1960 with the slim-line frame and the de luxe models. For these, the bulk of the mudguard became the tail section of the enclosure, but under this went a supporting stay and a front section of mudguard. Outside the enclosure, on the left, was a lifting handle.

The standard Jubilee in 1963 with its shiny hub embellishers

The 1959 Jubilee with massive front mudguard and full rear enclosure

The standard models also had changes for 1960, a one-piece mudguard being fitted with a new pair of stays. Again, these parts were available with a chrome-plated finish as an option.

For 1961 the standard mudguard and the de luxe tail section were modified to accept the clip for the Dzus fastener that now appeared on the rear of the seat. However, the other parts and the chrome-plating option remained and went on to the 650. In time, chrome-plating became standard, and for 1964 there was one more revision to the mudguard although the stays remained the same. From 1968 stainless-steel mudguards were also available as an option.

A further selection of mudguards, plus a forest of detail parts and fittings, were listed for the various hybrids. The P11 had a polished guard. Never an easy period to sort through as exact identification is a trying task.

The Commando began with a simple blade under its rear tail, which was altered for 1969 and joined by a chrome-plated item for the S. These were replaced by a new pair in 1971, one for the Fastback and another for the other models. For 1972 they were joined by a further blade in stainless steel for the Interstate. All three were replaced by a single part for 1973, which gained a mud flap for 1974. In 1975 the mudguard and the flap were revised once more.

At first the design on the 250 was similar to the de luxe models, having a tail section, which was part of the rear enclosure, and a mudguard section beneath and forward of the tail. The latter was amended for 1960 when it went on the de luxe big twins, and was altered for both machine ranges for 1961 to suit the Dzus fastener and clip. It also went on to the de luxe Navigator.

The standard small twins had a valanced rear

mudguard, which was also used on the 400 with the addition of a bracket to take the voltage regulator. Export versions of the 400 were chrome-plated. From 1964 this finish became standard on that model, and the smaller twins received a new type with revised number plate.

Rear enclosure

This form of styling was seen first on the Jubilee, enjoying a brief vogue from then to 1963. It also went on the de luxe Navigator for 1961–63 and the de luxe big twins for 1960–62.

It comprised a tail section (mentioned earlier under rear mudguard) and left and right side panels. The original tail was amended for 1960 so it could be used on the big twins as well as the small ones, and had a further change for 1961 when the seat mounting was altered.

The side panels for big and small twins differed, but only one pair was needed for each class of twin. Thus, one set catered for the 250 and 350 models and another served the 88, 99 and 650 de luxe machines.

Standard small twins lacked the full rear enclosure but did have a pair of styling panels in its place. These did not encompass the carburettor but ran just behind it to a join in front of the frame seat tube. Each one ran

down from the seat base to the rear-fork pivot area and was carried round to the side of the machine. On the left it blended into the toolbox and battery-carrier shell, and on the right into the oil tank. The same two panels were on all sizes and years of the standard small twins from 1961 on.

Tail section

This item was used on the first Commando, which later became the Fastback, and remained with it until early 1973 when it was discontinued. The first, used in 1968, was in green with a motif recessed in its top to the rear of the dualseat. This went for 1969 when several colours were listed, and the tail continued in this form until 1971 when it was modified, two grommets being added to the list of detail parts.

Another form of tail appeared on the John Player Replica. This was in a racing style and formed the single seat as well. Along with the special petrol-tank shroud and twin-headlight fairing, it went to complete the style of this individual machine, which was based on standard Commando mechanics.

Side panels

These are only to be found on the Commando models as earlier ones left the oil tank and toolbox-cum-battery-carrier lid to fulfil this function. While some of these do look similar, they are not (as described below).

The Commando panels were of two basic forms, triangular and rectangular, and finished in many colours. At first, only a left panel was fitted and the oil tank was formed to match it on the right, but from 1971 there were two panels for all as there had always been for the S and Roadster models. Early parts were made in fibreglass, but for 1972 steel ones were listed as well, taking over fully from 1974.

Despite there being only two basic shapes and two sides to the machine, there are no less than 25 different part numbers in the lists which, except for 1969, do not include colour variations.

The original Commando, R, Fastback, Interstate and Interpol machines have the rectangular panels. All others use the triangular pair, and in all cases these were made in left- and right-hands. Therefore, care is needed to make sure the correct parts are available. There is considerable variation in the transfers, so these need to be checked with care. Note that, while some 850 panels were distinguished by a double-line trim when introduced, this did not apply to the Interstate; also note that the red panels for this model were only made in steel, but the blue and black versions came in that material or plastic.

Front number plate

This is no longer a legal requirement in the UK, but many owners like to keep it and either display the registration number or the model type and year. The model 7 had a plate with a more rounded front end than that used on the singles, but the 88 kept to their form. Thus, the front edge aligned with the wheel spindle whereas that of the 7 was approximately vertical.

For 1955 the 7 plate was altered, its ends being curved out and away from the spindle line, but the 88 kept its early style until 1956 when it changed also. This form remained in use for many years. It went on to the small twins in 1961 with the exception of the de luxe Jubilee, which had a plate fixed to each side of its massive front mudguard.

The part number of the plate and its mounting details changed for 1964, although the shape did not, and it was joined by another part for the hybrids. In time, it went on to the Commando and continued on that model to the end.

Rear number plate

This is still required and is governed by local regulations, so in the end the firm just provided a mounting bracket below the rear light, leaving it to the local dealer to find and fit the necessary plate. Not so in earlier days when white numbers would be painted directly on to the plate. Later came transfers, plastic self-adhesive numbers, pressed-aluminium plates and finally the modern, reflective version in yellow.

The 7 and 88 used the same simple plate at first, but for 1955 a boxed-in type was fitted. This was revised a

ABOVE LEFT *Removal of the left side panel of a 1959 Jubilee to show the detail underneath*

BELOW *The hybrid 1965 model 33 AJS*

little for 1956. It continued in use until 1964 when it was altered to cater for the added letter of the registration number. At the same time, a second plate was listed for export models, and one more appeared for the P11.

For the de luxe big twins the number plate was made to be easily detachable from the rear enclosure, allowing the back wheel to roll out. The same plate went on the first Jubilee, but the standard small twins used the stock big-twin part at first. The 400 took the export plate, and all changed for 1964 with the big-twin part.

The plate was hung from the end of the tail section for the first year of the Commando and the Fastback. For the R and S there was a plate fairing running back from the mudguard to the support member to which the number plate itself was bolted. This fairing also carried a bracket for a pair of side reflectors, but these were transferred to the fairing itself for 1971. At the same time the support member was modified.

For 1972 there was a new number plate, and for the next year all the parts changed. A new, square-shaped rear lamp was used, which meant a new mounting for it and the number plate, together with a new fairing. These parts continued in use on to the Mk III models,

while the JPR had its own plate support to suit its tail fairing.

Battery carrier
Not all models have this as a separate part as for some it was combined with the toolbox. The model 7 did have one which was modified for 1950 and again in 1953 to suit the pivoted-fork frame. At first, the 88 had a platform on the left of the oil tank plus a strap to hold the battery, but for 1956 a box with lid was used. This went on the left and was styled to match the oil tank.

The box was amended for 1960 to suit the slim-line frame and joined by a tray with fittings for the de luxe models. There were part number changes for the assembly in 1964 and 1966, but all the details stayed as they were for the Featherbed to the end. Other carriers were listed for the hybrids.

The Commando used a battery tray that went behind its side panels and was amended, in one way or another, nearly every year. The exceptions were 1970 and 1973, while there were two listed for 1974.

The small twins began with a battery tray and brackets that were bolted to the right side of the frame beneath the rear enclosure. This part served all the de luxe models, but the battery went into the toolbox on

ABOVE *The Atlas scrambler of 1963 built for the US market*

LEFT *Undershield and prop-stand of a 1967 P11. Note the detail of the right footrest with its bracing to the frame*

the left side of standard machines. To give the Electra its 12 volts, a second battery was fitted into a tray under the seat where a heavy cable linked it to its companion.

Corrosion is one of the main enemies of battery trays and carriers, and where this is caused by battery acid the parts must be cleaned fully. The damage can be severe, but it must be repaired before the parts are finished and measures taken to prevent a recurrence.

Toolbox and tray
The model 7 had a toolbox mounted between the right chainstays of the plunger-frame models. For the pivoted-fork frame in 1953 it was moved into the left subframe angle, aft of the battery, and was modified for 1955.

The 88 had a tooltray under its seat, and this was a feature of all the Featherbed models. The tray itself was amended for 1959, and altered to suit the slim-line frame in 1960. The next year a second version appeared for the 650 models but, in time, the 1960 type was used by all. It was revised once more for 1966.

The hybrids had a toolbox on the left, three variations being listed in 1965 but only one in 1966, albeit a new one.

The Commando had a tooltray, but not until 1974 as prior to then the toolkit went either in the tail unit or a recess in the left side cover. The tray was revised for 1975. The de luxe small twins also had a tooltray which served both 250 and 350 models. It was under the seat, which was easily removed for access.

Battery and toolbox
Combining these two functions into one came first on the model 77 in 1957. It went into the left subframe angle and was styled to match the oil tank. Other models to have the feature were the standard small twins which introduced the part for 1961. It went on both 250 and 350 versions, a very similar part being used by the 400.

Chainguards
These are parts that are usually covered in grease, damaged by chains and bent or distorted by owners struggling to fit the rear wheel. So the first job is to clean what you have, and this may take several sessions before you get rid of all the grime. Then repair and finish as you would any other steel item, making sure it fits as it should.

If there is any doubt, replace the gearbox and rear wheel in the frame and check that the chain will run clear of the guard regardless of suspension movement. If it touches anywhere it will wear the finish away in no time and rattle constantly.

Chainguard and chaincase types

The original model 7 guard was altered for 1953 to suit the pivoted-fork frame, and that fitted to the 88 was similar in form. The latter was changed for 1957 and again in 1959, after which it continued for the Featherbed models while the hybrids had their own. The 77 used the guard from the pivoted-fork 7.

A full chaincase was listed as an option for the big twins in 1959, and was changed in detail for 1962 when nuts went on to the two front fixing screws. It continued in this form to 1967, and another was listed for the hybrids.

LEFT *Side reflector as fitted to the 1969 Mercury*

BELOW *The twin batteries and their mounting on a 1967 Atlas*

BELOW RIGHT *Tooltray, seat mounting and tank strap of a 1967 Atlas*

The Commando had a chainguard only, but for the first models this had an extension bolted to its inner side to increase protection. In 1969 it was joined by a skimpier, chrome-plated guard for the S. For 1971 both were replaced by a single part, which was amended for 1974 when a tail extension was added to it. The latter was altered for 1975.

The small twins had a top and lower chainguard which went on to all models and years. Also there was a full chaincase listed as an option for all, and for the standard models from 1961 an extension piece was added to the main guard between the chainguard and gearbox.

Footrests

These are sturdy items that usually can be repaired. For once you have something to get hold of, and the correct shape can be restored by heating the bent area and knocking it into place. Clamp it in the vice to do this. If the footrest is worn away, it may be necessary to build up the material again and reshape it with a file.

The early footrests were in the traditional Norton style, having half-moon end plates at the outer end of each rubber and long, thin screws holding the parts to the hanger. Serrations locked the hangers to the footrest tubes which, in turn, were mounted to the engine plates. This allowed some adjustment to the riding position. The same footrests went on to the early 88 model, the tubes being modified to suit the new frame and engine plates.

This design was simplified for 1957 when the rubber became a round section, much as many others, and was pushed on to the footrest. This part was new, but the hanger was unchanged. Other than an alteration to the mounting tube in 1958 to suit the alternator and its revised chaincase, there were no other changes for the Featherbed models.

From 1961 these machines had a rear-set option with the rests mounted in the pivoted-fork gusset plate. The right rest folded to allow use of the kickstart lever, and this arrangement plus suitable gear and rear brake pedals were listed for some years. The hybrids had their own footrest arrangements and parts.

The Commando footrest hangers were bolted to the

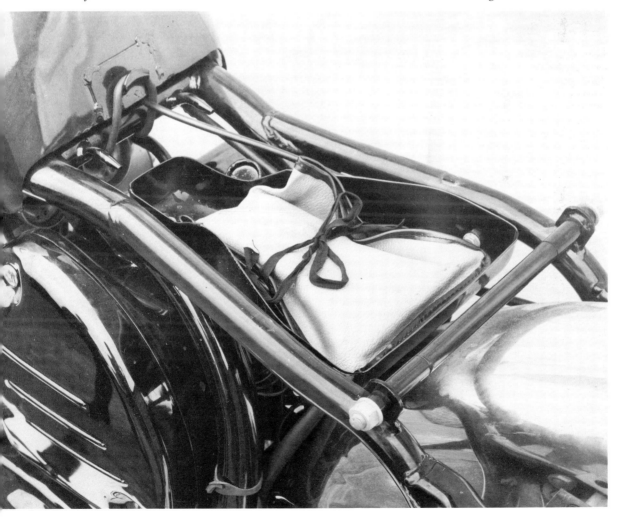

support plates and, at first, had the footpegs brazed into place. From 1972 the pegs were separate and screwed in, having a locknut on the inside. Either can break in a fall and both can be awkward to repair. The finish on the early type will be damaged if heat is used to mend it, while the later type usually snap off flush with the surface and have to be drilled out.

A solution, proposed by the owners club, is to make up pegs which have a flat next to the thread, so they can be screwed in tight with a spanner, and a groove outboard of that. This ensures that if a break occurs, it comes at a less awkward point, while the groove also helps to retain the rubber.

As well as the change to separate pegs for 1972, the hangers were altered for 1975 and the Mk III. That model had a right brake pedal, so the left hanger lost its pedal pivot and the right one gained two lugs for the master cylinder and one for the pedal. At the same time a spacer was added between the right hanger and its support plate to make room for the brake hydraulics. The JPR had its own pair of rear-sets, the left one supporting the rear brake pedal.

The small twins had simple hangers mounted on a crossbar, and these appeared on all models and years.

ABOVE *The engine room of a 1966 model which could be either an Atlas or a 650SS*

ABOVE RIGHT *Tail end of the 1966 88SS, its last year*

RIGHT *A 1963 model fitted with the Avon fairing which was an option for the SS machines used for production racing*

Footrest rubbers

It is best to replace these, if possible, as new ones will help to give the finishing touch to the restored machine.

The original pair were the same as those used by the rest of the road range, but the unique Norton shape went at the end of 1956. In its place came a round, anonymous rubber with little style. This went on all the big twins from then on, including the Commando. It was also fitted to the small twins from 1964 on, but they had their own part up to then.

Pillion rests

These need to be cleaned up and straightened if necessary, paying particular attention to the pivots

and threads. The pivot needs to be just tight enough to hold the rest in position without making it too difficult to move.

The plunger-frame model 7 had rests formed from sheet steel, oval-section rubbers and an eye bolt as a hinge. The pivoted-fork version and the 88 changed from this design to a solid rest, a new but similar rubber and a fork bolt to provide the pivot.

The rest changed in 1960 to suit the slim-line frame, and the parts were given new numbers in 1964 although, among the hybrids, the P11 retained the 1953 rubber. The 1964 rubber was used by all Commando models, but the pillion rest was new. It had a fork end and was fitted via small plates to an eye bolt attached to the silencer mounting plates.

The small twins used the 1953 rubber and their own rests pivoted from fork bolts. Like the big twins, the part numbers changed in 1964.

Brake pedal

Another part that is often damaged but is not too hard to repair. The pivot may need to be machined true and bushed if badly worn. Heat it to straighten and build up worn surfaces so they can be filed to shape.

Various pedals went on the early models, with one each for the plunger-frame 7, pivoted-fork 7, early 88, and Featherbed models of 1957 onwards. Others were listed for the hybrids, with at least three varieties, together with one for all the small twins. Also, from 1961, a rear-set pedal was listed.

The Commando pedal differed from the others in

ABOVE *The old-type black battery installed in its box on a 1957 model 88. Tools went under the seat*

ABOVE LEFT *A 1962 de luxe model fitted out with panniers, screen and front crash bar*

LEFT *A de luxe Featherbed 99 of 1960 with original pull-off seat. The rear number plate detached to let the wheel out for repair*

that it had a bracket for the stop-light switch welded to it. It was amended for 1969 and changed completely for 1975 when it moved over to the right and was linked to a hydraulic master cylinder.

Rear brake rod
These need to be straight, the thread for the adjuster and the fork hole being in good condition. Damage must be repaired. One rod served the plunger 7 and another the pivoted-fork version plus the 77, while a third went on to the Featherbed models.

The hybrids had their own sets of parts as did the small twins, which managed with one item for all. The Commando used a cable up to 1974 and then turned to hydraulics.

Legshields, crash bars, windscreen and panniers
All these items were options and none is essential for a restoration, but fitting an accessory from the correct period can set off a machine very well. Legshields and a windscreen were only listed for the small twins for 1961 on. Panniers were listed for them from the same year, and for the de luxe big twins for 1961–62.

Front and rear crash bars were listed for the big twins from 1959 on, and similar kits existed for the small twins from their introduction that year. The Commando had front bars only for 1968, but a rear assembly appeared the next year although neither continued into 1971.

Front crash bars are not necessarily a good idea on Featherbed or Commando models as a simple fall can result in bent or twisted frame tubes rather than scratched handlebar ends.

Oddments
These need as much attention as any other item. The parts list will show what is needed, and all must be collected, checked, mended and finished in the same way as for any larger part. Their fit can be important as they may align other pieces, so care with these details can pay dividends.

12 Wheels and brakes

This is an area where a good few operations have to follow one another in a definite sequence, and an early start is advised to avoid a hold-up later on when it may not be convenient. Once the machine is without wheels it becomes very hard to move about, unless reduced to parts. It might be worth considering slave wheels if this is a problem for you.

Restoration begins by removing the wheels, taking off the tyres and separating the brake backplate from the wheel assembly. Then each can be dealt with in turn.

Spoking pattern and rim offset

The wheel assembly comprises the hub assembly, spokes, spoke nipples and rim. Before doing anything else, get out your notepad, measure and write down the rim offset and draw the spoke pattern. This first is a vital piece of data and the second will give you real problems if you have to work it out from scratch. This can be done but it is not easy.

The rim offset is found by measuring between the edge of the rim and a straight-edge placed across the mouth of the brake drum. Just to make sure, also measure from a firm point at the other end of the hub and note the rim width. Take several measurements to see if there is any variation.

If the rim is buckled or has been removed from the hub, it is back to basics. You will have to work out where the rim should be in relation to the frame and there are two points of reference to help. First is that the wheels are normally central to the frame and forks. Second is the sprocket offset, which you can measure on the gearbox and wheel. Alternatively, find another machine and measure that, but consult the appendix notes on this matter first.

You may have to measure another wheel if you start with the bare hub and don't know the spoking pattern, but with a complete machine you can make notes. Consider each side and start by checking the rim to see which way round it is. No problem with a full-width hub, but when it is offset the spoke lengths and angles differ from side to side.

Now note where the valve hole is and check that the spokes on each side run away from it to give the best access. If they don't, the wheel has been built incorrectly at some time and you can expect to find most of the spokes bent near the thread. Note how the spoke to one side of the valve hole runs, whether its head points out from the wheel or into its centre, and any feature of the hub that will enable you to relocate that spoke in the same hole.

Relating the rim, spoke lay and hub for that first spoke will give the key to the wheel build, the remaining spokes falling into a pattern. Working round the rim, the spokes will alternate from one side of the hub to the other. Every third spoke will be laid the opposite way to the first and its head will face in the reverse direction, unless straight spokes are fitted. Every fifth will echo the first in angle and lay.

To finish the notes for side one, you need to work out the spoke cross pattern. On one side a spoke may cross one running the other way two, three or four times. Note the position of the first spoke and the one that crosses it nearest to the hub. Trace it to the rim and note its position in relation to the outer end of the first spoke.

Now note how side two relates to side one. Don't forget you reverse things if you turn the wheel over. One spoke on side two will give you the start to the pattern, but check it out anyway as a back-up for your notes for side one.

Wheel dismantling

If you want to repaint the hub you will have to take the wheel apart and rebuild it later. Hence the notes above. The rim is removed by undoing all the spoke nipples, which may be easy or could call for penetrating oil and a little heat. Note that there can be four types of spoke in each wheel, with differences in length and head angle, so these points need checking. Keep the spokes in batches, noting which goes where on your spoke diagram or you will have to sort out that as well. Note that for some wheels certain spokes will not come away until others have been removed. This sequence must be known as the rebuild has to be carried out in the reverse order.

You now have a rim, 36 or 40 nipples, batches of 10, 20 or 40 spokes (or 18 or 36 for some small twins), plus

ABOVE *A 1961 99SS with sports bars and ball-end levers*

ABOVE RIGHT *Same view of a 1967 Atlas with twin instruments*

the hub assembly with attendant brake drum and rear sprocket in one case.

Hub, drum and rear sprocket

Various forms of assembly were used by Norton for these items, their bearings and spindle. The bearing retaining rings need to be removed, some having left-hand threads, and all the parts dismantled, cleaned and inspected. Before removing the spindle, check the hub and brake drum for any run-out which will need correcting. This should not be attempted until the hub is on its new bearings to ensure accuracy.

Some Nortons used a built-up assembly of hub and drum, and it is as well to inspect all the parts individually. This construction does allow replacement of brake drums if scored and rear sprockets if hooked, but for many models the two were combined, so changing one means renewing both. Make sure the new parts run true when on their new bearings.

If renewal is not feasible it is possible to skim the brake drum, which will also deal with oval or belled drums. The sprocket teeth can be built up and recut by a specialist.

The hub itself should be inspected closely for any signs of damage. Repair can be awkward, depending on the construction, and should not be attempted unless you are confident that the result will withstand the loads placed upon it.

The parts will need masking carefully before finishing, and threads must be left clean or the locating rings may bind. Check this before assembly.

Front-hub types

The model 7 began with an offset, one-piece hub that contained a 7 in. diameter brake drum with $1\frac{1}{4}$ in. wide shoes. The hub was revised for 1951 to improve the waterproofing, but the size remained the same. It was also fitted to the model 88, and for both came an increase in diameter to 8 in. for 1954.

For 1955 there was a light-alloy, full-width hub with bolted-in brake drum of the same $8 \times 1\frac{1}{4}$ in. size for the 88, while the 7 stayed with the offset hub. The

full-width version went on to the 99 for 1956, and was used by the 77 for 1957–58. The 88 and 99 had a change for 1957, the iron drum being cast into the alloy instead of the bolted construction. This hub continued for all the big twins except the P11 and the Commando.

For the latter there was a new part number for what was, essentially, the same drum. This continued up to 1973. For 1972 it was joined by the disc-brake hub to which the disc was bolted. The hub was modified for 1975 when the method of retaining the bearing was amended to a circlip.

The small twins had full-width hubs for all models, and the 350 and 400 used the big-twin hub with its 8 in. brake. A hub with a 6 in. diameter drum and 1 in. wide shoes was fitted to the 250. It came from one of the AMC group of lightweights. The hub itself acquired two embellishing rings for 1962, and in 1963 the spindle was lengthened to suit a front-fork revision.

Rear-hub types

In nearly all cases, the drum and sprocket were made as one, the hub being a separate part. The two were joined either by three driving studs plus nuts or drive pegs set in rubber to provide a shock-absorbing effect on Commandos from 1971.

The model 7 began in this way with a 7 in. diameter brake drum, with integral sprocket and cooling fins, bolted to the hub. It was of the offset type, with $1\frac{1}{4}$ in. wide brake shoes, and was modified to a quickly-detachable form for the 88. This went into the pivoted-fork 7 for 1953. It continued for the 7 in 1955, but that year the 88 was equipped with a light-alloy, full-width hub to match the front. It continued to be quickly detachable.

Its construction was not altered much as the brake drum, complete with sprocket, continued to be separate, and the two halves were held together by three long sleeve nuts. The hub casting was open on the right, the side away from the drum, and the aperture was filled by a light disc retained by three drive screws. The disc had access holes for the sleeve nuts with rubber grommets to seal them. This hub continued for the big twins and the hybrids except the P11, which had its own arrangements. The number of drive screws holding the disc was increased to six for 1959.

The same design was also used on the Commando under a new part number up to 1970. For 1971 it was revised with rectangular recesses in the back of the hub for shock-absorbing rubbers. At the same time, the studs on the brake drum became tabs which mated with the recesses to transmit the drive. The aperture

FAR LEFT *The Jubilee in its first year, 1959, showing the front apron with horn mounting*

LEFT *A 1970 Commando Roadster pictured against the traditional dirty white sheet*

RIGHT *The standard disc brake developed by Lockheed seen here on a 1973 Roadster*

RIGHT *Development brake and fork leg on the 1970 Commando Production Racer*

disc was retained but did not have any sleeve-nut holes. This hub was amended in detail for 1974 and replaced by a hub with disc brake for 1975. The latter had a separate sprocket with a shock absorber between it and the hub drive.

The small twins began with a full-width hub and 6 in. diameter brake drum to match the front. There was a separate sprocket which was bolted into place, and the hub was amended for 1960. The next year it went on to the 350, and in 1962 acquired an embellishing ring to match the front. The firm used the hub with 7 in. brake from the big twins for the 400.

Wheel bearings

All models used ball races: a pair in the hub and a third set in the rear drum from 1971 on. There was little change as a double-row ball bearing went on the brake side and a single-row version on the other. The same two races were used in the big twins from 1949, with a part number change to the single-row type in 1964. The P11 was alone in using something different.

The Commando continued with the same bearings in both hubs but did have a change to the rear for 1971. That year there were two single-row bearings in the hub and the double-row version moved into the drum. For the Mk III in 1975 the single-row bearing in the front hub was changed, and in the rear hub there

LEFT *The twin-leading-shoe Norton brake with air-scoop and outlet holes, seen here on a 1968 Commando*

BELOW *A Jubilee special racer that should certainly be able to stop with that Manx brake*

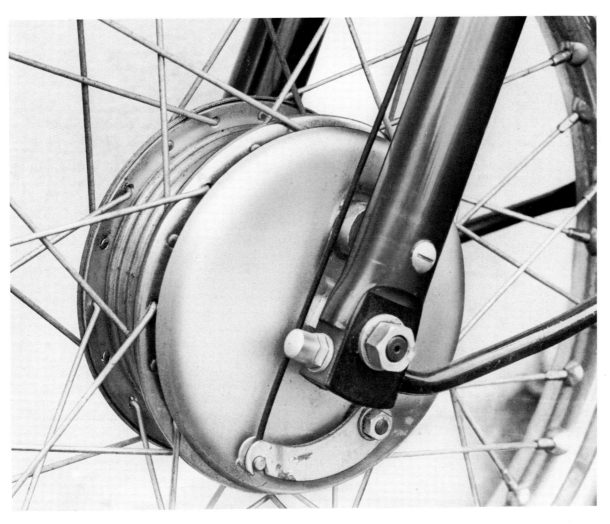

ABOVE *The Jubilee front brake in 1964 when the mudguard stay went under the wheel spindle*

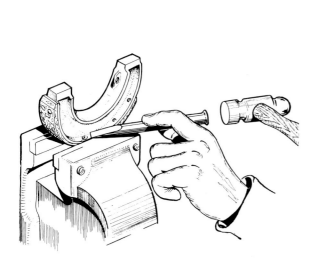

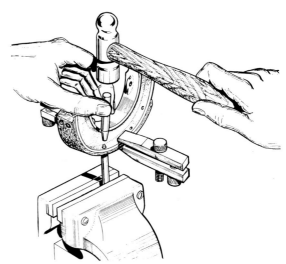

Renewing brake linings with the old rivets being cut away on the left and the new ones being peened over on the right

was the new one from the front plus another new bearing. The double-row bearing in the sprocket part of the hub continued as it was, but with a new number, and was common, as always, with the one in the front hub.

The 350 and 400 small twins used the same pair of bearings in their front hubs, the 400 having the same rear bearings as the big twins. Both 250 hubs and the 350 rear hub shared another pair of bearings for all models.

All ball races need to be a good fit in the hub, or drum, and on the spindle. The second is easy to replace if damaged, but in the former case it may be necessary to use Loctite to ensure it does not move. Races must be fitted square, and the drift or press used must bear directly on the race being inserted and not load the balls and their tracks.

Sometimes it will be found that the wheel spindle is tight when assembled. What can happen is that as you push the outer home, the inner is held back by the spindle and is forced out of line. To correct this use a hammer as a precision tool, tapping lightly in the required direction.

Brakes

Most are single leading-shoe, but regardless of type they require the same attention. Strip, clean and examine them for wear, damage, distortion or cracks. Repair as required. Check the fit of the backplate to the wheel spindle, the condition of the cams, the cam levers and the return springs. If the last are tired, replace them.

ABOVE LEFT *Rear wheel with embellished hub rim on a 1963 standard Navigator*

LEFT *A 1959 Jubilee demonstrating how the rear wheel could roll out from the rear enclosure*

ABOVE *The standard Norton front brake used for many years and seen here on a 1967 Atlas*

RIGHT *Ready to move off on a 1961 de luxe 99 fitted with full rear chaincase*

You are likely to fit new brake shoes or to reline the ones you have. With the former, check that the brake drum is of the standard diameter and has not been skimmed at some time. If it has not, still beware of pattern shoes as some have minimal lining material and will seem to be worn out even when new.

If you reline the shoes yourself you will need clamps to hold the linings in place, a drill and counterbore to form the holes, and riveting tools. Work out from the centre, chamfering the ends when finished.

Should you go to an expert he will, or should, want the wheel and backplate. He will check and skim the drum first, if this is needed, and reline the brakes with oversize linings which can be turned down to fit. This was normal practice on racing machines when they all used drum brakes.

Front-brake types

Most of the first model 7 front brake came from the road-single range, but not the shoes. The backplate was changed for 1951 to an alloy die-casting which matched the new hub to improve the water seal. This also appeared on the first 88, and for 1954 all parts, except the shoe return springs, were altered to suit the change to an 8 in. diameter drum.

The same parts were used by the 7 from then on, by the 77 during its short life and in the early full-width hubs. For 1957 the last of these had a changed backplate, lever and cam to go with a revised hub. This assembly continued in use on the Featherbed and hybrid machines until the end.

In addition to the standard brake, a twin-leading-shoe version was available as an option for these machines and was fitted as standard to the Commando. It featured a backplate with an air-scoop and three air outlets, a rod link between the two cam levers and a separate cam and pivot for each shoe.

The backplate and cams were modified for 1972 when a support plate was added inside to brace the cams and pivots. Reports suggest that the brakes varied in performance a good deal but that they could be improved. The first step was to bush the centre of the backplate to ensure a good fit on the spindle. Next was to cut off the air-scoop and to weld up or blank off the hole to stop water getting into the brake. The air-scoop would collect water even if its intake was blanked off, hence the need to remove it entirely.

Further possibilities were to fit a brake-stiffening kit, which helped to stop parts moving under load, or to fit AM4 green linings. These had to be fitted by an

LEFT *The full-width front hub of a 1957 model 88*

RIGHT *The Interpol model as built with the Tomos label for use in Yugoslavia in 1970*

expert, machined to suit the drum diameter and backed off well on the leading edge to avoid grabbing. It was suggested that the two combined could be too much for road use. The stiffening kit plus a 30 mm longer cam lever arm linked to the cable can also make the brake more effective.

From 1972 the Commando turned to a disc front brake, and for 1973 a conversion kit (from drum to disc) was listed. The disc was the same for all years, but the caliper was changed for 1974 when a disc scraper was fitted. As this made a dreadful noise and did nothing much to stop the inside pad wearing in the wet, it was dropped for 1975 when the earlier caliper returned but went on to the left fork leg.

The 350 and 400 small twins had the standard big-twin front brake, but the 250 had its own assembly. This was a conventional, single-leading-shoe type with the addition of a cover disc for the brake backplate. The latter was simply a styling item and was modified together with the backplate for 1960.

Rear-brake types

There was less change here as most models had a 7 in.

single-leading-shoe assembly, and the early model 7 used parts from the road singles. These were amended to suit the pivoted-fork 7 of 1953 and the model 88. The same assembly went into the full-width hub on the 88 of 1955 and the model 77. For 1957 the full-width hub had a brake with revised backplate, lever and cam. For the 650, in 1961, a second lever appeared, pointing upwards with a considerable offset. There were two reasons for this: to clear a large-diameter silencer fitted to US machines, and to enable the operating rod to clear the rear damper on its way to the lever. The silencer soon went but not the lever, which became the standard fit in 1964 and is best changed for the older type or the later Commando version, part 067755. The backplate was modified for 1966, and a further improvement can be made to stiffen it by using the Commando cam-spindle bush (part 060701), a narrower cover-plate spacer (part 060334), and lever return spring (part 060704). This is also a method of repairing a worn cam-lever bush. The G15 models had their own backplate, and the P11 its own assembly.

The Commando had an assembly similar to that of

the Featherbed, the only changes being to the shoes for 1973 and the backplate in the following year. For 1975 a disc brake and master cylinder were fitted.

The 250 and 350 small twins had their own smaller brake which was similar to the 250 front. This had a change made to the shoes for 1961. The 400 had the assembly from the big twins, and had an adaptor plus torque arm to fix the brake position.

Spokes and nipples

These need to be straight and have good threads. It is a false economy to replace only some if more than one or two are past redemption; better to re-spoke completely. Check carefully the length, gauge and head angle required before shopping and inspect what you buy to make sure you do get what you want.

If the spokes are being replaced, it is worth buying a new set of nipples as well. Remember that their diameter has to suit the spoke gauge and that the rim holes must match.

It is possible to buy stainless-steel spokes, although opinions vary as to how this material copes with the bending of the head angle and the stress pattern to which spokes are subjected. If made to really close tolerances they should be no trouble, but avoid anything cheap or poorly finished.

Wheel rims

All Norton twins have steel rims of the WM section form. Diameters used were 18 and 19 in. in width numbers one, two and three. All big twins had 40 spoke holes, while the 250 and 350 rear had 36. Security bolts were only listed for rear wheels, appearing from 1957 and on all Commando models. Light-alloy rims were listed as an option in 1964.

If the rim is damaged or rusty it will have to be replaced as you are unlikely to find anyone who can repair the former or who is willing to strip and replate to correct the latter. The first point to consider is the tyre size you will use. In many cases, it will be worth going to a WM3 section rather than keeping to the listed WM2 if you wish to fit a fatter type. If you do this, remember it will affect the offset dimension, which will need changing by half the alteration in rim width.

Next is the dimpling and the holes. For a really

strong wheel the spokes must lay at the correct angle in both directions, and to achieve this the rim must be pierced to suit. You also need holes for the tyre valve and any security bolts. Inspect the join in the rim; unless it is smooth you will never get the wheel to run true.

The rims used are set out in Appendix 12 along with the tyres fitted to each model and some modern equivalents.

The rim was either painted and lined, chrome-plated, or chrome-plated with a painted, lined centre. Unless you are very sure that you can produce the painted and lined finish really well, send it to an expert. This is an area where any flaw will be only too obvious, so the cost will be worth it.

Wheel rebuilding

This is an area that many people fight shy of, but with care and patience good results can be obtained. Your notes will make the job much easier and should be consulted to determine the order of assembly and the precise location of each item. The rim must be the right way round.

Simply fit the first spoke, starting its nipple so it cannot shift and scratch the rim. Then continue this process until all 40 are in place. Any mistake should be obvious as spokes either won't connect at all or will be at the wrong angle. As long as the first spoke is correct, the rest will fall into place.

Next you have to true the wheel, and you might consider sending the assembly to an expert for this important, final stage. Or you can do it yourself. To do so, set the wheel vertical with its spindle held so you can spin the rim. Place a marker clear of the rim and

spin it to check if it runs true. Adjust spokes to suit, but work to get the radial adjustment correct first and then go on to deal with the sideways error. If you start with a good rim and work carefully, you should not have much trouble. Make sure every spoke is nicely tensioned without being overstrained.

Tyres, tubes and rim tapes

Your first problem might be finding something to fit. Much easier with some models than others. You have the choice of 'old-fashioned' sizes (or some of them), more up-to-date, low-profile tyres, or the latest metric offerings which are low-profiles with their inches translated into millimetres.

Regardless of which you choose, do fit a good rim tape after you have checked the spoke nipples for protruding spoke ends. A new inner tube really is mandatory, don't even think of a patched example. The tyre itself must suit the rim section, and the front and rear must be compatible. The faster the machine, the more important are the condition and type of tyres, but they must never be ignored on any machine.

If you fit modern, wider-section tyres you must make certain that there is ample clearance in all positions of the rear suspension. Fit them with care and use slim, smooth, polished tyre levers. Don't forget the security bolt. Do forget the tyre-pressure table in the old manuals, which has no relevance to modern tyres. Establish the wheel loading and check tyre data tables for the correct pressure. Check the rolling diameter, or revolutions per mile, of the old tyre against the modern replacement in case it affects the speedometer reading significantly.

*Production Racer
on show in London
in 1970*

13 Cables, controls and instruments

There are few things that look worse on a restored motorcycle than cables drooping in loops because they are far too long or with their adjusters unscrewed fully and hanging on the last thread. There is nothing more dangerous than cables that are so tight that they might be pulled by the forks as they move.

The control cables should be of the proper length, be routed correctly and neatly clipped out of harm's way, and be in correct adjustment. They should also be of the correct gauge for the job or the throttle will feel heavy and the front brake full of sponge.

Every cable incorporates an assembly of inner, outer, outer ends and wire nipples, and normally all have at least one adjuster in their length. To these parts can be added end stops and fittings which attach the cable to its lever and the machine. In just about all cases the outer length determines the sweep of the final installation, while the inner must be chosen to suit the wear on the parts and the length of adjustment required.

Each end fitting needs to be checked over and repaired or replaced where needed. This operation should include any plating required. Nipples may be reused but must be cleaned fully first, and it is best to remove all the old solder using heat so you can assess the condition of the part properly. If beyond repair, they should be replaced. If the exact size is not available, a new piece may be machined from another larger nipple. Do make sure it is a good fit on the cable: free to slide into place but no more.

Soldering

This is the method used to attach the nipple to the wire, and the secret of success is clean parts. Solder will not adhere to surfaces that are dirty, tarnished or greasy.

The tools you need are soldering iron, solder and flux. The first may be electric, heated over a gas flame or heated by butane. The slim type used for electrical work will not hold enough heat for cables, and something of 60–70 watts is necessary. If you use a gas flame, clean up the iron tip with a file first and let the flame play on the iron an inch back from the tip to keep it clean. When hot, it should be dipped in flux to remove any oxidation and tinned with a thin coat of solder.

The solder needed comes in a stick. Do not use flux-cored, electrician's solder as it is not up to the job, being designed for electric wires, not steel cables. Use plumber's solder instead. The flux can be a paste in a tin or a liquid. My own preference is for the former as it is convenient to be able to open it and dip the iron or cable in. A match is handy for putting flux on to less accessible areas.

To cut an inner cable to length you need sharp, heavy-duty cutters, a cold chisel and block, or a hacksaw. Before cutting, you must tin the cable to stop it unwinding, the process being the same as any soldering. First clean the wire really well, next tin the iron, and third use the iron to tin the wire, adding solder if needed. Keep it to a minimum, avoiding blobs.

Now you can cut the wire and solder a nipple to the end. To do this successfully, you have to splay out the wire ends so they sit in the countersink in the nipple. This operation can be carried out as follows. Clamp the wire vertically in the vice with the nipple sitting on top of the vice jaw. Before tightening the vice fully, slide the wire down so its end is about level with the top surface of the nipple. Tighten the vice but don't crush the cable. Then tap the end of the wire with the ball end of a light hammer to splay the strands. This may be started with a tack if needed.

Now hold the wire lightly in the vice with a clothes peg between the nipple and the vice jaws. Leave the vice slack enough for you to pull down on the wire. Tin the iron and apply solder to the nipple to build it up as required. While it cools maintain a light pull on the wire and watch. The surface appearance will change as soon as it hardens. Leave the assembly for a short while and give it a good tug. Better it flies off in the workshop than on the road. File to shape, making sure it fits its lever and can turn if necessary.

Cable making

There are two ends to a cable, so there are two soldering jobs to do. As there are at least three, and sometimes four or five, cables to do, it takes some time to make a full set from scratch.

BELOW *First stage with a cable is tinning the wire and then cutting it to length*

ABOVE *The controls of a 1957 model 88 showing instrument mounting into the headlamp shell and the tank strap*

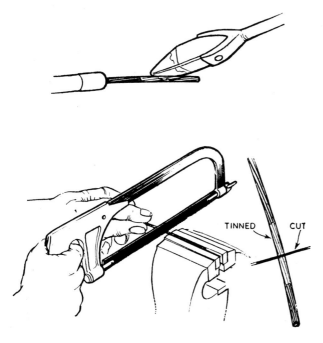

TINNED   CUT

Start with the outer, determining its run and, thus, its length. Fit its ferrules, having checked that they, in turn, will fit their housings at both ends. Solder one nipple to the inner and assemble to the outer complete with all fittings. Some owners like to lubricate the cable at this point, but the practice means that the end has to be cleaned again. My own preference is to assemble, clean, solder and then oil.

In either case, the important aspect is to ensure the length of the inner wire is correct. To do this connect the soldered end and offer up the other. No need to clip anything to the frame or even have the parts on the machine at this stage as long as the operation at the ends is correct. Set the adjusters to suit the controls. Thus, screw in the front brake adjuster fully if the brakes have been relined as movement will all be in one direction. The clutch is better in mid-travel as this will allow for wear and swelling plates if you have the latter problem. The throttle, air and magneto cables should be set to allow the controls to work to their integral stops without the adjusters hanging from their housings.

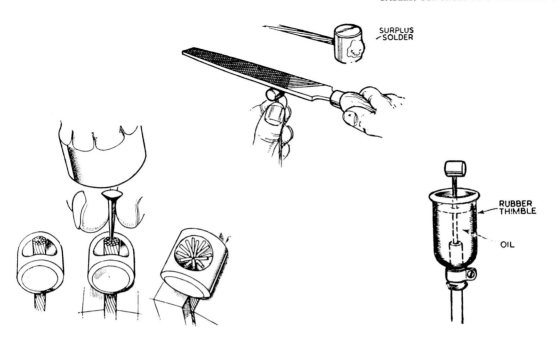

Now solder the second nipple in place and clean it up. Now the cable can be lubricated, and the only way to be sure the oil has gone all the way through is to pour it in one end until it comes out of the other. Funnels formed round the end are a common suggestion, but my own method is to use a pressure device which fits round the end and is pumped up with a bicycle pump.

Controls

The handlebars to which these are fitted varied to some extent and the list was extended to include a number of options. The original bars were altered for 1956 and the new form ran on for many years. The 77 used another bend, and in 1959 a pair of clip-ons was listed as an option as was a set of bars for the USA. The next year a straight-bar option appeared. For 1964 the standard bars were changed and were joined by a pair for one of the hybrids.

The Commando began with one bend for the home market and one for export. The latter was amended for 1969 but stayed in use from then on. It was joined by three more in 1971, with that for the Interpol continuing unchanged. The Hi-Rider bars were altered for 1973, and the third listing altered each year, appearing on the Street Scrambler for 1971, the Interstate for 1972–73 and as the Europe standard from then on. For the JPR in 1974 there was a pair of clip-ons and also a short length of dummy handlebar. This was held by the standard bar clamps and carried the air lever.

The small twins had bars for each capacity with welded-on clutch and brake-lever lugs for the 250 and 350. For these there were options of straight, US and flat bars in 1961. The first of these became the standard fit for the 250 and 350 in 1964. The 400 had a

ABOVE *Soldering the nipple into place and one way to oil the cable*

BELOW *A better if messy way of fully lubricating the cable*

ABOVE *Controls and instruments of a 1965 Matchless G15CSR with the light switch set between the two dials*

ABOVE LEFT *The 1969 Mercury with plate mounting for switch and speedo which can hardly be considered stylish*

LEFT *High-rise bars and correspondingly long control cables on a 1967 Atlas on show at Earls Court*

more conventional bar as used by the big twins.

The controls also varied over the years, and a careful study of the parts list needs to be made to ensure the correct item. Some machines had two controls mounted together, while the Commando used combined lever housings and electric switches. Beware of the Unified threads on the Commando fittings and cables which will not fit the older parts. These had cycle threads.

Each control needs to be stripped, cleaned, inspected, renovated as required and reassembled. Care will be rewarded by smooth operation and pleasant feel. Twistgrip and left bar grips should be replaced if required, the correct part enhancing the final result.

The handlebars themselves may well have been changed or bent. If the former, the criterion is whether they are comfortable for you or whether you want to change them to original. If bent, much the same applies, but beware of straightened bars as they have been known to snap due to the metal being stretched.

Instruments

The ammeter has been mentioned already, which leaves speedometer, rev-counter and oil-pressure gauge. The last was only fitted up to 1952 and was of a typical design with coiled pressure tube linked to the pointer. Repair entails instrument-mechanic skills and tools for the parts are smaller and lighter than the general run of motorcycle items. A magnifier and tweezers to hold things are well worth having. Treat the scale face with care but repaint the needle if necessary.

Two types of mechanism were used in the speedometers and rev-counters fitted by Norton, with the chronometric type being superceded by the magnetic in 1964. Generally, the former was held to be the more reliable in the long term, but it is a complex mechanical device that became too expensive for a mass-produced item. It has a camshaft, balance wheel,

ABOVE *Rear-set brake pedal on a 1970 Commando Production Racer*

ABOVE LEFT *Front end of a 1961 model 99SS with the usual Norton flat bars*

LEFT *1967 Atlas with twin dials and light switch between them, while the ammeter and warning light stayed in the headlamp shell*

gears, levers and springs. To get at these, you have to unscrew the bezel ring without marking it. This will allow the works to be removed.

If you are an instrument fitter you should be able to strip, repair and rebuild a chronometric speedometer. If you are an instrument mechanic it might be as well to stop at the mileage recorder which is easier to work with although it still needs a delicate touch.

The later magnetic type is easier to work on, but only once you get inside it for the bezel is rolled on. This means working with care and maybe a special tool to roll it off plus another to replace it. Once inside, it is much less complex but just as delicate as any other.

From the point of repair, the rev-counter is simply a speedometer mechanism minus the distance recorder. The case is basically the same and only the dial differs, having its own calibration.

In addition to the instrument head, its mounting and its drive must be considered. The first must be in good order. The second comprises the cable and the drive box; the cable needs to be inspected and replaced if either inner or outer is damaged, while the drive box must operate smoothly. For all models and years the speedometer was driven from the rear wheel. The rev-counter had two drive systems: one from the camshaft end and the other, used on the Commando from 1969, from a camshaft skew gear.

Speedometer types

The first point to consider on any speedometer is the direction of rotation of the needle, which must match the cable. Next is the maximum scale reading, then whether in miles or kilometres and, most important, the revolutions-per-mile figure. Normally, this is written on the scale just under the part number, and for many models a figure around 1600–1700 can be expected if it is calibrated in miles. This reduces to

LEFT Controls of a 1972 Interstate showing the Lucas bar switches and the light switch and warning lamps in the shell

BELOW LEFT Close-up of the left bar switch of the 1972 Interstate

BELOW The original Commando dials with green spots in 1968, the instruments being mounted in pods held by the fork top nuts

about 1000 for the metric version. The figure also represents the cable speed in rpm at 60 mph since at that speed travelling one mile takes one minute.

The final factors in speedometer selection are the presence of total and possibly trip distance recorders, the method of returning the trip to zero and the mounting of the instrument.

For nearly all models the speedometer was panel-mounted in one way or another. The early models 7 and 88 had a fork-mounted panel, but from 1956 the instrument moved into the rear of the headlamp shell. It stayed there until 1964 when an option became available to mount the speedometer and rev-counter side by side on a fork bracket. This arrangement became standard in 1967, but for 1969 and the Mercury there was the speedometer only on the right with a light switch on the left. The hybrids used

brackets, while the Commandos had instrument cups, one attached to each fork-leg top. The small twins kept to the headlamp-shell mounting.

The speedometer itself was listed in mph and km/h forms for most years, and it was changed for 1956 when the trip rewind was altered. Both were of the 120 mph or 180 km/h maximum scale reading and were joined in 1961 by a 150 mph unit, and its km/h equivalent, for the 650. All changed to the magnetic type in 1964, with one for the two SS models and the other for the Atlas and G15. The latter became the only fitting from 1966 and was fitted to all models.

The Commando had a change made to its speedometer head for 1971, and for 1973 Veglia heads were listed alongside the usual Smiths version. This practice continued.

Initially, the 250 had an 80 mph or 130 km/h head. This was changed to a 100 mph or 160 km/h type for 1961 when the 350 was introduced. For 1964 a white-faced instrument was fitted. The 400 used the same head as the 350 year by year.

When hunting for a replacement speedometer, most of the requirements are easy to determine and to check except for the important revs-per-mile needed to match the machine. For rear-wheel-driven machines, the factors are the tyre revs-per-mile and the ratio between wheel and cable. The latter is controlled by the speedometer gearbox, the ratio being usually around 2:1. If either changes so does the speed of the instrument cable, so adjustment is needed to allow for a change of tyre size or another gearbox.

The optimum cable speed can be found by calculation using the data available for the model in question, but applies only if the machine is to standard specification in respect of the features that affect it. If all is well, this is the figure to seek on the replacement speedometer, or something close to it.

On occasion, the calculation has to be used in reverse. If a good speedometer is to hand but has the wrong cable speed, it may be possible to achieve correct readings by using an alternative wheel gearbox. A calculator makes it easy to do the necessary sums once the data has been collected.

Rev-counter types

Both chronometric and magnetic types were used on the big twins, all driven from the camshaft. The fitment first appeared as an option for 1959 when the drive gearbox was bolted to the timing cover and driven from the end of the camshaft by a special nut. The timing cover specified with this arrangement was the pre-1958 type with the early pressure-release valve. Thus, any engines of 1958 onwards which had the rev-counter fitted also needed a change of timing cover. A blanking plate was listed to cover the hole left if the gearbox was removed later.

This arrangement continued with a gearbox change for 1964, and a new box for the Commando in 1968

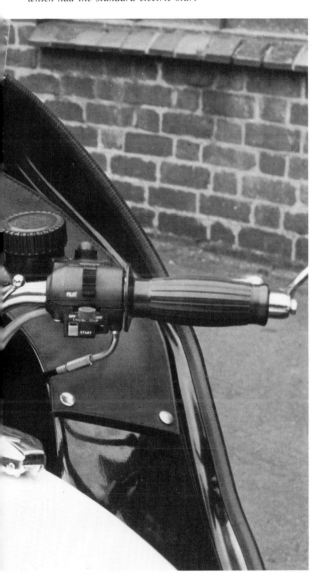

LEFT *Much improved layout of lights and switches as on the 1975 Mk III Commando*

BELOW *Controls and switches of the 1975 Mk III Interpol which had the standard electric start*

Cockpit of the John Player Replica with instruments and other items in the fairing and special bar for air lever

and early 1969. The rev-counter was a standard fitment from 1967 and, thus, appeared on all Commandos. When the points moved into the timing cover on the S, and later on all machines, the rev-counter drive had to move. A skew gear was cut on the camshaft and a mating gear housed in the front corner of the crankcase. There, it was tucked out of harm's way, but in practice proved to be prone to oil leaks.

There was no provision for a rev-counter on the small twins, but it should be possible to drive one from the exhaust camshaft by modifying the timing cover and making a suitable drive nut.

Instrument-bracket types

For years the mounting was either the fork panel or the headlamp shell, while the rev-counter was hung on a bracket bolted to the top of one fork leg. In 1964 a twin-head bracket became an option to hold the two instruments and a light switch. This became standard from 1967. For 1969 it was altered to carry just the speedometer and a light switch.

The Commando used a separate mounting cup, bolted to the top of the fork leg, for each instrument. The cups were changed for 1973 so they could be used for either make of head, using adaptor bolts in one case, and were given base covers for 1974 to keep the weather at bay.

14 Petrol tank

This has been mentioned already under Finishing. The tank is truly the crowning glory of any motorcycle, so its finish is important if you want the machine to look nice, but not to the extent that it does not match the rest of the machine. If the general paintwork is reasonable, but a touch shabby, a super tank job will stand out and show up against it. It may be better to leave the tank to blend in with the rest, or you may find yourself renovating all the paint you meant to leave alone for a season or two.

Any tank must be checked for damage that could prove dangerous. This means looking for splits and cracks, checking brackets, examining tap bosses and badge-screw threads, and looking closely at the bolt holes in the base. If bolts of too great a length have been used, or washers left out at any time, the base of the threaded hole may have been lifted and caused a small crack. All these faults must be corrected.

The fit of the tank cap should also be checked early on in case attention is needed in this area. Where there is no real damage but the tank interior is rusty, the corrosion needs to be removed as much as possible. If left, either the rust will block the carburettor or the affected area will develop a leak, or both. To remove the worst of the rust, drop a handful of small nuts and bolts, or sharp stones, into the tank and give it a good shake. Then wash out well. After this, a swill with a rust-inhibitor fluid is well worth the trouble and, when the finish is complete, the inside should be treated with Petseal. This two-part liquid forms a coat on the inside of the tank and seals any small pinholes, so it is well worth using in any tank which is suspect. However, do look on it as an extra insurance and don't expect it to hold a cobweb of steel together.

The tank's appearance is dependent on its external shape, and if dented it will require attention. This is specialist work, as has been mentioned already, and usually entails cutting the tank open for access and rewelding it afterwards. Before deciding what work is needed, remove all the loose items (such as taps, cap, badges and panels) from the tank. Then examine it to establish if it has any filled patches. If it has and you want a good job, they must be cleared away.

Usually, even minor work on the tank means a welding torch, and many are the horror stories on the subject. The problem lies in removing all petrol and its fumes before the torch is lit. Methods used are to wash it out with water or to allow a car exhaust to blow into it, or both. After this, many experienced workers will stand well back, light the torch and point it into the tank. The theory, and it works, is that if there is any vapour left you burn it then and there while expecting a bang.

You may not be disappointed, in which case you will remember to wash out the tank more fully next time. What you avoid with this method is an unexpected bang when welding close up to the tank.

Tank finish

This can be simply paint, embellishment coming from the badges and trim, or paint plus lining, or two colours of paint plus separating line, or, worst of all to cope with, chrome-plate plus painted panels and lining.

The last was used from 1949 to 1956 and is very specialized. The sequence of jobs is plate, paint and line. A good job will be expensive, but it will be worth the money.

As with any finish, preparation is all and for other than plated tanks follows the same lines as for any other steel item. The exception is the avoidance of polyurethane lacquer which would react with spilt petrol to lift the paint. Otherwise the final result will reflect the care with which the metal surface has been prepared and the skill with which the paint has been applied, rubbed down and polished. As with mudguards and the rear enclosure, a brush finish can be fine as long as you can keep the dust off it. Care will be repaid by a smooth, glossy surface. An internal coat of Petseal may be a good idea depending on what you discovered during your early examination. Protect the tank finish while applying, as a chip at this stage could be annoying.

Tank types

The plunger-frame model 7 tank is easy to recognize as it was the only one with a recess in its top for an oil gauge, which went on the left side. A new tank was

brought in for the pivoted-fork model in 1953. This had the same kneegrips, each held by two screws. The same tank was used for 1954, but for 1955 was amended to take the circular tank badge on each side.

The 88 tank followed the same route, the round badge appearing on its sides for 1955. Originally, it was held in place by a strap in the same way as the racing Manx models. This design, with minor amendments, continued until 1959. From 1957 the tank was painted all over, with separate, chrome-plated side panels being held in place by the tank badge and the kneegrips. Therefore, the tanks have

LEFT *Tank badge as first seen in 1955 and used then and in the late 1960s*

RIGHT *A variety of petrol taps with filters and reserve settings*

BELOW *Cleaning up the taper part of a tap prior to lapping it into the body*

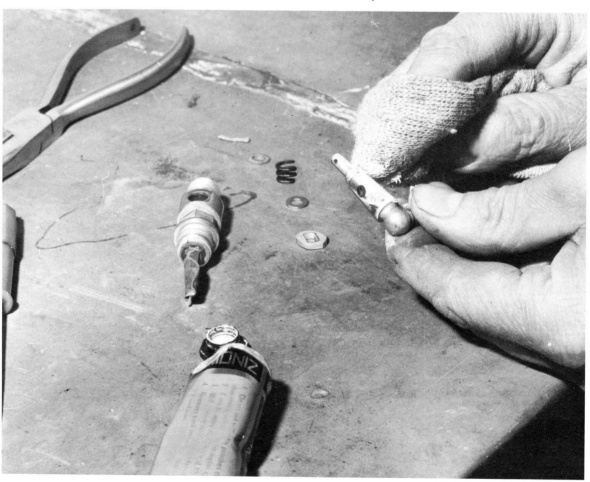

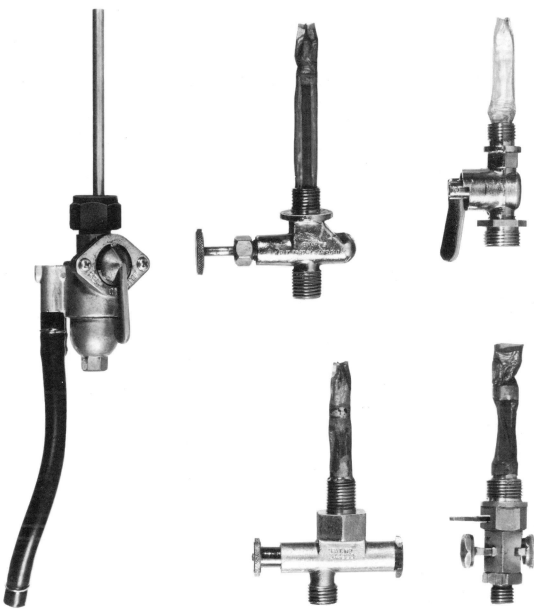

four tapped holes in each side. A similar style of tank
was used by the model 77.

For 1960 the tank style was revised to dispense with
the round badge and replace it with long styling bars
on each side. At the same time, the tank was amended
to suit the slim-line frame and it only had three tapped
holes in each side for the bar screws. It was held in
place with a new system so the fixing strap was no
more, after having done duty since the 88 was first
seen. This tank remained in use on all the Featherbed
models from then on.

The long, thin bar-style badge had been seen first in
a smaller version a year earlier on the Jubilee, which
had its own tank. This tank went on all the small twins
for all years.

The hybrids had their own arrangements to suit the

frames involved, three or four tanks being listed to
cover them all.

The Commando began with a fibreglass tank having
a badge on each side, but this was soon changed. For
1969 there was a smaller tank for the R and S in a
choice of two colours, and another for the Fastback in
four. All these had a 'Norton' transfer in place of the
badge.

For 1971 there was a long list of tank numbers to
cover the colour options, but the basis was one for
each model. The SS and Hi-Rider shared a tank, while
there were two listed for the Interpol, one of which
was recessed for a radio. Of the others, there were
three basic part numbers for Roadster models, plus
suffixes for the colour, and others for the Fastback and
LR models. The suffix numbers did not indicate the

same colour from one tank type to another, which may explain, in part, why all changed for the next year.

For 1972 some tanks were available in steel as well as fibreglass, and now the suffix numbers indicated the same finish for any tank. The Fastback and Hi-Rider tanks were in fibreglass only and the Interpol in steel only, but the Roadster and Interstate offered a choice.

The list was reduced for 1973 with only the Hi-Rider tank still in fibreglass and more code numbers for the finish and lining. There was a new tank for the Interstate for 1974, and this arrangement continued from then on. Also new for 1974 was a tank for the JPR. This went under a moulded shroud which bolted into the fairing.

Filler cap

The model 7 began with the wing-nut cap that had been on the road singles since 1946. It continued with this type up to 1954, while the 88 was fitted with a similar, but slimmer, version. For 1955 a change was made on both models to a quarter-turn bayonet cap. This remained in use on large and small twins up to 1963.

In 1964 it took a new part number and was joined by a wing-nut cap that went on some of the hybrids, with more appearing in 1966. The new part number also applied to the small twins from 1964 on.

The Commando was launched with a snap-action cap which remained standard on most models for all years. In 1971 the 1964 quarter-turn cap reappeared for the Interpol and Fastback LR, remaining in the list for the first of these up to 1974. For 1975 a second filler cap with a lock was listed alongside the original one. The JPR hid its cap under a cover mounted on the tank shroud and held down by a quarter-turn Oddie fastener.

Tank badges and panels

Handle with care. Check that they are not damaged and fit as they should. Make sure the fixing screws fit and don't bottom in their holes.

Badges were not fitted until 1955, and the following year a small replica appeared in the timing cover. One badge served all models and years up to 1959 although the fixing screws did change for 1957. That year chrome-plated side panels replaced the tank plating, one pair for the 77 and another for the two Featherbed models. Each sat on its own bead, and this was listed in gold as an option for 1959.

Matchless hybrid G15 of 1965 with Norton 745 cc engine and its own chaincase

LEFT *Midlands show with Andrea Lloyd from Walsall sitting on a 1974 829 cc Roadster Mk IIA Commando*

BELOW *A Fastback LR with its large tank at a Manchester show in 1972*

Bolting down the tank strap on a 1957–59 twin after which they all changed to the slim-line frame and other fixings

also used on late Featherbeds and hybrids to give corporate identity.

Kneegrips

These were a feature of machines from the 1920s, gradually becoming more common as speeds rose and the need for something to clamp on to became more pressing. As tanks fattened in the 1930s they also served to protect the finish.

The first model 7 types were each held by a pair of screws, being revised for 1955 and the round badge tank. All had the 'Norton' name embossed on them. Those of the 88 had a plain pattern and were stuck on, but for 1955 they altered to gain the 'Norton' name. They were changed for 1957 when the chrome-plated side panels were introduced, and the same pair also went on the 77.

Much smaller grips were introduced with the new styling bar for 1960, continuing in use on all Featherbed models. A similar, but smaller, pair was made for the small twins and remained in use on all models and years. Some, but not all, hybrids had their own kneegrips. However, none of the Commando models had them as such. What was provided, in their early days, was an extension of the dualseat, but only for the Fastback model.

Taps

For road use, Norton normally fitted taps with cork seals, but on the Commando you should find the taper-cock type. In either case, they need to come apart and have the sealing arrangements checked and repaired as required. Then check that the filters are undamaged and that the taps work freely. Before they are used on the machine, make sure the taps don't leak and can pass a full flow of petrol. Leaks at that stage are a bind, and they can cause a fire.

The model 7 began with a pair of push/pull taps from the early post-war International model, but for 1955 changed them for those from the more prosaic road machines. The 88 had just one tap, but of the two-level type, and this continued in use until altered for 1960 and again in 1961. The model 77 had its own tap and there were no more changes.

The Commando had two taper-cock taps, one with a reserve, which went on all models. There were detail changes for 1974 and 1975, but the use of twin taps continued. The small twins had a single tap with one type for the 400 and another for the two smaller models. This applied to all years.

For 1960 long styling bars were fitted to each side of the tank, and this design remained in use on all Featherbed models from then on. It was also used on all small-twin models and years, but the parts themselves were smaller than those on the big twins. The hybrids returned to the round badges of 1955, having either these or AMC versions to suit the model and marque the machine was being sold under.

The Commando began with its odd green blob on the tank sides plus a small Norton-Villiers badge. From 1969 on, the tanks carried transfers, just as the first model 7 had two decades earlier. The green blob was

15 Seating

Norton twin seating began as a saddle and pillion pad which was fitted up to 1952 and the end of the plunger frame. From then on, and for the 88 in 1952, all models had a dualseat although a saddle was listed as an option from 1960, being fitted as standard to the P11 and Interpol models. A handrail was available from 1961 to 1965 and from 1971 on.

Saddle

A saddle is an assembly and should be treated as such. On top is the cover which is sewn to shape and fitted with clips riveted around the edge. Under that is a felt underlay, and this tends to wear and fray on the springs beneath. With felt and cover removed, you are left with the main frame and a series of suspension springs which run fore and aft.

The two main springs were attached at the rear of the assembly and a pivot bolt went at the front. This was supposed to turn in a greased hole in the frame, but it is an area often neglected and the holes may well need repair. A good fit will allow the saddle to rise and fall on its springs as it should without any disconcerting side-sway.

The parts need to be refurbished as for any others and reassembled. Once complete, a new cover with underfelt can be fitted and retained by its clips. Fit the back first and work the material forward to the nose.

Saddle types

Only one saddle was listed for the model 7 for 1949–52, and this was a Lycett. A different single seat was listed from 1960 onwards for the Featherbed models, and others appeared for the hybrids and the P11. The P11A featured a dualseat. One further single seat was listed for the small twins for 1964–66.

Pillion pad

Separate passenger seats could be either sprung and built up like the saddle or simply a rubber pad with a cover. Norton listed neither, so owners would fit a variety of makes to the rear mudguard. Some of these were linked to the back of the saddle to form an embryo dualseat.

If a pad was fitted and water has got into the interior it is unlikely to be usable anymore, so replacement will be necessary. Again, if the cover is damaged, a new one will be needed. Make sure you have sorted out the fixing to the mudguard before that item is finished.

When the pillion seat is of the spring type, repair is carried out in the same manner as for a saddle. Again, the fixing to the machine needs to be finalized before finishing the mudguard and not after.

Dualseat

These can be more of a problem as there were a good few variations used by Norton over the years and they can be awkward to mend. They consist of a steel pan, which may rust, a moulded interior, which may rot, and a cover, which may tear or split.

The interior moulding is the greatest problem as replacement may be the only answer, and unless you can locate a suitable example you will not achieve the desired final seat shape. The pan can be refurbished as for any other steel part and the cover replaced by another which may be stitched from a suitable material.

Thus, restoration is a specialist job that you can expect to farm out in most cases as it is not practical for most owners. There are always exceptions, of course, depending on the size of the problem and the skills and resources of the person dealing with it.

Dualseat types

The first Norton dualseat went on to the 88 and remained the same up to 1959. It was shaped to provide distinct positions for rider and passenger, but this feature did not appear on the dualseat fitted to the model 7 for 1953.

For 1955 the model 7 seat was altered to give a step between rider and passenger and a form more on the lines of that fitted to the 88. With the advent of the 77 in 1957 it was back to a single-level seat with rather slab-like looks.

The year 1960 brought the slim-line frame and with it a new dualseat, which was used by both the standard and de luxe models, the latter with their rear enclosure. The new seat was a single-level type with a

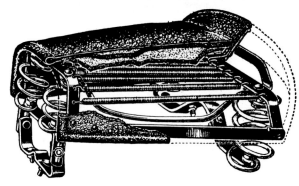

TOP *The seat fixing of this 1959–60 Jubilee allowed it to be pulled up for removal*

ABOVE *Typical built-up pillion seat sold as the Camden which a Norton owner might have bought around 1950 for his Dominator*

LEFT *'Torrens' of* The Motor Cycle *modified the seat on his 1952 model 88 to raise it but when the machine was passed on to Vic Willoughby it was soon back to standard*

ABOVE *The toolkit supplied with the 1960 model 99 all laid out for use*

LEFT *The seat of the Fastback Commando fixed to the rear unit mountings and the toolkit tucked into the rear tail*

Rear view of the 1968 Commando which was what many riders were to see in the years ahead

slight lift to the tail and was quickly detachable to give access to the oil filler and tooltray. Fixing was by two locating pegs at the front and spring clips at the rear, so removal was a case of pulling the tail up and then the seat back.

This arrangement lasted for a year as a new seat appeared for 1961. While it retained the locating pegs at the front, the tail fixing became a single, quarter-turn Dzus fastener into the rear mudguard. The seat was revised a little for 1962, but the fixing continued in its 1961 form. This arrangement ran on for the Featherbed models. For 1968 the seat grew a rear hump.

The hybrids had their own dualseats in various forms to suit the frames used. The P11 began with a single seat (really a very short dual one), but the P11A had a dualseat. The single seat was not new, for one had been listed as an option for the big twins from 1960.

The early 250 used the same arrangement as the de luxe big twins, with two pegs at the front of the seat and two spring clips at the rear. These located on to extensions of the top damper bolts to take the loads straight into the frame. For 1961 the rear fixing was changed to a single, central, quarter-turn Dzus fastener for the de luxe model. Another seat was listed for the standard machine; this used two pegs at the front and the damper bolts at the rear. From 1964 a single seat was offered as an option.

The first Commando had an orange seat that was extended at the front to form kneegrips on either side of the tank. The rather startling colour continued as an option to 1970 along with another in white, but the standard finish became black. This seat was used on all Fastback models and, thus, to 1972. It was held in place by a knurled knob on each side, and this fixing method continued until the Mk III models.

The R and S had their own seat of conventional shape with cross-ribs stitched into the cover. The same seat was used by the early Roadster models. It was modified for 1971, again for 1973 when it lost the ribs to become plain, once more for 1974, and finally for 1975 when it was hinged on the left side for the Mk III model.

The Fastback LR had its own seat as did the SS model. The Interstate came in with a ribbed seat for 1972 and changed to a plain top for 1973. It was modified once more for 1974, and became hinged and ribbed from 1975. The Hi-Rider seat was always rather special because of its shape, and it retained the twin-nut fixing to the end. The original of 1971 was ribbed, but it changed to a plain cover for 1973—it was further revised for 1975. The single seat supplied for the Interpol appeared in 1971 and was altered only once, for 1975. The JPR seat was, in effect, a padding attached to the tail fairing, and it accommodated only one person.

ABOVE *The right side of the 1969 Commando S looks rather bare with the exhaust system exiting on the left*

RIGHT *The Hi-Rider with its strange seat and handlebars in its 1973 745 cc form but hardly Norton style*

Handrail

This is a tubular, chrome-plated part that bolts around the rear of the seat. It first appeared in 1961 on the export 650 and later became an option for this model and the Atlas.

On the Commando models a grab rail was fitted to the Hi-Rider from the start in 1971 and was amended for 1973 when its clamp bolts changed. For 1973 grab rails were also listed for the Roadster and Interstate, a kit being available for older editions of these two models. For 1975 a single rail was introduced to suit both models, and this bolted to either dualseat.

16 Assembly

Often, this is the most satisfying part of a restoration or rebuild, culminating in that heady moment when you swing on the kickstarter and the engine bursts into life.

It is also a time for making haste slowly as rushing matters may easily damage something you have spent time, money and effort on. Slow and sure is best, with plenty of reference to your notes so you work in the right sequence. In the build-up to final assembly you should have checked the fit of bolts to holes as you went along, and all this work will pay off in the straightforward fitting of the parts without snags.

The greatest problem lies in protecting the finish you have lavished so much care on, so cover, pad and mask where necessary and work slowly to avoid damage. Think about the order in which you intend to assemble the parts and arrange the items of each stage so they are together. It is good practice to do this as it is a further check that you have everything and that each item has been reworked as required. It will also ensure that you are not caught off balance with something partly assembled and being short of a vital bolt and with no free hand to locate it. If this does happen, go back and dismantle rather than chance damage occurring while your back is turned.

Start the assembly with the frame, fitting the rear fork, the head race cups and the main stand. Now put the skeleton on your machine bench and prop up the front end. If you have any doubt at all about its stability, clamp the stand down. Fit the fork crowns and the forks themselves, adding the front wheel. If you fit the mudguard at this stage, it will need protection for sure, so it is best omitted for the time being.

The rear guard may well have to be fitted early on, and it may be necessary to add the wiring harness at this stage or at least fit the rear section, if this is threaded through frame and mudguard tubes and guides. If the machine is balanced on its centre stand, either fit the rear wheel or anchor the rear fork end to your bench.

Once you have a stable frame that is not going to rock about, fit the engine and gearbox while you have the most room in which to move. Don't forget to check that you have not left out anything that should have been fitted first. Sort out all engine fixings, plates and spacers in advance, placing them to hand. Spare rods on which to locate the unit may well be needed.

You are more likely to damage something while fitting the engine than at any other time, so protect everything you can. Don't try to lift the engine into place unless you have at least two helpers to take the load while you slide in the fixings. With only two people, something is sure to be scratched.

Blocks underneath are one way to take the strain, but better still is a means of lifting the engine from above. In view of the cost of a rebuild, it is well worth hiring or even buying a car engine hoist, which will be able to carry the load easily. Arrange the lifting sling so it is secure and holds the engine in the correct plane for its fixings to line up. If you have to tilt the engine to achieve this, you are more likely to have an accident and possibly crushed fingers. Better to adjust the sling so the engine drops into place.

Then fit all fixings and tighten. As with any assembly work, it is best to complete a sequence fully and not leave the final tightening for later in case you forget. However, this may not be always possible, in which case leave the nut undone and attach a marker to remind you.

Continue the assembly as you wish and as the design dictates, but leave the tank and seat as late as possible. Check wheel alignment once both are finally in place, and adjust the chain tension correctly.

Don't try to start the engine until all is ready, and keep the battery on the shelf until nearly finished. Before connecting it, use your meter to check that the wiring is not shorting to earth somewhere and make sure you have connected it correctly. It should be fine, but it is better to be sure than chance a spark at this

ABOVE RIGHT *The 1973 Commando Roadster with 745 cc engine and disc front brake*

RIGHT *In contrast, a 1961 standard Navigator with big front brake from the larger models but rear from the Jubilee*

Matchless G15CSR from 1965 with nice lines but not to a Norton fan who would prefer an Atlas or 650SS

BELOW *The 1965 Atlas the Norton man would go for rather than a hybrid*

ABOVE *Or he might prefer a special such as this one built by Bill Chuck in 1969 but with Norton engine*

BELOW *A decade or more earlier with a 1952 model 88 with a no-chrome (due to the nickel shortage), all-painted tank*

A 1957 Norton model 77 hitched to a Swallow Jet 80 sidecar to make a nice outfit

stage. Disconnect the battery while you fill the oil tank and check the gearbox and primary-chain levels.

If the machine is still up on the bench, you will need help to get it down safely. Take care that you don't drop it at this stage, giving yourself plenty of room in which to work.

The petrol tank should have been left off until the machine was on the floor. Fit it now, connect it up and pour in a small amount of fuel. Half a gallon or two litres is fine to start with. Turn on the taps and check for leaks. Connect the battery, open the workshop doors to allow exhaust fumes to escape and start the engine. Keep the engine speed low and check that oil is returning to the oil tank. When the rocker supply comes from the return line, hold your finger on the pipe in the tank to force some into the rocker box as soon as possible. Watch that the oil-pump pressure does not force the return line off its pipe or you could have a large puddle on the floor and a shortage of oil in the engine. Check that the generator is charging.

Next put the machine on its stand and run it up through the gears to make sure all is well in that area. Have a good look round the pipe connections to make sure there are no leaks and check the ignition timing with a strobe if this is called for.

Try the machine gently in your drive to check the operation of the clutch and brakes. If you have done your paperwork, are insured and the machine is still taxed after all this time, you can get your helmet and go for a ride. If not, you will have to put it away for the moment.

For most owners in the UK that first ride of a restored machine is the prosaic journey to the local dealer for its official test. Rather irksome after all your work, but look on it as a top mechanic may regard scrutineering at a race meeting—a check that nothing has been overlooked. It may help to go to a dealer who knows something of older machines and who will believe that, for instance, taper-roller-bearing wheels should have some side play and that a 7 in. sls drum brake may lack the bite of a double disc with hydraulic operation.

A chat when booking the appointment is well worth the effort and can smooth the way to a pass.

When the machine is legal, enjoy a ride. After a few miles check the oil level and give the machine a look over to see if anything has worked loose. Get some more petrol before you run short and roll off some miles.

Then take the machine back to the workshop. Check items such as chains, brakes and cables which may have settled down a touch. Do your carburation check.

Enjoy your Norton twin.

17 Paperwork

In this modern age, ownership and use of any road vehicle involves pieces of paper, some of which are documents issued by the authorities. This chapter concerns these in general and those specific to the United Kingdom in particular. Details for other countries will vary and must be checked as necessary.

The first piece of paper was mentioned in the opening chapter and is the receipt for the machine or the bundle of receipts for parts if that was the way you obtained your model. It is very desirable that they contain the engine and frame numbers so you have proof of ownership. Make sure they agree with what is stamped on the machine and beware of anything that looks altered.

The other documents you will need in the UK are registration form, test certificate and insurance certificate. The first is currently known as a V5, the second as VT20 and the last is obtained privately. With them you can tax the machine for road use.

You should consider insurance long before you get to the road as the parts, and the machine as a whole, need to be covered against fire or theft as soon as you get them. Try to obtain an agreed value for the machine and make sure you adjust this in line with the market. The insurance will need to be extended to cover road risks before you ride in public, and it is worth shopping round for a company that specializes in older machines. Otherwise your relatively sedate Norton 99 will be lumped in with modern 750 cc models of far higher performance and spares prices.

The V5 and VT20 are linked, to an extent, and also involve the number plate of your machine. Where a machine has been in use on a fairly continuous basis its original buff or green log book will have been replaced by a V5, which will record the correct engine and frame numbers along with the original registration number as displayed on the number plate.

As nothing is perfect there are even discrepancies when the documentation is all in order. For example, a Norton twin is bought from a dealer. It suffers an engine problem and the complete unit is changed, which is not recorded at the time. Eventually, the machine is withdrawn from use and, in time, sold off. The new owner rebuilds it and, on coming to register it, compares paper numbers with actual markings to find they don't tally—as they have not done for many years.

More difficult is a machine that has not been used for a period and has no V5. For the authorities to issue a form with a registration number appropriate to the machine's year, they need further proof, and the onus is on the owner to provide it. Only in cases of rare or historic machines, well-known past owners or some similar reason is there much hope of retaining the original number, but it is always worth trying with an application.

As part of this exercise to keep the original number, it helps to be able to link it to the machine. For this, old MoT certificates or old licence discs are acceptable. When these are not available, or to back them up, a letter from a recognized authority to confirm the date of the quoted engine and frame numbers, stating whether or not they were likely to have begun life together, should be obtained. Acceptable sources are the owners club, Vintage MCC, service-page writers from the specialist magazines (I am one of these) or the holders of the manufacturer's original records.

Normally, it is not possible to trace the original registration number from scratch as much of the official record exists no longer. The procedure needed would be to look at the firm's records to match engine and frame numbers. Then, if this is in order, the records will give the name of the dealer to whom the machine was sent. He, in turn, would need to be sought out and his records checked for the registration number. In practice, few dealers from those days are still in business, and fewer still will have kept such records for the 20 or 30 years likely to be involved.

So you have to call on your Local Vehicle Licensing Office and take all your documents with you. There you complete a form, as you would expect to do at any government office. This will trigger off a series of events that will culminate with the issue of a V5 if all goes well.

The first thing likely to happen is a visit from the authorities, or their agents, to inspect your machine. This is done to check that all the numbers agree with those quoted on the form and that the machine is what

*Stephen Spencer in the 1964 Manx Grand Prix on a model
88 with siamezed pipes*

ABOVE *Nice 1951 model 7 Dominator with Garrard S90 occasional two-seater sidecar*

LEFT *Possible twin of the future in the form of the Wankel-powered Norton*

you say it is and does exist.

This visit is not always carried out, but if it does take place the machine is best assembled to some degree. It is often desirable to register the machine long before the restoration is complete or there is any need to tax it for the road. At the very least, it allows you to finish the number plate.

After the visit, and if all is in order, the vehicle documents will be issued. If the evidence is good the original registration number, or mark as they call it, may, in rare cases, be retained and entered on the main computer at Swansea. Normally this is not so, but where there is evidence as to the age of the machine, the authorities will try to issue an appropriate number for the period. Should there be no way of linking the machine to any period, which may happen with a hybrid, a number with a letter Q prefix will be issued.

Following this, the machine will have to go for its official test as mentioned in the previous chapter. Book the test, make sure you have insured the machine for road use, pass the test (after all this, I would be most disappointed if you did otherwise), and you can then tax the machine for the road.

Keep all the paperwork in case there are any queries at any time and to go with the machine should you ever come to sell it.

Now you have to decide what to restore next year.

Track marshal Ted Andrews on his 1965 Atlas at Scarborough racing circuit

HM Queen Elizabeth passing the Bracebridge Street Norton works during a visit to Birmingham in 1955

APPENDICES

1 Engine and frame numbers

From 1946 to 1974 Norton machines had matching engine and frame numbers, each comprising two or three sections. The first of these was a year letter, which was only used up to 1960. Next came a number code to identify the model. After this came the serial number itself. These ran straight on without regard for whether the machine was a single or a twin or had side or overhead valves. Thus, while there were batches of models there is no certainty that successive numbers relate to similar machines.

The engine number is stamped on the left crankcase just below the cylinder barrel, but the position of the frame number varies. Initially, it could be found on the left side of the tank support lug near the headstock, but on Featherbed frames it went on the left rear frame gusset above the fork pivot. In this position, the number was stamped in a vertical line with the model number and year letter in a horizontal line above it. Commando frames were numbered on the headstock, a riveted-on plate appearing for 1969. The small twins had their frame number stamped on the right frame lug, which carried the pivoted fork up to 1963. From then on the number was moved to the pillion footrest bracket.

Model code number

12	Dominator 7
122	88
14	99
15	77 and Nomad
16	Nomad
17	Jubilee
18	All 650s
19	Navigator
20	Atlas
20M3	Commando (distributor)
20M3S	Commando (camshaft points)
EL	Electra

Suffix D means de luxe
Suffix SS means Sports Special

Year letter code

D	1949	E	1950	F	1951	G	1952	H	1953
J	1954	K	1955	L	1956	M	1957	N	1958
P	1959	R	1960						

Serial numbers

From 1946 to 1960 the year letter is a better way of determining the age of a machine than the number. This is because there is some overlap of dates and numbers in the factory records, and those tables that do exist show some variance.

The year letter was also a feature of the parts list up to 1956; until then the part number would include an indication as to when the part was first used and the model it applied to, while the detail number was common.

An example is the gearbox shell, which for the model 7 was numbered D12/299: D indicates 1949, 12 the model 7, and 299 the part. For the model 88 the part number became H12-2/299, indicating 1953, model 88 and a similar item.

Another example of this is the fork lower crown which was B2/172 for the 7 and F11M2/172 for the 88. Thus, the former comes from a 1947 model 16H and the latter from a 1951 Manx.

Once the year code was dropped, the number provides a means of checking the year. Numbers and approximate dates used are set out for each model below:

Model	Date	Number	Note
Jubilee	Nov 1958	79866	first machine
	Aug 1959	84525	
	Sept 1960	92485	de luxe
	Nov 1960	93773	standard
	Sept 1961	99598	
	Sept 1962	103446	
		106838	new gearbox
	Sept 1963	107988	
	Sept 1964	111026	
	July 1966	117825	last machine
Navigator	Nov 1960	94573	first machine
	Sept 1961	99110	
	Sept 1961	99172	de luxe
	Sept 1962	103275	standard
		106838	new gearbox
	Sept 1964	106980	
	Aug 1965	114519	last machine
Electra	July 1963	650	first machine
	Sept 1964	6201	
	Aug 1965	7961	last machine
500 cc	Oct 1960	93235	standard
	Oct 1960	93385	de luxe
	Mar 1961	96539	88SS
	Aug 1962	97227	last de luxe
	Sept 1962	101918	standard
	Sept 1962	102911	88SS

Model	Date	Number	Note
500 cc	Sept 1963		last standard
	Sept 1964	109512	88SS
	July 1966	118151	last 88SS
600 cc	Aug 1960	92270	standard
	Sept 1960	92460	de luxe
	Mar 1961	96496	99SS
	Aug 1962	103392	last 99SS
	Aug 1962	103801	last de luxe
	Aug 1962	103929	last standard
650 cc	Oct 1961	100200	first machine
	Aug 1962	104121	last de luxe
	Sept 1962	104123	650SS
	Sept 1962	104267	650 standard
	Sept 1963		last standard
	Sept 1964	110375	650SS
	1966	115871	
	1967	119760	
	July 1967	123164	
	Feb 1968	126124	
	Sept 1968	129147	Mercury
	Feb 1970	129894	last Mercury
Atlas	Feb 1964	108000	first UK Atlas
	Sept 1964	111377	
	1966	115871	
	1967	119760	
	May 1967	120323	N15CS
		121307	Concentric carbs, coil ignition
	May 1967	121665	P11
	Aug 1967	123364	
	Jan 1968	124372	P11A
	Sept 1968	128646	P11A Ranger
	Nov 1968	129145	last Ranger
Commando 750 cc	Aug 1967	123666	first model
	Feb 1968	126125	first production machine
	Mar 1969	131180	Fastback
	Mar 1969	131257	S with camshaft points
	Sept 1969	133668	Fastback with camshaft points
		134108	first Wolverhampton engine (engines with P suffix from Plumstead)
	Mar 1970	135140	Roadster
	June 1970	135088	last S
	Sept 1970	139571	Fastback Mk II
	Jan 1971	141717	last Fastback Mk II
	Jan 1971	141783	Fastback Mk III
	Jan 1971	142534	Roadster Mk II
	Mar 1971	145234	SS
	Apr 1971	144343	Fastback LR
	May 1971	146074	Hi-Rider
	Oct 1971	150723	last SS
	Jan 1972	200001	Fastback Mk IV
	Jan 1972	200001	Fastback LR Mk IV
	Jan 1972	200001	Roadster Mk IV
	Jan 1972	200001	Hi-Rider Mk IV
	Jan 1972	200001	Interstate

Model	Date	Number	Note
750 cc		200976	first Combat engine
		211110	first detuned engine
	1973	212278	Interstate
	Mar 1973	220000	Roadster Mk V
	Mar 1973	220000	Hi-Rider Mk V
	Mar 1973	220000	Interstate Mk V
	Oct 1973	230935	last 750 Commando
Commando 850 cc	Apr 1973	300000	first 850
	Sept 1973	306591	Mk IA 850
	Jan 1974	307311	Mk II and IIA 850
	Feb 1975	325001	engine number Mk III
		F125001	frame number Mk III

The Norton Owners Club have checked the factory records and confirm the overlap of numbers at the year end. However, they have published the following as a guide which is reproduced here with their permission and included on the same basis. It should be treated as such and used with all the other data.

1948	13792	1956	66511	1964	107900
1949	20701	1957	71359	1965	112000
1950	27118	1958	77284	1966	115871
1951	35490	1959	80484	1967	119760
1952	42210	1960	87031	1968	124370
1953	48706	1961	94335	1969	130021
1954	55071	1962	101060	1970	134700
1955	60700	1963	104930	1971	141900

2 Model charts

First chart:

Capacity	Model	1949	1950	1951	1952	1953	1954	1955	1956	1957	1958	1959	1960	1961	1962	1963	1964	1965	1966
497 cc	7	—	—	—	—	—	—	—											
	88				—	—	—	—	—	—	—	—	—	—	—	—			
	88 Nomad													—					
	88 dl													—	—	—			
	88SS														—	—	—	—	—
596 cc	77									—	—								
	99								—	—	—	—	—	—	—	—	—	—	—
	99 Nomad										—	—	—						
	99 dl												—	—	—				
	99SS													—	—				

Second chart:

Capacity	Model	1961	1962	1963	1964	1965	1966	1967	1968	1969	1970
646 cc	650	—	—	—							
	650 dl	—	—								
	650SS	—	—	—	—	—	—	—			
	Mercury								—	—	
745 cc	Atlas		—	—	—	—	—	—			
	Atlas MX		—								
	N15CS'N'			—	—	—	—	—			
	N15						—				
	N15CS						—	—			
	P11						—				
	P11A						—				
	Ranger								-		
	G15				—	—	—				
	G15 Mk II							—	—		
	33				—	—	—	—			
	G15CSR				—	—	—	—			
	33CSR				—	—	—	—			
	G15CS						—	—			

		1959	1960	1961	1962	1963	1964	1965	1966
249 cc	250 dl	—	—	—	—				
	250 std		—	—	—	—			
349 cc	350 dl	—	—	—					
	350 std		—	—	—	—			
383 cc	400			—	—	—	—		

1959 1960 1961 1962 1963 1964 1965 1966

Commando		1967	1968	1969	1970	1971	1972	1973	1974	1975	1976	1977
745 cc	Model 20	—										
	Fastback		— 2	3	4 —							
	R		—									
	S		—									
	Roadster		— 2		4	5 —						
	Street Scrambler		—									
	Production Racer		—	—								
	Fastback LR			— 4 —								
	Hi-Rider			— 4	5 —							
	Interstate				— 5 —							
829 cc	Roadster						1	2A —				
	Hi-Rider						1	2 —				
	Interstate						1	2A —				
	Roadster							1A	3 —			
	Interstate							1A	3 —			
	JPR								—			

1967 1968 1969 1970 1971 1972 1973 1974 1975 1976 1977

3 Model alterations

These notes have been compiled from the main text as a quick guide for checking the year of a machine. The starting point should always be the engine and frame numbers, and the following is mainly concerned with external details that can be inspected when purchasing.

The notes run on and, in general, are applicable to later models of the same series. If in doubt, refer to the main text.

Dominator, Featherbed and hybrid

1949 **7**—start, iron cylinder head, dynamo, magneto, type 6 Amal, laid-down gearbox, plunger frame, 21 in. front wheel, saddle, oil gauge in tank top.
1951 New front brake with die-cast backplate.
1952 **88**—start, duplex frame, **7** engine and gearbox, dualseat, pear-shaped silencers, underslung pilot.
1953 **7**—pivoted-fork frame, dualseat, no oil gauge, pear-shaped silencers, underslung pilot, 19 in. front wheel.
1954 **7** and **88**—8 in. front brake.
1955 **7** and **88**—alloy cylinder head, Monobloc, boxed-in rear number plate, round tank badge, reflector below number plate.
88—welded-on subframe, full-width alloy hubs.
7—end.
1956 **99**—start, as **88** with 596 cc engine.
88 and **99**—new oil tank, battery case, no underslung pilot, switch panel in headlamp shell, Armstrong rear units.
May 1956 AMC gearbox for **88** and **99**. First on machines 68761/68828 and then from 68931 on.
1957 **77**—start, pivoted-fork frame with single downtube, tubular silencer, 596 cc engine, 1954-type 8 in. front brake.
88 and **99**—petrol tank with separate chrome-plated panels, Girling rear units, new cylinder head, new dualseat, tubular silencer with no tailpipe, new front hub, headlamp with items mounted directly into top surface, round footrests.
1958 **99 Nomad**—start, off-road model with 596 cc engine, twin carburettors, magneto, alternator, siamezed exhaust, **77** frame, undershield, 21 in. front wheel, alloy mudguards, trail tyres, lights.
77—no change, as 1957.
88 and **99**—RM15 alternator, distributor and coil ignition, cover over front engine plates. During year—options of twin carburettors, high-compression pistons, sidecar forks, steering damper, stiffer forks and rear units.

77—end.
1959 **88** and **99**—rear chaincase option.
1960 **88 Nomad**—as **99** version, both with coil ignition.
88 and **99 de luxe**—models with rear enclosure based on standard machines.
88 and **99 standard** and **de luxe**—slim-line frame, new long tank badge, new seat, valanced front mudguards, new inlet manifold, new silencers, two-tone finish.
88 Nomad and **99 Nomad**—end.
1961 **650 Manxman**—start, new model as others with 646 cc engine. As **Manxman**, for export with twin carburettors, downdraught head, magneto, siamezed exhaust. **650** as **88** or **99**.
88, **99** and **650**—new seat location.
Apr 1961 **88SS** and **99SS**—start, twin carburettors, siamezed exhaust, ball-end levers, folding kickstart.
1962 **650 de luxe** and **650SS**—start, as others.
88, **99**, **650** in **standard**, **de luxe** and **SS** forms—RM19 alternator.
88SS—new cylinder head with downdraught, parallel inlet ports cast in, magneto with manual or automatic advance.
99SS—old head, twin splayed carburettors, coil ignition.
All **SS**—Avon GP rear tyre.
Mar 1962 **Atlas**—start, 745 cc engine, one carburettor, breather from camshaft end, magneto.
Late 1962 **88 de luxe**, **99**, **99 de luxe**, **99SS**, **650 de luxe**—end.
Aug 1963 **Atlas MX**—start, 745 cc engine in AMC CSR frame, Norton forks and wheels, twin carburettors.
Late 1963 **88** and **650**—end.
1964 **88SS**, **650SS**, **Atlas**—wider forks, 12-volt electrics, steering lock.
Atlas—twin carburettors.
N15CS'N'—created from **Atlas MX**.
1965 **88SS**, **650SS**, **Atlas**—$\frac{3}{8}$ in. rear chain.
G15, **33**, **G15CSR**, **33CSR**—start, Atlas engine in AMC frame, Norton forks and wheels.
1966 As 1965.
Late 1966 **88SS**—end.
1967 **650SS** and **Atlas**—RM21 alternator, Concentric.
G15, **33**, **G15CSR**, **33CSR**—Concentric.
N15—start, **G15** with Norton tank, Concentric.
Mar 1967 **P11**—start, Atlas engine, Concentric, coil ignition, Matchless G85CS frame, AMC forks and brakes, waist-level silencer.
Apr 1967 **G15CS**—start.
Late 1967 **33** and **33CSR**—end.
N15CS—created from **N15CS'N'**.

G15 Mk II—created from G15.
1968 P11A—created from P11.
All-capacitor emergency ignition.
Late 1968 Mercury—created from 650SS with single carburettor.
Ranger—created from P11A.
N15CS—end.
End 1968 Atlas and Ranger—end.
Early 1969 G15 Mk II, G15CSR, G15CS—end.
Mid-1970 Mercury—end.

Lightweight

1959 Jubilee—start, rear enclosure, 249 cc twin, 6 in. headlamp.
1961 Navigator—start, as 250, 349 cc engine, Roadholder forks, 8 in. front brake, 19 in. front wheel.
Standard versions of 250 and 350—no rear enclosure, side oil tank.
All—7 in. headlamp.
1963 Electra—383 cc model with electric start, 12-volt electrics, no rear enclosure, 7 in. rear brake, indicators.
Late 1963 250 de luxe and 350 de luxe models with rear enclosure—end.
1964 All—flat bars, wider rear number plate.
Late 1965 350 standard and Electra—end.
July 1966 Jubilee—end.

Commando

Apr 1968 Commando—start, Atlas engine inclined in frame with Isolastic mounts, seat sides extended forward as kneegrips, tail unit, silencers without tailpipes. Points in magneto position.
1969 R—as Commando with normal dualseat and rear mudguard, no tail unit.
Mar 1969 Fastback—was original model.
S—timing cover points, twin pipes at waist level on left, silencers with conical ends, no fork gaiters, normal dualseat, no tail unit.
Mid-1969 R—end.
Mar 1970 Roadster—start, as S with low-level exhausts.
June 1970 Combat engine available.
S—end.

Sept 1970 Fastback Mk II—tilted exhausts with reverse-cone silencers.
Jan 1971 Fastback Mk III—no fork gaiters, alloy levers.
Roadster Mk II—exhausts as Fastback.
Mar 1971 Street Scrambler—small tank, waist-level exhausts, reverse-cone silencers, braced bars, undershield.
Apr 1971 Production Racer—disc front brake, half fairing, rear tail, special seat and tank, silencers with no tailpipes.
Fastback LR—as Fastback with big tank.
May 1971 Hi-Rider—chopper-style, high-rise bars, short seat with high tail, grab handle.
Oct 1971 Street Scrambler—end.
Jan 1972 All—new crankcase with rear breather, cartridge oil filter between engine and gearbox, disc front brake and Combat engine options.
Fastback, Fastback LR, Roadster and Hi-Rider—became Mk IV models.
Production Racer—reverse-cone silencers.
Interstate—Combat engine, front disc brake, long reverse-taper silencers, longer seat, 5-gallon tank.
June 1972 Combat engine and disc front brake standard.
Mar 1973 Fastback and Fastback LR—end.
Roadster, Hi-Rider and Interstate—became Mk V models.
Apr 1973 850 Roadster, Hi-Rider and Interstate—with 829 cc engine, exhaust balance pipe, double styling lines, grab handle.
Sept 1973 850 Roadster and Interstate—also in Mk IA form with revised air filter and black cap silencers.
Oct 1973 750 Roadster, Hi-Rider and Interstate—end.
Nov 1973 John Player Replica—special seat, tank and fairing, 829 cc engine usual, 749 cc option.
Jan 1974 850 Roadster and Interstate—became Mk IIA models.
850 Hi-Rider—became Mk II model.
Feb 1975 Roadster IA, Roadster IIA, Interstate IA, Interstate IIA, Hi-Rider II, John Player Replica—end.
Roadster and Interstate Mk III—electric start, rear disc, front disc on left, left gear pedal, right brake pedal, new ignition switch and warning lights, RM23 alternator.
Oct 1977 Roadster and Interstate Mk III—end.

4 Colours

Dominator, Featherbed and hybrid

1949 **7**—black frame, forks, mudguards, oil tank, toolbox, headlamp shell, wheel hubs, brake backplates, chaincase and chainguard. Petrol tank chrome-plated with silver panels on top and each side. Each panel lined with $\frac{3}{16}$ in. wide outer black and $\frac{1}{32}$ in. wide inner red lines with $\frac{1}{8}$ in. gap between them. A very few early models had a wider $\frac{7}{16}$ in. black line. Black 'Norton' transfer on each side panel, gold with black outline 'Norton' transfer on tank top. Wheel rims chrome-plated with black centres, lined red. Chrome-plated headlamp rim, exhaust system, handlebars and upper part of fork slider after early models. Timing cover engraved 'Norton'.

1950 **7**—small 'Norton' oval badge on timing cover.

1951 **7**—die-cast front brake backplate.

1950–52 **7**—for export a few machines were produced having a chrome-plated tank with polychromatic blue or post-office red panels, both lined in black and gold.

1952 **7**—due to the nickel shortage tank finished in silver all over with normal lining.

88—polychromatic grey frame, forks, mudguards, oil tank, chaincase, chainguard, hubs and headlamp shell. Petrol tank chrome-plated with polychromatic grey panels on sides and top, lined as model 7. 'Norton' transfer on tank sides in black with white outline to each letter. Wheel rims chrome-plated with grey centres, lined red. Timing cover with oval Norton badge. Chrome-plated exhaust system, headlamp rim, upper fork sliders and handlebars. Polished fork sliders. During year 7 and **88** wheel-rim centres finished in silver, lined red. Some export **88** models having chrome-plated tank with blue panels, lined black and white, plus 'Norton' transfers on sides in black with white outline.

1953 **7** and **88**—no change.

88—optional finish with black frame, mudguards, oil tank and toolbox. Petrol tank chrome-plated with silver panels, lined black and red; rims as standard with chrome-plating and red-lined, silver centres.

1955 **7** and **88**—as before except round plastic 'Norton' tank badges, more chrome-plating on details and some nuts and bolts, chrome-plated wheel rims.

7—with polished fork sliders as **88**.

1956 **99**—as **88**, both with small round plastic 'Norton' badge in timing cover.

1957 **88** and **99**—petrol tank painted grey with separate chrome-plated side panels and plastic beading on edge.

77—as **88** or in black with grey tank on lines of earlier model 7.

1958 **77**, **88** and **99**—no change.

99 Nomad—black frame, part forks, oil tank, battery cover and headlamp shell; polished headlight brackets and lower forks; polished light-alloy mudguards; tank red with chrome-plated side panels and white lines at panel edges; seat with white top and black sides.

1959 **88** and **99**—as 1957 with options in metalescent blue, Norton post-office red or black and silver on lines of 1953 option. Option of chrome-plated front and rear mudguards, front stays and rear lifting handles.

99 Nomad—as 1958 with chrome-plated chaincase.

1960 New, long tank badge together with $\frac{1}{8}$ in. wide white line for road models to give divider to tank and allow the use of two colours.

88 and **99 standard**—Norton grey, red or black for upper tank, fork shroud, headlamp shell, oil tank, frame, chaincase and chainguard. Dove-grey mudguards, rear units and lower tank. Option of chrome-plated mudguards as 1959.

88 de luxe and **99 de luxe**—Norton grey, red, Tunisian blue or forest green for upper tank, fork shroud, headlamp shell and upper part of rear enclosure. Dove-grey lower tank, front mudguard, lower part of rear enclosure, chaincase, chainguard, rear chaincase, frame and oil tank.

88 Nomad and **99 Nomad**—as 1959.

1961 Specific colours for each model in 1960 pattern.

88 and **88SS**—green upper tank, frame, fork shroud, headlamp shell, oil tank, battery cover, chaincase, and chainguard. Dove-grey mudguards, lower tank and rear units. Option of chrome-plated mudguards as 1959.

99 and **99SS**—as **88** except polychromatic grey in place of green.

88 de luxe—as 1960 in red and dove grey.

99 de luxe—as 1960 in blue and dove grey.

Manxman—polychromatic blue frame, tank and forks, chrome-plated mudguards and chaincase.

650—as **standard 99**.

1962 **88**, **88 de luxe**, **88SS**, **99**, **99 de luxe**, **99SS**—as 1961.

650—all polychromatic grey.

650 de luxe—as **99 de luxe** in blue and dove grey.

650SS—black, silver tank, option of chrome-plated mudguards.

Atlas—as 650SS with chrome-plated mudguards as standard.

Option of chrome-plated mudguards for 88, 99, 88SS, 99SS, 650 and 650SS as 1959.

1963 88—as 1961 in green and off-white.

650—as 1961 in black and polychromatic blue.

88SS—as 1961 in black and silver.

650SS—as 1962.

Atlas—red, black and chrome.

1964 88SS—as 650SS in black with all-silver tank and chrome-plated mudguards. Option of black mudguards.

650SS—as 88SS.

Atlas—as 88SS with red or black option for petrol tank, no mudguard option.

Atlas scrambler—silver petrol tank with wide black outer and thin red inner side-panel lines, silver oil tank and battery cover, chrome-plated mudguards, black frame, forks, headlamp shell and rear units, polished fork legs.

1965 88SS and 650SS—as 1964.

Atlas—black with cherry-red petrol tank.

G15 and 33—black frame, forks, headlamp shell; chrome-plated mudguards; petrol tank in red for G15 or blue for 33 with chrome-plated sides and zigzag double line between on tank shoulder, thick lower and thin upper lines in gold; oil tank and toolbox in red or blue to match.

G15CSR and 33CSR—as G15 and 33 except light-alloy mudguards; chrome tank sides below smooth lining; chrome-plated headlamp shell, rear chainguard and instrument panel; red or blue tank top, oil tank and toolbox.

1966 88SS, 650SS, G15, 33, G15CSR and 33CSR—as 1965.

Atlas—tank in burgundy, otherwise as 1965.

1967 650SS, Atlas, G15CSR and 33CSR—as 1965.

G15 and 33—petrol tanks black for G15 and blue for 33.

P11 and N15—black with chrome-plated mudguards, round tank badge as used in 1955.

1968 650SS, Atlas, G15 Mk II, G15CSR, P11A, Ranger and N15CS—as 1967.

G15CS—black with candy-apple red tank and chrome-plated mudguards.

1969 G15 models—as 1968.

Mercury—black frame, forks, headlamp shell; silver tank; Atlantic blue chaincase, mudguards, oil tank and battery cover; optional stainless-steel mudguards.

1970 Mercury—as 1964 88SS in black and silver with chrome-plated mudguards.

Commando

1967 Launch model—silver tank, tail unit, side cover, oil tank, chainguard, frame, headlamp support and barrels. Chrome-plated wheel rims, front mudguard and headlamp. Polished-alloy chaincase and lower front forks. Seat in orange at Earls Court Show. Petrol tank had green globe disc on each side with small Norton disc just in front of it. Small green globe disc on each side of tail unit level with seat hump.

1968 Black frame and barrels. Petrol tank green with Norton disc badge on each side. Tail unit green with disc badge on top and reflector on each side in place of green

globe. Green dots on both instruments. Silver side cover and oil tank. Chrome-plated rims and front mudguard. Polished-alloy chaincase and lower fork legs. Black seat.

1969 Black frame, silver barrels, oil tank and side cover, chrome-plated headlamp common to all models.

Fastback—black or chrome-plated fork shrouds; petrol tank and tail unit in Grenadier red, British racing green, fireflake silver and, in a few cases and to special order, Burgundy red and silver. 'Norton' transfer on tank sides.

R—petrol tank in fireflake red or sapphire blue with 'Norton' transfer, black or chrome-plated fork shrouds, chrome-plated rims and mudguards, silver side cover and oil tank.

S—as R except no fork shrouds and side covers to match tank, chrome-plated chainguard.

1970 Colours of signal red, canary yellow or British racing green as solid and in fireflake as royal blue, purple, emerald, bronze or silver for petrol tanks of all models and side covers of S and Roadster. Fastback side cover and oil tank remained in silver. Roadster with chrome-plated chainguard. Otherwise as 1969.

1971 Black frame and oil tank, silver barrel, chrome-plated rims, mudguards and headlamp supports.

Fastback LR—tank in British racing green or signal red with black 'Norton' transfer on each side. Side covers in black, rear tail unit to match tank.

Fastback—as LR plus tank and tail unit also available in fireflake royal blue or golden bronze.

Roadster—usually in black with gold panel line on tank sides and 'Norton' transfer in gold with black edge. Black side covers with matching '750 Commando' transfer. Tank and side covers also listed in signal red, canary yellow, signal orange and fireflake royal blue, golden bronze and Roman purple.

SS—tank in canary yellow or tangerine with side covers in any Roadster colour.

Hi-Rider—tank and side covers as SS plus tangerine option for covers.

1972 Combat engine with black barrels.

Fastback, Roadster and Hi-Rider—as 1971.

Interstate—tank and side covers in black with gold lining, blue with silver lining or red. Stainless-steel mudguards. Transfers in gold with black edge for black or red items, silver with black edge for blue Interstate and all black.

1973 850 models with double line on tank and side covers; silver barrels. All models with stainless-steel front mudguard.

Roadster 750—in canary yellow, black or fireflake royal blue for tank and side covers plus golden bronze for covers only. 850—in bronze, blue, black or candy-apple red.

Interstate 750—in black or blue with single lining. 850—the same with twin lines and also in candy-apple red.

Hi-Rider 750—in black, yellow or tangerine. 850—in black only with double line.

1974 As 1973 except 850 only, Roadster also in dayglow white with wide blue stripe along tank side and across top in front of filler cap, blue stripe repeated on side cover. Hi-Rider in tangerine but no lining.

John Player Norton—black frame, barrel and side covers; matt-black exhaust pipes and silencers; chrome-plated wheel rims, rear mudguard and chainguard; polished fork sliders and chaincase. Front mudguard, fairing, petrol tank and seat unit white. Black 'Norton' transfer on each tank side. Fairing finished in two styles. One based on works race team with horizontal stripes of red and blue spaced apart, with red above, model name above top stripe and owner's name just below screen. Second style had red upper and blue lower tapered lines running back from headlamp recess to turn down at ends in broad bands with thin white separation, model name just below on fairing side and owner's name as above. Both styles had yellow reflectors on fairing, mounted low down on sides. Tail unit with red upper and blue horizontal bands separated by white band with Union Jack.

1975–77 Interstate—black frame and barrels, stainless-steel mudguards, chrome-plated wheel rims, chainguard, headlamp and its supports. Tank and side covers in black or red, also in Manx silver with 'Norton' transfer in black on tank sides, which were lined in black and red.

Roadster—as **Interstate** in black, red or white, the last as in 1974 with wide blue stripe.

Lightweights

1959–60 Jubilee—two-tone with red, forest green or Tunisian blue for upper tank, forks, headlamp shell and upper part of rear enclosure. Dove-grey lower tank and enclosure, front mudguard, frame, chainguard, optional chaincase, oil tank and tooltray. White dividing line, $\frac{1}{8}$ in. wide, between colours. Chrome-plated wheel rims. Seat cover: grey check top, grey sides, white piping.

1961–62 Jubilee de luxe—as 1959 in blue and dove grey.

Navigator de luxe—as **Jubilee** in black and dove grey.

Jubilee standard—red upper tank, forks, headlamp shell, oil tank and toolbox lid with remainder in dove grey.

Navigator standard—as **Jubilee standard** in blue and dove grey.

1962 Option of chrome-plated mudguards, front stays and rear lifting handles for **standard 250** and **350**. Rim embellishers fitted to both sides of **250** front hub and one side of **250 and 350** rear hub.

1963 250 de luxe—blue and dove grey or black and off-white (possibly a match for dove grey) in 1959 style. First is likely to have been Bracebridge Street production and the second Woolwich.

250 standard—red and dove grey in 1961 style or flamboyant burgundy petrol tank, oil tank, mudguards and toolbox lid with black frame, forks and details.

350 de luxe—black and dove grey as 1961.

350 standard—blue and dove grey or polychromatic blue petrol tank, oil tank, mudguards and toolbox lid with black remainder as **250 standard** model.

Electra—black frame, forks, headlamp shell and chainguard, silver grey petrol tank, oil tank and toolbox. Chrome-plated mudguards standard for export, optional for home market, for which black was the stock finish.

Standard models—option of chrome-plated mudguards as for 1961.

1964 250 standard—as 1963 in flamboyant burgundy and black.

350 standard—as 1963 in polychromatic blue and black.

Electra—chrome-plated mudguards standard, otherwise as 1963.

All—seat black with white piping.

Option of chrome-plated mudguards for **250** and **350**.

Option of coloured rear mudguard for **Electra**.

1965 250, 350 and Electra—as 1964.

1966 250—as 1964.

5 Pistons

Capacity	Bore	Left	Right	Ratio	Years
497 cc	66 mm	D12/702(LH)	D12/702(RH)	6.7	1949–55
		L12-2/702(LH)	L12-2/702(RH)	7.8	1956
		19785	19786	7.8	1957–58
		22504	22505	7.8	1959
		22504	22505	8.1	1960
		23179	23180	8.5	1961–63
		23185	23186	9.45	1961–66
		L12-2/702HC	L12-2/702HC	9.0	1958
		T2233/C	T2234/C	9.0	1959–60
596 cc	68 mm	L14/702(LH)	L14/702(RH)	7.4	1956
		19406	19407	7.4	1957–58
		21339	21340	9.0	1958–60
		22512	22513	7.4	1959
		22512	22513	7.6	1960
		22518	22519	8.0	1959–60
		23182	23183	8.25	1961–62
		23189	23190	8.9	1961–62
		23187	23188	10.2	1961–62
646 cc	68 mm	24022	24023	8.9	1961–65
		25387	25388		1966
745 cc	73 mm	24246	24247	7.6	1962–65
		25389	25390	7.5	1966
		061185	061186	8.7	1968–70
		062459	062462	8.9	1971
		063338	063339	9.0	1972
		063348	063349	10.0	1972–73 Combat

The 1972 and 1973 pistons are the same shape, and the higher compression ratio of the Combat engine came from machining 1 mm from the cylinder head. Ratios of Commando engines are approximate in all cases as they depend on the head used along with the head and base gaskets. See also the 'Commando Service Notes' from the Norton Owners Club. The only difference between the last two pistons is that the 1972 versions had a slot under the oil-ring groove. While fine in an Atlas, the top can come off at the Commando's higher ratio, especially if the engine is run much above 5000 rpm.

The pistons above are all handed with valve-head cut-outs machined into the crown. The small twins and the 850 Commando have the same piston in each bore so are not handed. The details for these are as follows:

Capacity	Bore	Piston	Ratio	Years
249 cc	60 mm	20703B	8.75	1959–60
		23191	8.75	1961–66
349 cc	63 mm	23972	8.75	1961–65
383 cc	66 mm	24708A	7.9	1963–65
829 cc	77 mm	063838	8.5	1973–77

6 Camshafts

Camshaft	Years	Timing data	Check at	Inlet	Exhaust
D12/790	1949–56	22/57.5/57.5/22	0.01	0.003	0.005
17413	1957–58	22/57.5/57.5/22	0.01	0.003	0.005
21225 (QR)	1959–63	49/77/79/47	0.013	0.003	0.005
22729 (SS)	1961–70	50/74/82/42	0.013	0.006	0.008
061084	1969–74	50/74/82/42	0.013	0.006	0.008
062608	1975–77	50/74/82/42	0.013	0.006	0.008
061404	R or S	59/81/86/54		0.01	0.01
063536 (2S)		59/89/88/60		0.01	0.01
063761 (3S)		59/89/88/60		0.016	0.016
064858 (4S)		65/83/88/60		0.016	0.016

22729 may be marked X1 or X2, the latter having double the hardness depth.

See also 'Commando Service Notes' from the Norton Owners Club and *Norton Tuning* by Paul Dunstall.

The small twins have two camshafts as follows:

Model	Inlet	Exhaust	Timing	Check at	Inlet	Exhaust
250	22253	22254			0.002	0.004
350/400	22831	22832	30/54/59/25	0.01	0.004	0.006

250 valve gaps increased to 0.004/0.006 in. for high-speed running.

7 Sparking plugs

Model	Year	Listed recommendation KLG	Lodge	Champion	Plug equivalents Original Make	Type	Modern NGK	Champion
500 (iron)	1949–55	F70			KLG	F70	B5HS	L86
500, 600, 650 std	1956–65	FE80	2HLN	N5		FE70	B5ES	N8
Atlas, G15	1962–65	FE75				FE75	B6ES	N4
650, 750	1966–70			N4		FE80	B7ES	N3
Twin carbs and SS	1959–66	FE100	3HLN			FE100	B8ES	N2
SS–running in	1961–66	FE75			Lodge	2HLN	B7ES	N3
2 carbs–running in	1959–62	FE70				3HLN	B8ES	N2
Commando	1968–70			N6Y	Champion	N4	B7ES	N4
Commando	1971–77			N7Y		N5	B6ES	N5
250	1959–60	FE100				N8	B5ES	N8
250, 350	1961–66	FE80				N6Y	BP8ES	N6Y
400	1963–65	FE80				N7Y	BP7ES	N7Y

8 Carburettor settings

Model		Year	Type	Size	Main	Pilot	Slide	Needle pos.	jet
7		1949–54	76AK	1	170		$6/3\frac{1}{2}$	2	.107
		1955	376/19	1	240	30	$3\frac{1}{2}$	2	.106
88		1952–54	76AK	1	170		$6/3\frac{1}{2}$	2	.107
		1955–56	376/18	1	240	30	$3\frac{1}{2}$	2	.106
		1956–63	376/66	1	240	30	$3\frac{1}{2}$	2	.106
88 Nomad		1959–60	276GX 276GY	1	110		6/5	3	.106
88 de luxe		1960–62	376/247	1	240	30	$3\frac{1}{2}$	2	.106
88SS		1961	376/220	$1\frac{1}{16}$	250	25	3	3	.106
		1962–66	376/288 376/289	$1\frac{1}{16}$	250	25	$3\frac{1}{2}$	3	.106
88 Clubmans	(2)	1955–56	T15GP	1	190		4	2	.107
88 twin carbs	(2)	1959–60	376/219	1	240	30	$3\frac{1}{2}$	2	.106
	(2)	1959–62	376/66	1	240	30	$3\frac{1}{2}$	2	.106
77		1957–58	376/67	$1\frac{1}{16}$	250	25	3	3	.106
99		1956–62	376/67	$1\frac{1}{16}$	250	25	3	3	.106
99 Nomad		1959–60	276/GV 276/GW	$1\frac{1}{16}$	130		6/5	3	.106
99 de luxe		1960–62	376/248	$1\frac{1}{16}$	250	25	3	3	.106
99SS	(2)	1961–62	376/220	$1\frac{1}{16}$	250	25	3	3	.106
99 twin carbs	(2)	1959–60	376/220	$1\frac{1}{16}$	250	25	3	3	.106
	(2)	1959–62	376/67	$1\frac{1}{16}$	250	25	3	3	.106
650		1961–63	389/71	$1\frac{1}{8}$	320	25	3	2	.106
650 (one carb option)		1961–62	389/64		320	25	4		
650 de luxe		1962	389/72	$1\frac{1}{8}$	320	25	3	2	.106
650SS		1962–64	376/288 376/289	$1\frac{1}{16}$	250	25	$3\frac{1}{2}$	3	.106
		1965–66	376/317 376/318	$1\frac{1}{16}$	270	25	$3\frac{1}{2}$	3	.106
		1967–68	R930/17 L930/18	30	280	25	3	2	.107
650 Mercury		1969–70	930	30					
650 twin carbs		1961–62 ⎫	⎧ 376/274	$1\frac{1}{16}$	250	25	$3\frac{1}{2}$	3	.106
650/99 (USA)		1965–66 ⎬	⎨ 376/275						
650/99		1967–68	R930/19 L930/20	30	260	25	3	2	.107
750 Atlas		1962–66	376/294	$1\frac{1}{16}$	400	20	$3\frac{1}{2}$	4	.106
		1963–64	389/87 389/88	$1\frac{1}{8}$	420	20	3	3	.106
		1965	389/218 389/219	$1\frac{1}{8}$	350	20	3	3	.106
		1966	389/241 689/241	$1\frac{1}{8}$	420	20	3	3	.106
(export)		1966	389/236 689/236	$1\frac{1}{8}$	350	20	3	3	.106
		1967–68	R930/7 L930/8	30	220	25	2	2	.106

Model	Year	Type	Size	Main	Pilot	Slide	Needle pos.	jet
N15CS	1964	389/210 389/211	$1\frac{1}{8}$	380	20	3	3	.106
	1966	389/237 689/237	$1\frac{1}{8}$	380	20	3	3	.106
P11	1967–68	R930/7 L930/8	30	250	25	3		.107
33 and G15	1965	389/87 389/88	$1\frac{1}{8}$	350	20	3	3	.106
33P and G15P	1965	389/87 389/88	$1\frac{1}{8}$	420	20	3	3	.106
33CSR and G15CSR	1965	389/222 389/223	$1\frac{1}{8}$	360	20	3	3	.106
	1966	389/242 689/242	$1\frac{1}{8}$	360	20	3	3	.106
33CS and G15CS	1966	389/237 689/237	$1\frac{1}{8}$	380	20	3	3	.106
G15P	1966	389/241 689/241	$1\frac{1}{8}$	420	20	3	3	.106
G15 and G15CSR	1967–68	R930/5 L930/6	30	230	25	2	2	.106
33 and 33CSR	1967–68	R930/7 L930/8	30	220	25	2	2	.106
Commando*	1968	R930/26 L930/27	30	220	25	3	2	.106
	1969	R930/30 L930/31	30	220		3	2	.106
	1970	R930/46 L930/47	30	180		3	2	.106
	1971–72	R930/68 L930/69	30	220		3	2	.106
Combat	1972	R932/19 L932/20	32	220		3	1	.106
	1973	R930/82 L930/83	30	220		3	2	.106
Combat	1973	R932/26 L932/27	32	230		3	1	.106
Roadster/850 Mk I 1973 / 850 Mk I and II 1974	1973 } 1974 }	{ R932/29 { L932/30	32	260		$3\frac{1}{2}$	1 or 3	.106
Interstate/850 Mk IA 1973 / 850 Mk IA and IIA 1974	1973 } 1974 }	{ R932/31 { L932/32	32	230		$3\frac{1}{2}$	2 or 3	.106
850 Mk II option	1974	R932/35 L932/36	32	260		$3\frac{1}{2}$	3	.106
850 Mk IIA option	1974	R932/33 L932/34	32	220		$3\frac{1}{2}$	2	.106
850 Mk III	1975–77	R932/33 L932/34	32	230		$3\frac{1}{2}$	1 or 2	.106
Jubilee de luxe	1959–63	375/36	$\frac{25}{32}$	130	25	$3\frac{1}{2}$	3	.1065
std	1961–66	375/43	$\frac{25}{32}$	130	25	$3\frac{1}{2}$	3	.1065
Navigator de luxe	1961–63	375/47	$\frac{7}{8}$	170	25	$3\frac{1}{2}$	4	.105
std	1961–65	375/48	$\frac{7}{8}$	170	25	$3\frac{1}{2}$	4	.105
Electra	1963–65	375/54	$\frac{7}{8}$	190	25	3	4	.105

*Note: 1970 Commando main jet is 220 with early megaphone silencer and 210 with modified megaphone. With the restricted megaphone, jet size was 180. 1972 Commando main jet is 210 and the needle position 1 with the mute fitted. The 1972 Combat engine was the same when the mute was fitted.

9 Commando cylinder heads

These are identified by part number and a code stamped on the right exhaust rocker-box face.

Code	Part no.	Model	Ratio	Inlet dia.	Remarks
RH1	060988	750	9.0	30 mm	Standard up to 1972
RH2	061427	750	10.25	32 mm	AMA racer
RH3	063327	750	10.0	32 mm	1972 Combat
RH4	064038	850	8.5	32 mm	1973 850 model
RH5	064048	750	8.9	32 mm	1973 low ratio
RH6	064097	750	9.3	32 mm	1973 preferred item
RH7	064854	750	10.0	32 mm	1973 short-stroke std
RH8	064884	750	—	32 mm	1973 short-stroke race
RH9	065213	850	10.5	32 mm	1974 high performance
RH10	065062	850	8.5	30 mm	1974 850 model

Carburettor adaptors used on Commado engines were:

062819	30 mm from carb to port
062711	32 mm from carb to port
065196	tapered from 32 mm at carb to 30 mm at port

Note that some RH6 heads carry a suffix S which indicates that they are fitted with the preferred 850 valve guides. Useful.

10 Petrol tank capacity

Model	Year	Size	Model	Year	Size
7	1949–55	3.75	Roadster	1970–72	2.25
88, 99	1952–59	3.5	Roadster (steel)	1972–77	2.5
77	1957–58	3.0	Hi-Rider	1971–73	2.0
Nomad	1958–60	2.25	Interstate	1972	5.25
88, 99, 650, 750	1960–70	3.62	Interstate (steel)	1972–73	5.5
Commando	1968	3.25	Interstate (steel)	1974–77	5.8
R	1969	2.25	250, 350, 400	1959–66	3.0
S	1969–70	2.25			
Fastback	1969–72	3.25	(Size in UK gallons)		

11 Transmission

Sprockets, boxes and overall gear ratios

Model	Year	Sprockets				Overall ratio	Box type
		E	C	G	R		
7	1949–55	19	42	19	43	5.003	Norton
77	1957–58	21	42	19	43	4.526	AMC 1
88	1952–56	19	42	19	43	5.003	Norton
	1956–59	20	42	19	43	4.753	AMC 1
	1960–63	19	42	19	43	5.003	AMC 2
88SS	1961–63	19	42	19	43	5.003	AMC 2
	1964–66	18	42	19	43	5.281	AMC 2
99	1956–59	21	42	19	43	4.526	AMC 1
	1960–62	20	42	19	43	4.753	AMC 2
99 (2 carbs)	1959	20	42	19	43	4.753	AMC 1
99SS	1961–62	20	42	19	43	4.753	AMC 2
650	1961–63	21	42	19	43	4.526	AMC 2
650SS	1962–68	21	42	19	43	4.526	AMC 2
Mercury	1968–70	21	42	19	43	4.526	AMC 2
Atlas	1962–68	21	42	19	43	4.526	AMC 2
7 sidecar	1949–55	18	42	17	43	5.902	Norton
G15	1964–65	23	42	19	43	4.133	AMC 2
	1966–69	22	42	19	43	4.321	AMC 2
N15, P11	1967–68	21	42	19	43	4.526	AMC 2
Commando 750	1968–72	26	57	19	42	4.846	AMC 2
	1973	26	57	21	42	4.385	AMC 2
Commando 850	1973	26	57	21	42	4.385	AMC 2
	1974–77	26	57	22	42	4.185	AMC 3
US Commando	1975–77	26	57	20	42	4.604	AMC 3
250	1959–63	22	46	17	55	6.765	250/350
	1964	22	46	17	55	6.765	400–1
	1965–66	22	46	17	53	6.519	400–2
350	1961–63	22	46	19	52	5.722	250/350
	1964	22	46	19	52	5.722	400–1
	1965	22	46	19	52	5.722	400–2
400	1963–64	22	46	19	52	5.722	400–1
	1965	22	46	19	52	5.722	400–2

Options for Commando: 19 to 24 teeth for 1972–75 plus 16 and 17 teeth.

Continued overleaf

Gearbox internal ratios

Gearbox	Used	Mainshaft				Layshaft				Gear ratios		
		4	3	2	1	4	3	2	1	3rd	2nd	1st
Norton	1949–56	24	22	18	13	18	20	24	29	1.212	1.778	2.974
AMC 1	1956–59	24	21	18	14	18	21	24	28	1.333	1.778	2.667
AMC 2	1960–73	23	21	18	14	18	20	24	28	1.217	1.704	2.556
AMC 3	1974–77	23	21	19	14	18	20	24	28	1.217	1.614	2.556
250/350	1959–63	28	25	21	16	18	21	25	30	1.307	1.852	2.917
400–1	1963–64	30	27	23	17	21	23	27	32	1.217	1.677	2.689
400–2	1965–66									1.24	1.75	2.76

Chains

Camshaft 0.375 × 0.25 × 0.225 in. with 38 links
Ignition 0.375 × 0.25 × 0.155 in. with 42 links
Electra starter 0.375 × 0.25 × 0.225 in. with 66 links

Primary: Big twins 0.5 × 0.335 × 0.305 in.
      Commando 0.375 × 0.25 × 0.225 in. triplex with 92 links
      Small twins 0.375 × 0.25 × 0.225 in. duplex with 66 links

Final drive: Big twins 0.625 × 0.4 × 0.255 in. for 1949–64
      0.625 × 0.4 × 0.380 in. for 1965–77
      Small twins 0.5 × 0.335 × 0.305 in.

Primary

7	1949–55	76 links
88	1952–64	75 links
88SS	1965–66	74 links
77	1957–58	77 links
99	1956–59	76 links
	1960–62	75 links
650	1961–70	76 links
Atlas	1962–68	76 links
G15	1964–69	68 links
N15, P11	1967–68	68 links

Final drive

Model	Year	Links	
7	1949–52	90	
	1953–55	91	
77	1957–58	90	
88	1952–60	98	
	1961–66	97	
99	1956–59	97	
	1960–62	98	
650	1961–70	97	
Atlas	1962–68	97	
G15	1964–69	97	
G15CSR	1965–69	98	
P11	1967–68	100	
N15	1967–68	97	
Commando	1968	98	
	1969–73	98	(19T)
	1969–73	99	(21T)
850	1973	99	
	1974	99	(21T)
	1974	100	(22T)
	1975–77	99	(20T)
	1975–77	100	(22T)
250	1959–66	121	
350, 400	1961–65	120	

12 Wheels, brakes and tyres

Brake diameters

Big twins	1949–53	$7 \times 1\frac{1}{4}$ in. front and rear
	1954–73	$8 \times 1\frac{1}{4}$ in. front, $7 \times 1\frac{1}{4}$ in. rear
	1972–74	10.7 in. disc front, $7 \times 1\frac{1}{4}$ in. rear
	1975–77	10.7 in. disc front and rear
250	1959–66	6×1 in. front and rear
350	1961–65	$8 \times 1\frac{1}{4}$ in. front, 6×1 in. rear
400	1963–65	$8 \times 1\frac{1}{4}$ in. front, $7 \times 1\frac{1}{4}$ in. rear

Tyre sizes

Model	Year	Front	Rear
7	1949–52	3.00×21	3.50×19
	1953–55	3.25×19	3.50×19
88, 99	1952–56	3.25×19	3.50×19
	1957–66	3.00×19	3.50×19
77	1957–58	3.25×19	3.50×19
650	1961–70	3.00×19	3.50×19
650 US	1961	3.25×19	4.00×18
Atlas	1962–68	3.25×19	4.00×18
Commando	1968–71	3.00×19	3.50×19
	1972–77	4.10×19	4.10×19
250	1959–63	3.25×18	3.25×18
250 std	1962–63	3.00×18	3.25×18
	1964–65	3.25×18	3.25×18
	1966	3.00×18	3.25×18
350	1961–65	3.00×19	3.25×18
400	1963–65	3.00×19	3.25×18

Rims

WM2 in all cases except:
Some early model 7s with 21 in. front wheel had WM1 rim;
US variants, Atlas and hybrids for scrambles or off-road had WM3 rim.

Wheel-rim offset
Front wheels have the rim central to the hub and backplate in both narrow and wide forks. The rear wheel of the Featherbed has the rim central to the complete rear hub, including the brake plate and spacer on the left and the speedometer drive with its spacer on the right. This centralizes it in the rear fork.

The Commando has its rear rim offset about $\frac{3}{16}$ in. to the right to allow for the engine plates being offset by that amount to the left. Thus, its wheel is not central in the rear fork.

Some figures which are to hand are:
Jubilee with WM2 rims: front, offset from face of brake drum to rim edge is $\frac{5}{16}$ in., rear is $1\frac{7}{8}$ in.
Navigator with WM2 rims: front, offset from drum face to rim edge is $\frac{1}{4}$ in., rear is $1\frac{7}{8}$ in.
88, 99, 650 and Atlas with WM2 rims: front, offset from face of bearing boss on brake side to rim edge is 0.276 in., rear is 1.253 in.
Note that if a different rim is fitted it alters the dimension by half the change in rim width.

Tyre equivalents

Section

Original	Low profile	Metric
3.00	3.60	90/90
3.25	3.60	90/90
3.50	4.10	100/90
4.00	4.25/85	110/90

Revolutions per mile

3.25×18	839	4.10×19	816
4.00×18	812	3.50×19 s/c	803
3.50×19	795		

Data from Avon Tyres Ltd.
Sidecar tyre included for reference.

13 Frame and fork dimensions

Frame-head angles taken between steering head and lower frame tubes, in degrees:

Manx	26
Wide-line	26
Slim-line	24
750 Commando	27
850 Commando	28

Fork stanchion lengths, in inches:

Long Roadholder	23.312
Short Roadholder	21.843
Commando	23.161
Manx	20.375

Fork spring lengths, in inches, with part numbers in brackets:

Long Roadholder	(18809)	11.781
Long for sidecar	(19481)	11.0
Manx	(15312)	9.25
Short Roadholder	(18813)	18.687
Short for sidecar	(15906)	18.15
Commando	(18813)	18.687
Navigator	(23015)	18.187
Electra	(23015)	18.187

14 Commando side panels

Early machines, the Fastback from 1968 to 1970 and the R for 1969, had a left panel only. All other models have a panel on each side. Panels came in many colours, as detailed in Appendix 4, and in two basic shapes.

The original shape (1) used by the first Commando is broadly rectangular. It appeared on the Fastback, R, Interpol and Interstate models.

A second type (2) is smaller and more triangular. It was used first on the S and then went on to the Roadster, SS, Hi-Rider and JPR models.

The following table gives part numbers and usage; refer to Appendix 4 for the colour. See parts lists for suffix number used to call up colour.

Model abbreviations

FB	Fastback	LR	Fastback Long Range
R	R	S	S
Ro	Roadster	Pol	Interpol
SS	SS	Hi	Hi-Rider
Int	Interstate	JPR	John Player Replica

Year	Shape	Left	Right	Models
1968	1	060854	—	
1969	1	061175	—	R
1969–70	1	061119	—	FB
1969–70	2	061202	061213	S (in red)
	2	061198	061209	S (in blue)
1970	2	061513	not listed	Ro
1971–72	1	061785	061675	FB, LR
1971–72	1	062227	061675	Pol
1971	2	061687	061693	Ro, SS, Hi
1972	1	063176	063177	Int
1972–74	1	063505	063506	Int (steel)
1972	2	063503	063504	Ro (steel)
1973–74	2	063503	063504	Ro, Hi (steel)
1974	1	064081	064136	Int
1974	2	064079	063218	JPR
1974	2	064996	—	Ro
1974	2	—	063220	Hi
1975	1	066329	064136	Int, Pol
1975	2	066330	063504	Ro, Hi

15 Headlamp, ammeter and switches

These varied and moved about over the years, and while the data given below is to be found in the main text as well, a summary may help.

1949–52 **7**—small panel in headlamp shell carrying ammeter and light switch. Speedometer in fork-top panel, oil gauge in petrol tank.

1952–55 **88**—plain headlamp shell, speedometer in fork-top panel with light switch to left and ammeter to right.

1953–55 **7**—as 1949 except no oil gauge.

1956 **88** and **99**—deeper, larger shell with small panel carrying speedometer, light switch ahead to the left and ammeter to the right.

1957 **88** and **99**—as 1956 with items fitted directly into the headlamp shell.

1957–58 **77**—as 1956 models.

1958–63 **88**—as 1957 with ignition switch in centre of lighting switch.

1958–62 **99**—as **88**.

1959–60 **250**—shell with speedometer aft of ammeter, separate lighting and ignition switches to left and right of ammeter.

1961–66 **250**—as 1959 but in larger shell to accommodate 7 in. light unit.

1961–65 **350**—as **250**.

1961 **Manxman**—as 1957 model **88**.

1961 **SS** models—as 1958 model **88**.

1961–63 **650**—as 1958 model **88**.

1962 **99SS**—as 1961.

1962–66 **88SS**, **650SS** and **Atlas**—as 1957 model **88**.

1963–65 **400**—as 1961 **250**.

1967–68 **650SS** and **Atlas**—light switch between separate instruments.

1969 **Mercury**—panel with speedometer on right and light switch to left. Ammeter and warning light in headlamp shell.

1970 **Mercury**—as 1969 or as 1967 **650SS**.

1968–70 **Commando**—ignition switch ahead of left side panel, headlamp shell with ammeter, light switch and warning light. For 1969–70 **S** and **Roadster** ignition switch in top, front corner of left side panel.

1971–74 **Commando**—four-way ignition switch, shell with light switch and three warning lights.

1974 **JPR**—light switch between instruments with three warning lights above, all mounted in fairing. Lights were red on left, green on right (both with shields), and amber in centre.

1975–77 **Commando**—main switch on fork top with four warning lights.

Picture indexes

These are compiled in date order, by machine and by item to give the maximum benefit. Owing to restrictions on space, it is not possible to have a picture of each side of every model for every year, but by using these indexes it is often possible to find a picture that helps. This is because the cycle parts were often common for several models in any one year, so any picture from that year will help. Thus one of an 88 will help with a 99 while a Roadster can assist an Interstate.

So look for your model and year but also check other models of the same year. It can also be worth looking at the same model in the years before and after as the feature you are checking may not have changed. Some of the references are for detail parts only so check the index, list the relevant pages and have a look at each to see if it helps.

Picture index by year

Commando models

Picture index by model

Component picture index

Index

Books in this series are
BSA Singles Restoration
BSA Twin Restoration
Matchless & AJS Restoration
Norton Twin Restoration
Triumph Twin Restoration

Hardback motorcycle marque books series are
AJS & Matchless - the postwar models
Ariel - the postwar models
BMW Motorcycles
BSA Gold Star & Other Singles
BSA Twins & Triples
Honda - the early classic motorcycles
Kawasaki - Sunrise to Z1
Kawasaki - Z1 to Ninja
Norton Singles
Norton Twins
Royal Enfield - the postwar models
Suzuki Two-Strokes
Triumph Singles
Triumph Twins & Triples
Velocette Flat Twins
Villiers Singles & Twins

Motorcycle Buyer's Guides series are
Illustrated BSA Buyer's Guide
Illustrated Norton Buyer's Guide
Illustrated Triumph Motorcycle Buyer's Guide